Diary of a Lone Twin

David Loftus is an internationally acclaimed photographer. His images have brought recipes to life in more than 150 cookbooks and he has been named one of the most influential photographers of all time. David grew up as the joint eldest of four siblings in Carshalton Beeches in South London. He lives with his wife in London, when not travelling and photographing the world. You can find him on Instagram @davidloftus where he shares imagery and art from his adventures.

DAVID LOFTUS

Diary *of a* Lone Twin

bluebird
books for life

First published 2019 by Bluebird
an imprint of Pan Macmillan
20 New Wharf Road, London N1 9RR
Associated companies throughout the world
www.panmacmillan.com

ISBN 978-1-5290-1128-9

Typeset in Haarlemmer by Jouve (UK), Milton Keynes
Printed and bound by CPI Group (UK) Ltd, Croydon, CR0 4YY

Visit **www.panmacmillan.com** to read more about all our books
and to buy them. You will also find features, author interviews and
news of any author events, and you can sign up for e-newsletters
so that you're always first to hear about our new releases.

To my three graces, Ange, Mother and Pascale,
and their d'Artagnan, Paros.

WINTER/SPRING

'You can't get to the meadow of happiness
without climbing the cliff of hardship.'

OLD TIBETAN PROVERB

Monday 1 January

Riad El Fenn, Marrakech

New Year's Day, and thus begins my personal diary of the year, an odyssey in which I will try to come to some sort of understanding of the events, thirty years ago, that so shaped my life: the death of my identical twin Johnny. It shouldn't read as vengeful or vitriolic, but I want to tell the truth in as few pages as possible, over 300 days, from New Year's Eve to the anniversary of John's death. I will try to be as honest and open and transparent as I can, leaving myself psychologically and emotionally bare, telling the story as faithfully as I can and showing the ultimately positive and cheerful me that lives and breathes today. There's no point in this painful journey unless the truth, and the telling of it, helps others who have lost loved ones, not just identical twins, but brothers, sisters, partners, friends and children.

Today I'm in a rather sad and contemplative state. I can't be sure as to whether I will complete the first day of this journey, let alone the whole year. Where to start? Sitting here in the shadow of the Koutoubia Mosque in ancient Marrakech, a place I have come to call my 'home from home', seems as good a place as any. As does the first day of the year. I have just watched the sun set over the palms beside the mosque's melodic call to prayer, disturbing the sparrows as they rush to their nightly evensong conventions in the trees and vines of the riads. Half an hour of incessant chatter and then blissful silence. I watch and listen nightly.

3

How to start? Last year was the thirtieth year since John died. Thirty years of surviving as a singleton after spending nearly half my life as an identical twin. And what do I hope to achieve by dedicating myself to this year of exploring the loss? Will this be a cathartic experience, a voyage of self-discovery, or will it end in sadness? Time will tell. The desire to write something has been with me for many years, fuelled by a deep sense of injustice surrounding the nature of Johnny's death, alongside a festering guilt around the events that led to it. Plus a feeling that this has to be confronted and faced.

Since John died one of the simplest of everyday tasks has become one of the most heartbreaking for me: the act of shaving. I had shaved John while he was in hospital and the contours and blemishes of his face were so familiar to me, akin to looking in the mirror. After that, the task of shaving myself became an impossible chore. That feeling has never left me, and the feeling I have on day one of this journal is of facing a very large, very clear mirror, for the first time since his death.

Tuesday 2 January

I'm here in Marrakech to see in the New Year with Ange. My day has been spent sunbathing. No longer deemed fashionable or indeed safe, tanning to both John and I was deemed quiet, solo, 'me time'. A time to liberate ourselves from the use of our primary sense, sight. I was thinking today of the combined hours, indeed weeks and months, we spent in that semi-catatonic state of rest, listening to the sound of the sea and the wind in the olive and casuarina trees on the Greek island of Paros, drinking in the smell of drying oregano and thyme in the intense Aegean heat. To many it might seem wasted time, but some of our best ideas came from these sun-baked, silent moments. Today as I listened to the mosque's call to prayers, smelt the cinnamon and spices in the air and watched the high-flying storks sailing in the winds from the Atlas Mountains, I started thinking about John's early joy of writing poetry. Aged eight or nine we were both often to be found at my father's desk or at the dining table drawing and painting, but occasionally he would wander off and hide to write a poem, usually addressed to our parents. I found one recently:

Beautiful Things by John Loftus

Beautiful things that look a sight
Make the world nice and bright
The red is the sun, the white the moon
The black is the night, the pink is the noon
Colourful butterflies in the air
On a plate, a golden pear

Little red berries on a hawthorn tree
And an elegant bumble bee,
The nice little ducks are on a flight
And a child's flying kite
The coloured shirts of a football team
Freshly pulled vegetables, mostly green

Blue is the sea, the river too
On the grass, a silver dew
The daisies and buttercups are very small
The people like them one and all
Don't forget the purple heather,
And the grass that is as light as a feather

The owl is known to be very wise
Bird watchers watch him with beady eyes

All things are beautiful
Not like a beastly bull
All these things, God made them all
All these things, great and small

Finding this was a glorious reminder of the innocence and simplicity of our youth. John and I would kneel and say our prayers nightly, either side of the bed. We'd pray for our parents and maybe our little sister and brother if they hadn't annoyed us too much. We'd pray for an end to wars, we'd pray that there wouldn't be another Ice Age, and we'd both pray that we'd never, ever get a brain tumour.

Wednesday 3 and Thursday 4 January

Last night at Riad El Fenn, Marrakech

Flying home from Marrakech with Ange, I'm thinking about brain tumours . . . what made our young minds fear them so? The Ice Age fear stemmed from a very early dream I'd had, when creeping down from the North Pole came a wall of ice hundreds of feet high, crushing everything in its path. But brain tumours? I can't remember why. Mother, being a doctor, would occasionally talk over tea with my father about her day's events, but we were normally ignorant of the medical phrases we'd hear, like spina bifida and toxic shock syndrome.

Our first encounter with brain cancer was on our first 'solo' trip abroad as twins. Unaccompanied by our parents, at fourteen or fifteen years old we were sent to stay in Ontario during the summer of 1976, the UK's great drought. We stayed with our Uncle Almond, best known for being the country's leading nuclear scientist, but more interesting to us boys as the inventor of the 'bluey whiteness' chemical in Daz's washing

powder. Alison and Lesley, his twin daughters, were fascinating to us, and us to them – our first experience of non-identical twins. They were fiercely different and often fought like cats and dogs, but John had a crush on Cousin Alison and I had a soft spot for Cousin Lesley.

They introduced us one night to a boy called Billy. He must have been about eighteen or nineteen and we were both drawn to his recklessness. He owned a silver Ford Pinto, a car more akin to an episode of *Thunderbirds* than the boxy, sensible cars of home. He'd souped-up the engine and on the first Sunday of every month he took it to the local diner to hang out, and occasionally to drag race up a mile of open road. One time John and I lay side by side, holding hands in its weird space-age boot as he took part in one of those illegal contests. We were both terrified but didn't admit it to each other for days. Billy was bonkers, wildly irresponsible and – to us – as cool as a cucumber. It was only later, during a long and uncomfortable lecture from Uncle Almond, that we learned his abandon stemmed from the removal of a very serious tumour from his brain and the insertion of a metal plate in the part of the brain believed to govern sense or reason.

Flying into Montreal that summer, our first landing in a plane other than a few turboprop European jaunts, was scary. Our descent took place during an extraordinary flash storm, with lightning hitting the plane twice, but it was accompanied on our starboard side by the most beautiful double rainbow.

It was the first of three times in my life that I have flown through a rainbow, the other two when I was flying co-pilot. As one nears the rainbow, it seems to shrink, with the arc getting tighter and tighter, until, for a few moments, it forms a perfect 'halo' around the aircraft, moving at the same speed, bathing the cockpit in an extraordinary kaleidoscopic glow. If one had to visualize the ideal 'gates to heaven', this must surely be it.

The Mews

'A reader lives a thousand lives before he dies.
The man who never reads lives only one.'
—George R. R. Martin, A *Dance with Dragons*, 2011

Lying here at home in the Mews, contemplating a rather uneventful photoshoot today, I gaze at my bedside wall covered in a collage of front covers and pages from the magazine *The Graphic* from the 1870s. Scenes range from a newly discovered parakeet from an exotic land to a map of Paris, surrounded by the Prussian artillery. Browned or bleached by the sun, worn by over a century's page turnings, the pages are collaged together to create a wallpaper of antiquated typography and engravings.

One of them depicts my hero Alexandre Dumas. Somehow I had always imagined Dumas as the handsome and courageous hero Edmond Dantès in *The Count of Monte Cristo*, but handsome devil he is not. Portly, moustachioed and sporting what can only be described as a wild afro, he stares down at me now, challenging me to write, to keep going onward, regardless.

For many years *The Three Musketeers* was the benchmark novel I compared all other books to, until I read *The Count of Monte Cristo*, which remains my desert island book. When I told John I had finished it, he told me he had already read it, but refused to be tested on it. I didn't believe him for a minute. Competitive reading lasted all our lives. In the early years it was who could read *Janet and John* without being corrected. Later it was who could read *Emil and the Detectives* faster or *Asterix the Gaul* in French. I once gave him a copy of Tintin's *The Black Island* in Greek and fibbed that I had translated it into English. Later in life the competitiveness grew, but it was more, 'my author is better than yours'.

Where he read Mervyn Peake, I read Michael Moorcock. Where he read Tolkien, I read Camus and Kafka.

Now I can't remember a single character's name from Michael Moorcock. John the Elder was right there. For fifteen years I refused to read *The Lord of the Rings*. Why would I read what was considered a children's book when I could be reading Jack Kerouac? Orcs? Or cool chicks in berets smoking unfiltered Gauloises, listening to abstract jazz and driving in old convertible Cadillacs across the States?

Four years after John's death I took his copies of *The Lord of the Rings* to Paros, the Cycladean island John and I had shared as a summer holiday destination for many a year. He had two copies, almost identical, paperback and tatty. One had been read by him four times, and the other three. He'd read *The Lord of the Rings* seven times! Not only that, but he had read it each time without reading anything else, so back to back. Like painting the Forth Bridge; finish the book, and start again.

For three and a half weeks I caught the little caique fishing boat across the bay from Parikia port to Livadia. I would wander the sun-baked pathway, passing the solitary nudist on his rock (we nicknamed him 'Adonis the Bronze'), to our little beach at Agios Fokas. It was always deserted, because it was stony rather than sandy, and facing out into the deep Aegean blue, I would sit under the casuarina trees and read about hobbits, orcs, fairies and dwarfs.

Jane Apostopolous was our landlady in Paros for many years. At the end of John's last stay he trudged up the mountain to the Yria potteries in Lefkes and bought Jane a little blue pottery bird, a love bird. It was part of a pair; there was a light and a dark blue one, but he could only afford one. Jane adored it, popping it on one side of her mantelpiece. Two weeks later, I also came to stay at Jane's with my oldest chum, Peter Hornsey. We roasted ourselves at Agios Fokas, him reading Stephen King, me with my Beat novels, sharing cassettes of The Cure and Nick Cave. At the end of our three and a half weeks I also trudged up the mountain to Yria in Lefkes and purchased a small dark blue bird that had been part of a pair. When I presented it to Jane she burst into tears and placed it next to its other half. I hadn't known that John had bought the lighter one. Sadly, John would never return to Paros.

I left one of the copies of *The Lord of the Rings* on her mantelpiece, next to the two birds, and haven't been back to Paros since.

Tuesday 9 January

The Mews

Having passed my first week of writing without slipping into a pit of depression, I have begun to assess how much I can mentally cope with in this Year of Living Retrospectively. A to-do list, I think, must begin with a return to Paros. When my son was born I wanted to give him a name that somehow honoured the memory of my dear twin, but to call him Johnny seemed too much, so we called him Paros, after the island of our shared adventures. Paros Erik (after my father) Loftus was born 21 June at Chelsea and Westminster Hospital.

Wednesday 10 January

Apparently the bluebirds over the white cliffs of Dover were actually swallows and house martins, which, upon close inspection, have a blueish sheen to their black plumage. I saw my first true bluebird in summer last year, in the Catskills of upstate New York, an identical pair of vibrantly iridescent males.

I've been drawn to birds since I was nine or ten. I didn't know until recently that, as the younger twin by an all-important ten minutes, I was often following in John's footsteps in many of my hobbies. By that age he was already showing signs of being a much more talented artist than me. And while I was struggling with my piano scales, John was a natural on the ivories, soon Scott Joplin-ing away on our mother's Steinway. Unbeknownst to me, my parents were quietly discussing their worries that I didn't have quite as many hobbies as John. He was not only winning Blue Peter gold badges for artistic endeavours, but also researching and hand-painting entire battalions of Napoleonic soldiers, creating exhibitable LEGO structures and transporting all these and more in his perfectly maintained Hornby train set. Maybe, in hindsight, he was trying to cram more into his life.

I was drawing and reading like a demon, but I struggled to be passably good in so many of the things he excelled at. Only now do I see that my father's wanderings through Richmond Park with a pair of binoculars, trailing a cold and puzzled me, were a (successful) attempt to interest me in ornithology. Later, too, the gifts, firstly of a little Kodak box camera, and then an Olympus Trip, along with second-hand copies of *Camera* magazines, were his successful attempt to interest me in photography. One (photography) is now my chosen career, the other (ornithology) one of my greatest pleasures. To sit in a garden, field or wood, to close one's eyes and just quietly listen to the sound of birds is music for the heart and soul.

Thursday 11 January

The Mews

Fraternal, or non-identical, twins come from different eggs within the mother's womb. The eggs happen, by chance, to be fertilized by different sperm from the father at around about the same time. Both eggs – or ova – then begin to divide and develop at about the same rate. They can be the same sex or they can be brother and sister and they will look as similar as any other brother and sister – they just happen to share the same womb for nine months.

Identical twins are a different kettle of fish. A single ovum is fertilized by a single spermatozoon. This, by a freak of nature, doubles and then separates into two separate embryos sharing parts of the same foetal membrane. These identical embryos grow entwined and bonded by this extraordinary and still hardly understood oddity in human development.

* * *

When I first altered my career course from illustrator to photographer, *Traveller* magazine sent me on a commission to photograph an article celebrating Greek Orthodox Easter in Cephalonia. It was a beautiful piece by Louis de Bernières describing the slaughtering of goats, midnight processions of priests and ancient icons, feasts and firework fights in the streets. It must have been four or five years since John had died and I flew to Cephalonia and jumped in my Durell-esque taxi to the small fishing port of Fiskardo. From there it was a short boat ride to Ithaca, Homer's home for Odysseus. An hour's walk along the deserted seafront of Vathy and I arrived at my little pension. It was stunning, a deep Tuscan yellow, clad in bougainvillea, with deep green wrought-iron chairs looking out over the blue Ionian Sea.

When John was twenty years old he travelled out to Paros alone, his first time away by himself, accompanied only by his Tolkien and an old scouting tent. Worried sick that he hadn't called to catch up on cricket scores (a twice-a-week habit) or written a beautifully illustrated postcard (a once-a-week habit), I travelled to Paros to find him. Twenty-four hours later I discovered him reading in his tent near Agios Kokus, malnourished, dehydrated, suffering migraines and tearful. After tea and cuddles and a good souvlaki or two he quietly buried his head in his hands and made me solemnly promise to 'never go travelling on my own'.

Now here I was, on my own, unlocking the door to my room all these years later. I threw my camera bag and notebooks all over the bed and sat quietly for a few moments. I moved to the wicker chair in the corner, then I moved to the stool by the window. I didn't know what to do. I didn't know where to sit, and I didn't know how to act. I remembered my promise to John and it dawned on me I was about to spend my first night alone, not only since John had died, but since we had been conceived.

John and I loved each other immensely, immeasurably, but I probably only appreciated how immense this love was once he was gone. In the unreal, unbelievable silence that followed his dying, dawned the unimaginable truth that he, who was the wiser, the more talented one, and my leader by ten important minutes, was gone. I was in the state most people are in, for the first time since conception and cellular division: a singleton.

It's impossible to quantify love until you are so deeply 'in love'; then the all-encompassing feeling is of limitless joy, unity and calm. My love for John was different still. He would drive me mad. Sometimes he'd get so angry with me he'd ignore me for days and I would lie crying in my bedroom, despairing of his apparent cruelty.

Personally, I rarely show anger; I don't swear and I don't lose my temper. I'm always good cop to someone else's bad cop. I don't really dislike, I certainly don't hate, I am needy and I hurt easily. In the last years of John's life this was one of the few ways that we differed. It was years later that I discovered that many of his tempers and mood swings were caused by pressure on the brain from the tumour slowly developing in the centre of it. Those days when I was exiled to the 'Coventry' of my bedroom seem like such a wasted time now.

Our father was the quintessential gentleman, beautifully dressed, mild of temper and impeccably mannered. He retired many years before my mother, but would always put on a tie and shave and groom for my mother's return from the surgery. John would, invariably, get up from dinner before cheese or dessert and ask to be excused, much to my father's disappointment.

As he left the room, he would say, without fail, 'But Papa, life is so short.'

As ever, he was right.

Friday 12 January

Cheam, Surrey

I spend the morning with Mother (Mutti, la Mere, Dr Jean). Such an extraordinary and formidable woman who has saved so many lives, including the resuscitation of her own husband and her own daughter Jean-Marian, as well as her own granddaughter, after they suffered pyrexial convulsions.

We lived in a house called The Beeches, in Carshalton Beeches, Surrey. My mother had a GP practice nearby, and my father was a stockbroker in the city. Growing up, beside the phone in the hallway was a lump of wood, loosely carved into the shape of a truncheon. If my sister had 'one of her episodes', often caused by the slightest raise in body temperature, John was to run to the phone, dial for an ambulance then run several doors down to our kind artist neighbour Mr Frank's house and bang as hard as he could on his heavy oak door. Mr Frank would know what to do. The first time Jean-Marian had one of these convulsions and we made the run, my mother kept her alive with mouth-to-mouth and heart massage until the ambulance arrived, while John and I ate leisurely scones and lemonade with Mr Frank.

Father (a.k.a Papa, Padré, Eric, Eggit, Farter) used to take John and I in his little Aston Martin to Nonsuch Palace, very near where Mother lives now. Behind a long walled garden of Henry VIII's last pleasure palace there was a small enclosure of the most beautiful peacocks. John and I would run as fast as we could to see them, weaving, pretending to be Spitfires strafing the arboretums, and stare agog at their majestic beauty. Father used to delight in telling me stories about them, stories of immortality and royalty, but we didn't really listen. I still often dream of our running up and down the avenues of trees in Nonsuch Park.

Mr Frank once gave my parents a painting of the walled garden of Nonsuch. From afar it was a beautiful, if slightly naïve, oil of the arched entrance into the garden. On closer inspection there are two little boys, in full-tilt charge, both in blue and white sailor's uniforms. One (me), wearing my little blue and white peaked sailor's hat, and the other (John), wearing my father's red wartime beret with yellow piping and two shiny brass buttons.

Saturday 13 January

The plum tree at The Beeches, Carshalton Beeches

I have many memories of us running, charging, chasing, flying through the air on our wooden 'shuggy boat' – a swing Father built from wood that could seat four of us. It was a beautiful soft blue and would swing so high from the old plum tree at the bottom of the garden that I'm sure the childhood shrieks could be heard for miles. John and I would spend hours in that plum tree, knees grazed from its rough bark. We would pick overripe plums and catapult them over into the neighbouring tennis court, the players looking to the air to spy which bird had dropped them. Luckily our immediate neighbours, the Mugglestones, had an old dovecote so they were usually falsely accused. But we were once spotted by a fat, bald man with an extraordinarily powerful serve for someone who looked so unfit. He shouted at us up in our tree, not as invisible as we thought, and called us 'a pair of wankers'.

I asked my father what that meant. He said he didn't know, but was later heard to shout at the television during a news item about Enoch Powell: 'We fought the war against wankers like him!' Amazingly, for us, my mother did know what it meant and none of us uttered it again. Well, not in front of my mother.

15/16 October 1987 was the night of 'the Great Storm'. It was also the night John suffered his bout of meningitis, and was rushed from Oncology to the neurology unit at another hospital. That night I sat in the front window of our home, watching the giant beech trees creak and groan and sway like never before. We'd been angry the week before that the tree surgeons had trimmed the trees back so violently, however it was the pruning that saved them that night; where they bent and twisted they could have broken. I couldn't sleep for worry. Earlier, John was barely awake when I saw him, but was responding to my touch, so I think he could feel that I had been there.

Sadly, the ancient plum tree did not survive the Great Storm. It came down with an almighty crash, destroying the path, our old sandpit and the neighbours' fence. I never did tell John.

That plum tree gave us an annual harvest of fresh red and orange plums, making several jars of plum jam to stir into our semolina and rice pudding. Its wasps would sting us regularly, its bark would graze us and its blossom would grace our dining table. Its roots would hide our Action Men in battle, its branches hold our swings, our tree house and our blue 'shuggy boat' swing. That tree held many a secret and was, to us, the best tree in the world.

Sunday 14 January

Marmalade Cake

Sitting with my mother yesterday has delivered me into a deep sadness. Growing up in London and Surrey, she was the hardest-working mother I had ever come across – a full-time general practitioner with over 4,000 patients at a time when 'on call' meant she was essentially almost always working. If not working, she was always rushing. Now, suffering from osteoporosis and poor circulation, she has just been diagnosed with breast cancer at the age of eighty-seven. She sits calmly in her corner chair, as I sit in mine, uncomplaining and chirpy, as usual covering subjects as diverse as marmalade cake, Aristotle, the use of mnemonics in the teaching of anatomy, and the feeding habits of birds – 'her tits on their nuts'. We did chuckle.

While watching a pair of blackbirds, we remembered that at The Beeches there was a blackbird that liked to follow John as he helped Father water the garden. I preferred the job of trying to clean Father's garden shed, which was an impressive Victorian mock-Tudor folly filled with a Harry Potter-esque collection of tools, machinery, bicycles, birds' nests and bats, all under a thick layer of dust. I loved the smell, a mixture of Father's cigars, oil paints and wood shavings. The little mullioned windows looked out from under the old plum tree, past the greenhouse, to the garden beyond. In that perpetual summer of our youth I can see John now, watering the tomatoes with Father looking on, pulling on one of his coconut-smelling pipes. I can't remember why, but John gave the blackbird the name Marmalade Cake. Maybe he fed the bird some; neither of us could abide peel in cakes.

The one time I managed to get John home from hospital during the three months of his illness, I walked him out to the garden and sat him in a chair under the purple hazelnut tree. It was probably the most serene moment of his illness and a rare moment of calm. Amazingly, while I was inside making him a pot of tea, Marmalade Cake paid him a visit, bringing a smile to his face. It was his last visit home.

Tuesday 16 January

Shooting Rachel Khoo's new cookbook in northern Sweden

It's so eerily quiet here. I'm in Sweden, after a 3a.m. alarm call and a journey through snow-filled landscapes of shades of grey. Sky, trees and more trees, all grey, framed by lakes of pure snow white. The silence here is deafening and I really don't like it. I miss the birdsong of my youth.

John and I grew from shared womb to shared birth to shared cot and pram and bed, to bunk beds, and eventually separation in twin beds and then the big move to separate bedrooms. This is when my separation anxiety took hold and the nights went from calm, unbroken sleep to nights of restlessness, dreams and often nightmares and fearful awakenings. I often dream now of wandering into Johnny's room at the end of the corridor, knowing that he is no longer alive, but wanting to visit. I open his door to find the shape of his curled body beneath his duvet and I feel such joy as I notice the movements of his breathing and realize that he is not dead after all. Of course, I'm always mistaken. Often he is like a pale shadow of himself and when I reach out to touch him he is not solid and my hand passes through him. Sometimes he turns and looks at me, terribly sad and grey, and he tells me he still has a headache and it won't go away. I always cry; deep sobs but without a sound, though I am desperate for my mother to hear me and come and comfort me.

When I was first moved to my own room I'd sometimes try and crawl as quietly as possible into his bed. He wasn't, by then, the most receptive cuddler – that extra ten minutes of age was beginning to kick in: 'I'm older and wiser, you are but a small child so give me some space.' Dejected, I would stumble back to the other end of the corridor and stealthily sneak in next to my mother, the warmth of her body giving me the comfort I yearned for. She would sleep in the enormous matrimonial bed far from my father's slumbering form, nearer to the phone so as to cut off any 'on-call emergencies' before they awoke him.

I wouldn't really sleep, but would lie, perfectly straight, awake but content, until the first sign of morning when I would quietly sneak back into my bed. I did this for years, until I was gently persuaded that maybe I was a little old to share my parents' bed. Eventually I replaced them with a little blue and silver transistor radio, tuned in to Radio Caroline or Radio Luxembourg, which accompanied me until morn. There I would await the first tweet and twitter of morning. The following chatter of songbirds at break of dawn would bring me such an overwhelming sense of serenity, I could finally relax. The night was over and a new day had dawned.

Birdsong. There is none here. What a deafening darkness. Not even a whisper of the wind in the bulrushes by the lake, just ice, snow and bone-aching coldness.

Wednesday 17 January

A night in my cabin on the lake, endless quietness and blackness, from afternoon to mid-morning. The only light seems to be a blueish glow from the snow and the only sound the crunch of two passing deer in the wee hours. It is too much for me. Madness seems to grip me easily in the night, like a fever without a fever, along with a terrible loneliness and paranoia. I've grabbed a lift into Stockholm and the cackle of a group of hyperactive girls next to me is somehow better than that aching quietness.

For many years the upstairs corridor at The Beeches was our playground. There were three pieces of furniture there: a large old Victorian mirror, a chest of drawers and, best of all, my father's wonderfully grand gentleman's armoire, which was a cavern of sartorial elegance. It was full of many small drawers, like you'd find in a gentlemen's tailors. One for underwear, one for handkerchiefs, one for socks and so on, all bearing his initials, E. J. L. It smelt of hair tonics, eau-de-cologne and mothballs and there was a rail on the inside door for ties. He must have had a hundred: stock-exchange ties, club ties, ties with pheasants, planes, boats, none gaudy of colour or kipper of shape, all elegant and narrow and stylish. Racks of suits, morning suits, walk-in-the-city suits, lounge suits, even desert suits. But it was the elegantly smooth-opening drawers that held the most attention, smelling of cherry wood and age. The bottom drawer was a small boy's nirvana; it contained my father's medals in a beautiful moss-green velvet box, along with letters, mementos, a bullet, a star-shaped brooch, a small box of poison with ancient Chinese calligraphy, and two pistols, one ancient and musket-like, and one newer and shooting-at-Germans-like.

Thursday 18 January

Flying home from snowbound Stockholm to London,
exhausted, creatively replenished, sad but inspired

At least once a week there would be a call from one of us to 'Swap Shop'. My sister Jean-Marian, menace little brother Ian, John and I would congregate in the middle of the hall with an army of swappable items, a Tonka for some crayons, a puzzle for a yo-yo. Jean-Marie always cried because no one wanted doll's clothing. John would often instigate a game of 'car-hee', a version of 'It' using Matchbox cars. The skill was in not zooming the car too fast and putting pressure on the wheels to get an element of curve to the propulsion. Under the armoire legs was the best place and at the time it felt pretty damn skilful. Alas these games often ended in tears, particularly for the younger ones, who always wanted to use Tonkas (too big) and not Matchbox cars (more skill).

The corridor also became the 'cricket pitch'. As a child, when lightness came, slowly but surely, I would hear the patter of Johnny's slippers on carpet as he ran, pretending to be Dennis Lillee, bowling a pair of tucked-together socks at my head, waking me for a day of mischief and play.

If you stood in Jean-Marian's room, much to her chagrin, you got quite a decent run-up to bowl full tilt and full toss at the wicket marked on brother Ian's door. Father's silky socks, four of them, rolled up inside each other, made the perfect soft cricket ball, especially for 'bodyline' bowling tactics (aimed at the head). Over the wardrobe was a six, down the stairs was six and out, worth it for the fun of it. Into my room was a four, John's a six, Jean-Marian's – which meant launching a shot over the advancing bowler's head – was also six and out. Ian could rarely play for more than ten minutes without crying off to Mother with whimpers of 'not out', and as a result was banned from what we came to call a game of 'sockit'.

Father, who would sit quietly on the loo for an hour or two's peace, reading *Asterix* or *Tintin* (you could hear the chuckles, but no flush) would occasionally sit with the toilet door slightly open. He never batted an eyelid as he watched his rolled-up silk socks fly first one way, then the other, with calls of 'Catch it!' or 'Howzat!'

Today, while walking in the snow in Stockholm I saw the most beautiful pair of jays. Such gorgeous plumage, the flash of blue wing vibrant against the skeletal greys of the snow-laden woods.

Growing up we had the most wonderful Mrs Tiggy-Winkle of a nanny called Molly Wrigglesworth. Molly was from County Durham, about four feet tall, and possibly one of the most generous, loving women ever born. I don't think she ever had a boyfriend; she treated us as her family and had been present for not only our four births, but also the birth of my mother. With Father working as a broker in the City and Mother a full-time GP, it was often Molly's task to keep us dressed, fed and bathed. We loved Molly. When John was in his twenties and working as a designer in Thames Ditton she would often bake one of her famously tasty apple pies and bike it to him at work. Every one of our friends knew and loved Molly. When we were sick she nursed us, when we were stressed she calmed us. She was four feet of unflappability.

Molly was with me the day my mother called, early on 11 November, to tell me that John had just died. Poor Molly, she was shaking like a leaf in autumn and shocked to her core. We held on to each other, too uncomprehending to cry. Molly watched sadly as my world fell apart in front of her eyes. Poor Molly Wrigglesworth of County Durham, she never really recovered.

Friday 19 January

The Mews

> 'Piglet sidled up to Pooh from behind. "Pooh,"
>   he whispered.
> "Yes Piglet?"
> "Nothing," said Piglet, taking Pooh's paw,
> "I just wanted to be sure of you."'
> —A. A. MILNE, THE HOUSE AT POOH CORNER, 1928

I sometimes wonder if identical twins remember more of early life than singletons. As the two little identical beings grow in the womb, so they begin to communicate with each other, forming the unbreakable bond of twinhood, sharing everything from breathing space to their mother's heart. If I look at my skin closely enough in the mirror, I can see crescent-shaped scars. Apparently John used to hold onto my face with both hands, so tight that he drew blood. I didn't reciprocate but neither did I cry, I accepted his hold on me and now feel glad that these small scars of babyhood haven't faded away.

One of my earliest memories was from our birthday on 31 October 1967. The image is as clear as crystal: us on the deck of a ship, with our parents, just off Southampton Sound. We were waving our handkerchiefs at the passengers on the deck of the RMS *Queen Mary* as she sailed off on her last voyage to California. I was so upset when my favourite little polka-dot handkerchief fluttered from my tiny grip and disappeared into the green-blue wake of the departing liner. Johnny was so upset for me that he dropped his too, so that they could be together forever. A red polka-dot and a blue polka-dot hankie, tossed by the swell. We watched as they got smaller and smaller, no longer upset by our loss. We had just turned four years old.

Sunday 21 January

Gidleigh Park, Devon

Shooting today at Gidleigh Park, I arose early and wandered down through the early-morning mist to the banks of the river Teign rushing in full spate through the grounds. It's a damp, messy wonderland of ponds, rooks, pools and waterfalls. Just me and a pair of wrens, every moss and blade and bare branch dripping with dew, so peaceful, even with the crashing of water over stone. I wanted to lie there today, needing some time to think. Concerned my client might fear for my sanity, I followed the wrens back up to the main house for tea and crumpets; a comfort of sorts.

Back home now at the Mews, I'm sitting in my little ship's bunk room, what I call my 'Cabinet of Curiosities'. It's a deeply personal room that I share only with Ange, my darling wife of just over a year, and Paros and Pascale, my children – now young adults. It's an unconsciously curated jumble of memories and tokens and mementos of my life, and particularly of my life with John.

Obviously there are photos from childhood to adulthood. Plus paintings, drawings, beachcombed shells, rocks, cards, clay pipes, statuettes, sketchbooks and all manner of eclectic things, somehow fitting together in a visual tableau of our lives. What is lovely now is adding in the 'new' trinkets. A Koran pencil from Morocco, a metal blue tit from a midsummer walk in Kew, drawings by Paros and Pascale. My love of Ange has somehow broken the 'spell' that this was an untouchable shrine, and now it feels so much brighter and more positive. As does the Mews. A breath of fresh air has wafted through, brightening every nook and corner and cranny.

Monday 22 January

The Mews

I finished my shoot early today and hopped in a taxi to visit my mother. She was frail and tired but chirpy as I held her by the shoulders to kiss each paper-thin cheek. She seems so petite, her body bending backwards as if being pushed forward, then back and then forward again, the fragile 'S' shape. She's been sitting up in her library, sorting and collating old family photographs to make a collage of memories for my little brother's fiftieth birthday. She's frustrated she can't find his graduation photos, but he's graduated so many times I find a back-up shot that works. She smiles at the memories, so proud of Ian and his medical achievements; like mother, like son. Ian was a medical student of twenty-one when John died and the circumstances of John's death nearly made him abandon his studies. John, the doctor's son, was killed by a medical error. In hindsight, it is extraordinary that Ian carried on.

Ian called me one Sunday night and we spoke for hours about taking each day as it comes, slowly but surely. He is living proof of what my mother also demonstrated over and over again, that there are some truly wonderful and caring doctors out there for whom the Hippocratic oath is solemn and binding, standards that seemed to have been forgotten in the careless treatment of John.

I'm going to sit in the library over the weekend and look again at some of her albums. There were a few images of John and me that I hadn't seen before, particularly through our early teens, when 'being different' seemed so desperately important to us both. And such lovely pictures, square and black and white, shot on an old twin Yashica by Father. Some are with the camera turned on himself, and these are mostly slightly out of focus; it was a beast to focus. He looks so suave, beautifully dressed, the same age as I am now, but in the blurriness of time seeming somehow younger and yet more mature. Wedding pictures of him and Mother in his old Aston Martin outside Carlisle Cathedral; early pictures of him, chuffed to bits, with a twin on each knee; us in our cots on our balcony in Knightsbridge; the 'leaving hospital' shots of Mother and Father and two little boys, first with Jean-Marian and then Ian. Fifty years ago this coming weekend. In among the pile was a tiny contact shot of Ian laughing, age six or seven, head thrown back, black t-shirt against a pure white sandy beach. I remember this shot so well, but it's the first time I've seen it in over forty years. It was the first picture I ever took with my new Olympus Trip, the one my father gave me to pique my interest in photography. Thankfully it worked.

The Ponds

Miserable January day, wet, windy and foul, photographing food and interior at Patron, a cool French bistro and bar in Kentish Town with a wonderfully upbeat and excitable team of Frenchies from Brittany or Provence. My spirits are lifted – got nearly 1,500 shots, always a good sign.

As I was coming back from Mother's in Cheam last night I passed Carshalton Beeches, close to our old home. I asked the cabbie, a local chap, not to go past The Beeches itself. (I haven't passed it since John died.) I did, though, pass the Ponds for the first time in over twenty years.

The Ponds, along with Nonsuch Palace, were one of our early playgrounds. I don't really remember moving down from London, but I do remember John and me paddling around the Ponds in our baggy pants, waving our nets through the lavender to try to catch red admirals, or poking them under the lily pads to catch sticklebacks and tadpoles to hurry to an early airless grave in our jam jars. There is a grainy but beautiful film of John and I feeding the ducks on Carshalton Ponds, shot on my father's Super 8 camera. Channel 4 used the film in a documentary called *Identical Twins* that filmmaker Rebecca Frayn made a while ago and, though painful to watch, it was as fascinating as it was heartbreaking. In films and pictures, before we were eight or nine, I have no idea which one of us is which.

Wednesday 24 January

The Mews

Missing my father today. He died several years before John. It's hard to admit, but it was possibly best he didn't witness the terrible suffering

John went through. My father was so different, so sensitive – his first-borns were his *raison d'être*, his life. He had been a happy enough bachelor at forty-nine, living a life of fast cars, parties and fine wines in Knightsbridge, but he had missed out on love. He worked hard as a stockbroker and raced his Aston Martin at the weekend, but while his brother Patrick and cousin Derek married young model beauties, he was shy among women.

At a party one night in Knightsbridge he spied a beautiful and enigmatic young doctor, Jean, on her first trip to London from Carlisle. She was so shy that she spent the evening playing the baby grand rather than talking to the glamorous Chelsea folk. My father was smitten at first sight and, no doubt bolstered by a champagne or two, he slipped a note into her music, proposing to her, asking for her hand in marriage. My mother was far too shy and shocked to even acknowledge the presence of what was, to her, obviously a joke.

But it wasn't. He was in love, and the following Friday he jumped into his car and sped up north to Carlisle. Through my godmother Jane he discovered that my mother was a doctor covering the Northern Lakes in Brampton, and she lived, oh so romantically, in a tiny wing of Naworth Castle. Father drove to the house, slept fitfully in the car, and waited for her to rise. When she came down in the morning to fetch her milk, there he was, milk in hand, leaning against his little Aston. I can't imagine how nervous he must have been. They married several months later in Carlisle Cathedral, only the hundredth couple to ever do so. My mother, to 'prove her virtue', had to live in the Cathedral close with the Dean's family for a month before the big day.

We were born soon after, identical twins, one for each of his knees. As he would have said, he was 'chuffed'.

* * *

Today, going through the papers, I came across an old copy of the *News of the World*. Ironic that the paper John so hated would be the only one brave enough to state the truth. The headline reads:

DOC'S BLUNDER KILLS BOY CURED OF CANCER

followed in bold type by

Brave John is injected with massive overdose

I know, I was there.

* * *

In my work diary I see I have a meeting at 2p.m. at Nucleus Design in Thames Ditton. John was a graphic designer at Nucleus, under his boss and mentor Peter Matthews, and I worked as an illustrator under the watchful eye of my twin. The building is now named after him: John Loftus House.

Arriving at Nucleus, I see not a lot has changed in twenty years. John's signature is still etched into the glass at the building's entrance: John Loftus House. The silver birch planted in his memory looks out over the graveyard of the beautiful Norman church, nearly thirty feet high, bare of leaves but strong and tall. My legs felt heavy on the steps and I spent a few minutes walking through the graveyard, round to the Thames. John was so happy at Nucleus. He attended Kingston Art College and studied Graphic Design and was offered several great jobs at his degree show, but it was Nucleus that won him over. His boss, Peter Matthews, became one of his dearest friends.

For lone identical twins there is often a complex feeling of deep loneliness, but also an air of unease and unsettlement. It's akin to a feeling of being watched, but not in a comforting way. I felt it here by the water. Today I felt uneasy and in need of home.

From *Twins, Triplets and More,* a book by Dr Elizabeth Bryan – a consultant paediatrician known as the 'pioneer of twin studies'. She's also the person who introduced me to my best friend, Tim. Here she is describing my experience:

For an identical twin the constant reminder in himself of his twin may be deeply painful. One young man [me] whose identical twin had died, described the agony of his daily shave – 'looking at my twin'. Three years [since we spoke] and it was still the most painful part of the day.

Early adulthood seems to be a particularly difficult time to lose a twin. Many such twins will not have yet embarked on independent lives. Some may be starting careers. One identical twin in his early twenties had shared an art and design studio [John's bedroom] with his brother. Although their styles differed, they were in harmony with each other and had sometimes done joint designs. More importantly, they had a constant source of companionship, under-standing, stimulation and encouragement. For this young man, as for many, his twin was not only his closest relative but also his best friend, and the bereavement doubly hard to bear.

Thursday 25 January

The Mews

Yesterday's trip down to Johnny's old office was a more profoundly moving experience than I had expected. His office was unchanged; the same pictures on the wall, even a couple of the same staff members sitting at the same desks. I spotted their heads nervously peering around at me as I sat awaiting Peter. Some of the wine labels John and I had worked on still adorned the shelves; illustrations by me, typography hand-painted by John.

I found a postcard yesterday, dated 27 May 1981, Parikia, Paros. John wishes our mother a happy birthday, then goes on:

> It's so nice to see Greece without all the tourists, when the sun isn't as hot as when the islands are greener. All the wild flowers are out on the hills. Wamfi's [his girlfriend Samantha] leg looks like the Battle of the Somme (mozzies?) and my back looks like the Russian Flag. (Sun?) Jane's giving us the room on the cheap and is very jolly as usual, looks forward to seeing David and Peter [Hornsey]. David, I hope working for Nucleus is just as good and easy as when I am there. Give my love to the Crates [my sister's married name] and the dustbins, hee hee, and Ian and anyone else. Lots of love to Mum, see you all soon, xx John and Wamfi
>
> P.S. David, you can buy 'The Independent'! Good news about the cricket!!

It's strange to think how worried he was about me working at Nucleus without him. We always worried about each other. Separation anxiety; I guess mine is somehow a permanent form of that now. He knew that without him there to watch over me at my drawing board I wouldn't be doing as good a job as if he was there, and he was right, I wasn't. It's good to read Wamfi's name again, I think about her often, but haven't seen her for over a decade. Now married with children and living in the Kent countryside with the loving husband she met a couple of years after John died, she was for a long time a shadow of her former self, like a bird with broken wings. She eventually learned to fly again, thank goodness. Wamfi used to paint letters to look a bit like wood-block printing, but in watercolour, with little hearts and kisses painted inside the letters. She and John were the masters of illuminated letters to each other, and if you were lucky, to yourself. Sweet Samantha, they were perfectly suited and I am glad she is settled now and happy. When I saw her last she said she found it hard to remember great tracts of time, particularly towards the end. I found it rather upsetting to hear, but ultimately maybe it's a good thing. One of my most heartbreaking memories is of her holding John's hands at his bedside when he was no longer breathing, talking to him as if he was still alive, refusing to believe he was no longer with us. It's impossible to describe the gut-wrenching wretchedness of that moment. For the first time I understood the expression 'it's like having your heart ripped out.' Truly awful and heartbreaking.

Saturday 27 January

The Mews

I think it was around our fifteenth year that John and me began to dress differently. It coincided with my interest in punk music. John was listening to Simon and Garfunkel and I'd started listening to Siouxsie and the Banshees and it suddenly became very important to both of us that we had differences; not small ones but distinct, polar opposites. This remained so for all of the rest of our short lives together.

I'm looking at a photo now of Johnny wearing a vintage American short-sleeved shirt, bought from Kensington Market in the vintage surplus store where all the punks used to buy their old army uniforms. It cost £8. I know, it was mine. He's wearing it on holiday in southern Ireland, with Samantha. I would have been furious if I had known, but I was probably wearing the greyish-blue handmade shirt he bought in Camden Market, and he would have been a lot angrier than me! Funny now, thinking back. We were convinced that we were so different but then kept nicking each other's clothes whenever we could.

When filmmaker Rebecca Frayn was making her Channel 4 documentary about identical twins, she asked me several times if I would agree to appear. Rebecca was mum to identical twin babies, Jack and Finn, and was fascinated by the unbreakable bond of identical twins. After some gentle cajoling I agreed, because I was persuaded that appearing could potentially help other sole surviving twins. And to this day she has become one of my dearest friends.

I can barely remember what I said or what the team filmed, and I couldn't finish watching it. It felt like I was watching not me, but John's ghost. I had had no idea that while I was concentrating on our differences in taste, in clothing and art and music, everything else – our mannerisms, our turns of phrase, our gesticulations, the minutiae of facial expressions, a faint lisp here, a slight slope of the shoulders there – was identical. Until I saw the programme, I had absolutely no idea how truly alike we were.

Monday 28 January

On the train to Bodmin Parkway, Cornwall

Contemplating over the last few days, I'm sad to admit that I have, in recent years, distanced myself somewhat from my brother and sister and nieces. I can't, at the moment, fully explain why, but there does seem to be a yawning gap between us, a gap that shows no sign of narrowing. My bond to my mother is still strong, lovingly intense and unbreakable, but since John died, Jean-Marian and Ian and me seem to have drifted further and further apart. Deep down something feels gravely wrong. I think it may come from an unaired belief that the wrong twin died. It might sound extreme, but during the hours and days following John's death, when emotions were running so high, I was very aware that some of John's friends thought this way. John was the elder, John was the more talented, John didn't really drink. John was the more studious, and John took fewer risks.

Tuesday 30 January

Bodmin, Cornwall

Bodmin Parkway station is wonderfully caught in a time warp, with old signal box houses, The Signal Box Café and posters advertising coastal steam-train services and 'love-ins' at the local owl sanctuary. The express leaves Bodmin, trundles over coastal inlets and rolling hills to Plymouth and, after twenty minutes of four seasons' worth of sunshine, showers, rainstorms and hailstorms, enters a long tunnel to emerge moments later bathed in blinding sunshine, wind-smoothed and bulbous cloud formations and a turbulent, aqua-blue sea crashing against rocky beaches. I always try to snatch a pic on my phone, but that fraction of a second delay between pressing the button and capturing the picture means that I never 'get the pic'. Nowadays I don't even try, I just sit back and enjoy the ever-changing spectacle.

John loved trains and had a really beautiful Hornby train set in his youth. He'd make trees and hills out of moss, and paint every detail from station master to signal box. His locomotive was lovely, of 'OO' gauge I seem to remember, much akin to the Flying Scotsman. We once travelled together up to Scotland on a sleeper and he brought his trainspotters' handbook with him. I refused to allow him to get his *i-SPY on a Train Journey* book out, I was so embarrassed. I think I was probably quite mean. Later that night, unable to sleep in our juddering bunks, we took turns to stick our heads out the window into the cold and inky darkness, daring each other to keep them out longer and longer. The game ended when someone further up ahead flushed the loo. If you've never been hit by a lukewarm mixture of someone else's high-speed urine and poop in the mouth and nose and eyes, I promise you that it's something that comes back to haunt you in later life. John thought it was the most hilarious thing he had ever witnessed! He named the train The Flying Shitstorm. My pyjamas never recovered; I sealed them tightly in a plastic bag, left them in the bottom of my rucksack and promptly forgot about them. It was my poor mother who released them from their fermented and foul-stinking wrapping, crusty and mouldy, three weeks later, on our return home.

Wednesday 31 January

The Mews

I'm at home with my dear wife Ange, flu-bound and feverish, and as someone who is rarely ill, frustrated and bored. 'Windmills of Your Mind' is playing on Spotify, the Terry Hall's The Colourfield version that John loved so much and that Ange and I played at our wedding. John chose it as a song to animate while studying design at Kingston School of Art. He sat up all night at his trestle table, painting what were then called 'cells' – painted layers on clear acetate that are then layered over each other to create a subtle moving image. It took over a month to create a couple of minutes of film of a little boy in a hot-air balloon, sailing over a toytown scene of bubbles and clocks and balloons and waterwheels. I haven't been able to watch Johnny's film, but I can listen to the song now because I can relate it to much happier memories. I still have all of the original cells, beautifully painted in block colour gouache, meticulously precise. I now realize that the boy in the balloon, sailing across the dreamscape, is John. He painted himself. I know it's him and not me because he's wearing the red cap, not the blue.

Thursday 1 February

Shooting Clarence Court eggs at the Mews

Lovely evening with my daughter Pascale and one of her friends. They are free in their openness and questioning, including ones about 'Uncle Johnny'. It is fascinating how little my children, Paros and Pascale, really know about my twin. It saddens me that Johnny will never meet them and they will never meet him.

Saturday 3 February

Flight to Mumbai

A lingering headache behind my eyes, I'm on a flight watching a blood-red sun setting over the blue, snow-capped Zagros Mountains, halfway between Baghdad and Tehran. Apparently it's −73°C outside and the air is clear and dark. Every little town in the valleys and hills seems to have a pyre burning, forming a vivid pattern as far as the eye can see. They must be enormous to burn so very bright.

My destination is Mumbai to shoot the lovely food writer Meera Sodha with art director John Hamilton in the markets and bazaars of the city. I'm always slightly nervous flying to a city I've never been to before, particularly so far from home. Carrying a camera can single you out for rough treatment and I've had my unfair share of scrapes. Terrifyingly, in Morocco I was accused of being a Tunisian spy and in New Orleans I had my head slammed into a silver burger van; my beloved camera punched from my smarting eyes and stamped into pieces. The New Orleans police force not only witnessed the beating, they ignored it, later claiming that if they had intervened I would probably have been shot. Ironically, recovering from the concussion, I was actually shot two days later by a huntsman as I tried to photograph him shooting an alligator in the head. Getting a little too close to the action, he fired a small Colt pistol at an alligator trying to untangle itself from a chicken-trap. The bullet ricocheted off the critter's skull, scraping across the top of my head. I looked down to see my favourite white shirt sprayed with blood and turned to see his stunned-looking face: 'I think you might have shot me!'

* * *

Now flying over Muscat, just the Indian Ocean left to cross – an inky darkness outside. My head pounds and I break out the Solpadeine (or 'Solps' as we'd call them), thinking to myself that I must work on kicking my painkiller habit. It's hard after so many years. Johnny suffered awful headaches that would send him under his duvet for hours. Of course, his last terrible headache was the one from which he wouldn't recover. I remember a trip he had taken with his first girlfriend, Liz, to Florida. They must have been about seventeen. He'd suffered a terrible, crippling migraine that lasted several days. When John had his operation, years later, the surgeons found some dried blood on his brain, which, extraordinarily, they had been able to date to that holiday in Florida. He had suffered a brain haemorrhage, unbeknownst to anyone, probably caused by a slowly growing malevolence in the centre of his brain. He must have been in so much pain. It's a shame, in a way, that he met it with his normal brave stoicism and didn't make more fuss – a calm trait inherited from our mother.

Sunday 4 February

In Mumbai watching the Eagles soar

3p.m. arrival at the hotel with a 6a.m. call time – hells bells! I'm in Mumbai shooting the Sassoon Docks, which proved to be as terrifying as predicted. Within three minutes I am threatened with a severe beating, being thrown into the sea and the destruction of my new Leica. Located on a filthy promontory jutting into an equally rancid-looking sea, the smell is undeniably foul. Rats scurry about freely in the filth as boatloads of fish are auctioned and quite literally fought over by some of the fiercest and most menacing women I have ever come across. Photography is not encouraged since the Mumbai terrorist attacks but I manage a few shots before being forced to give up by the sheer stinking crush of it all, the noise, the chaos, and the outright hostility. Of course my dear art director, who remains 'ashore', immediately says 'I hope you got the shots'.

The filth is hard to cope with. This morning I photographed the early newspaper sorters at Victoria station. Everyone in India still seems to read a paper and there are so many dialects and languages. The editions all arrive by train, and are then thrown onto the side of the road opposite the station. Somehow, through the chaos and the darkness, they are sorted and bundled and dispatched to their destinations, by overloaded bicycles or by foot.

Whole families openly sleep in the gutters, millions of commuters every day stepping over and past them. I find it hard. Why them, not me? Although I am staying at possibly the grandest old hotel, my job over these few days is to photograph the 'real' workers of new Mumbai – the tiffin wallahs, the paper wallahs, the street-food vendors, the fishermen and women, the flower and vegetable stall holders. All live in utter, abject poverty. Just the price of my camera alone makes me feel wracked with guilt.

I wonder what Johnny would think. He was on my mind a lot today as I journeyed to one of the ancient Koli fishing villages that jut out like ugly crab pincers into the grey murk of Bombay's waters. As I walked through the slum-like alleyways out to where they sort the fish and repair the boats, I was reminded of a drawing I have of Johnny's of Paros, Naousa, of the old Kaiki boatyard. I wonder if it still exists. I will go there to draw this summer. Knowing John, he would have produced beauty even out of the horror, the privilege of the artist. Sadly for my client, hard as I try today, the camera does not lie easily.

Wednesday 7 and Thursday 8 February

2.20a.m. flight from Mumbai to London

Ange's face waiting for me at the Mews brings an overwhelming feeling of love and relief. Home feels good. Seeing the horrors of Mumbai has left me hollow and dry. Witnessing the injustices, the corruption and the extraordinary gap between rich and poor has left a truly foul stench in my mouth. Here I am, writing about my own demons and loves, and the process of trying to access some sort of acceptance and understanding of what I have been through, and it now seems like a perverse indulgence, a privilege. Yesterday I was stepping over distressed and undernourished babies and parents and grandparents, literally living in the gutters of the fastest-growing city on earth. I try never to swear, but it is quite simply fucked up!

Saturday 10 February

Riad of the Storks, Marrakech

Here in Marrakech to shoot a Moroccan cookbook, I have arrived at the Riad of the Storks under the walls of the El Badi Palace where storks perch precariously upon an intricate nest of jungle-like constructions. At the dawn's call to prayer they tilt their beaks and delicately rearrange enormous high-rise nests that lean impossibly exposed. Hawks constantly circle the nesting pairs, I assume looking for egg-stealing opportunities. I'm instantly missing home.

As I left early this morning I grabbed a handful of papers. One of them is a testimony of the sequence of events that led up to 11 November 1987, written in legalese. As the year progresses and anniversaries (operation, recovery, birthday, injection, sickness and death) come and go, I want to approach those moments conscious of their full emotional impact on me. I've only read this document once, soon after the coroner's controversial handling of the case. A psychologist would probably say being hugely overtired and stressed is the wrong time to reread it, but I'm not sure there is ever a right time for these things.

The mosque's call to prayer has awoken the storks and they are a-clacking!

Sunday 11 February

This evening I walked past the Berber Market and round the city walls, past the Koutoubia Mosque and round to Riad El Fenn in the dying light of day. The roads were crammed with horse-drawn carriages, buses, motorbikes and cycles. Often when I walk in a city in the early evening, wherever I am in the world, I feel strangely detached from reality. If you've ever suffered déjà vu, you might understand the unreal and discombobulated state; almost like being tipsy without drinking. For many identical twins who have lived and worked together, as we did, the death of a twin can leave the surviving twin feeling so utterly bereft as to doubt whether they have the ability to ever function as a complete person. Many feel they have become half a person. Some are able to absorb the strengths of the lost twin and endeavour to become stronger as a result. I have done this to a limited extent, but mostly I have always felt a half-person, walking in the shadow of my lost brother. It's almost akin to an out-of-body experience, as if I'm somewhere else, watching myself walking through the overcrowded streets. One thing is clear, I don't feel that it is John watching over me.

John and I spent a great deal of time during our youth mucking about in the Lake District. Our parents loved it in Cumbria and we had many a *Swallows and Amazons*-style birthday in the Lakes. After John died I didn't venture out for a while, but Peter Hornsey, my oldest chum, persuaded me that a long, boozy weekend in the Lakes was just what I needed. We decided to walk from the banks of Wastwater at Wasdale Head, up the valley to climb Red Pike, one of the tallest Lakeland mountains. While everyone bundled into the pub after a long walk, I wandered over to St Olaf's Church, which is rumoured to be the smallest in England. I'd never been in, but knew that the graveyard, surrounded by beautiful yew trees, contained many a climber who had lost their lives in the surrounding fells and that the beams of the roof are made from the wood of Viking longboats. It seemed as good a place as any to get away from my friends for some peaceful reflection. The door was open and no one was within so I sat quietly at one of the pews in front. Prayer did not come to me and I no longer felt even an inkling of belief, but I sat there for a while thinking about the disastrous events of the past months.

As I sat there I felt a presence in the tiny church. I turned, but the heavy door was still closed behind me, and the nave was cold and silent. I rested my head again. I was desperately, overwhelmingly sad and broken. Within seconds I felt a presence, like a hand on either shoulder. Every hair on my body stood on end and I shivered violently. The pressure remained only for seconds but what initially felt so cold and terrifying ultimately became warm and comforting. It's the only time since his death that I sensed that maybe, just maybe, I had somehow felt the presence of John. Writing about it now, having never told a soul, it seems slightly fantastical and makes me wonder if it was my overemotional tiredness that conjured up this mythical moment. But I don't think so. John is buried with my father in a ghastly communal graveyard in Sutton. The place has no meaning to any of us, but it seems dying in London doesn't guarantee a space anywhere but the council cemetery. When my time eventually comes, maybe I'll make all my chums row me out onto the waters of Wastwater and scatter my ashes within full view of St Olaf's Church and its centuries-old yew trees.

Monday 12 February

Waking up to the ever-present 'clacking' call of the storks and my tiny, damp garret room bathed in a stained-glass yellow light, I romantically imagine myself as a real writer, a Hemingway or Dumas, working in conditions of relative discomfort.

For a long time after Johnny died I barely put pen to paper. The last thing John wrote was probably his birthday card to me. John was killed while we were opening our birthday presents and his last birthday card lies on the top drawer of an old desk on my houseboat, which is a kind of refuge for me. The drawer is filled with his small paintings, letters and postcards, and that last card.

After the operation on his tumour he found his sight was badly affected, slightly cross-eyed, and needed a lot of retraining. This upset him greatly and his tears upon opening his eyes are seared into my brain. His card to me reads very simply, but powerfully, as it's obviously written with his left hand. 'Dear David. Love Johny x, I. O. U. 1 prezzie.'

Even seeing it now, after all these years, tears me apart. The wobbly nature of each letter and the concentration and effort it must have taken to write it.

This was 31 October, our birthday. I had given John and Samantha a joint present of train tickets on the Orient Express to Venice, returning on Concorde, and had collaged a card with images of his toy trains and old Venetian postcards and stamps. The departure was booked for the following Easter, by which time the experts in the neurology unit believed he would be fully fit to travel again. He loved his present and was so happy. Easter didn't feel that far off in the grand scheme of things. Sadly, within eleven days he would be dead, cancer-free, but with a brain violently struggling under the effects of a fatal dose of the antibiotic gentamicin.

Thinking of that wobbly but carefully written birthday greeting reminds me of a moment at the breakfast table many years before. Bounding down the stairs we would lean forward, holding on to the banisters on both sides, attempting to get down while touching as few stairs as possible. Our record was five, but that day John, bragging about his all-important ten-minute age gap, somehow managed to complete the task in four. For the next hour I tried and tried to do the same, but failed, much to my dismay. Finally admitting defeat, I sat down for porridge and honey at the dining table. Facing John, I was immediately aware of a difference. I wasn't sure if it was his wry smile of superiority, but something was off. It was only when he went to butter his toast that I realized what was wrong. He was using his left hand, and dextrously so.

'Johnny boy, you are so not left-handed.'
'Oh Davy boy, I most certainly am.'
'Since when?'
'Since forever, born and bred.'

That teenage desire to be different must have meant hours and hours of training himself to be left-handed. Poignantly, the only time he ever needed that skill was upon our last birthday together, writing 'I. O. U. 1 prezzie'.

Tuesday 13 February

Riad of the Storks and El Badi Palace, Marrakech

I was looking at my mother's deposition last night; it left me desperately sad at the thought of her being dragged through a coroner's inquest and giving evidence, alone, post John's death.

One event missing is the beginning of the whole sorry train of events that led to John's death: the cricket match in Richmond Park. I had just met a new girlfriend and was keen to introduce her to John, so I'd accepted an invitation to the Nucleus staff get-together. It was one of those perfect late-summer days really – deer roaming the park, the smell of cut grass and barbecue, and enough space to indulge in a cricket match without spoiling a family's picnic spot. I introduced John to Debbie, my new girlfriend, and there was that inevitable moment of disbelief at the similarities and differences between us, the slightly forced chumminess and platitudes. John had been with Samantha for a while by then and we had all assumed that an engagement couldn't be that far off. I knew immediately that he wasn't sure about my new girlfriend, but there was always a 'cooling period' upon introduction. He had thought that a previous girlfriend had been the bee's knees, whereas I had known her to be a total nutter with terrifyingly violent interludes, so he could hardly show me the way to girlfriend enlightenment.

John and I were competitive cricketers; we both believed passionately that we could out-bat and out-bowl each other even though most of our cricketing experience was either from our on-the-upstairs-landing-rolled-up-socks cricket matches or from watching and listening to Grandmother eulogizing about Derek Randall's Test match-batting acrobatics. We were both on good form – me showing off my stylish new girlfriend, he showing off that he had a 'real job' and new work chums. I have to admit, I was actually very jealous; he was surrounded by such lovely people. His boss, Peter, was charming and had also brought half a cellar of fancy wines with him – this was no ordinary office party but a classy picnic that we would always remember. Sadly, of course, I remember it not for its poetic late-summer haze, but for the moment someone, I can't remember who, tonked an attempted six into the outfield. The ball flew high and fast into the ebbing sun . . . John ran one way to catch the ball, Mandy, his chum and work colleague, ran the other way, both with eyes on the ball, both unaware of each other's trajectory. They collided with an almighty crash of heads, thumping into each other and collapsing side by side. Mandy was bruised but okay, but John was much worse. He lay there for a while, stunned and slightly unaware, and was slow to recover and return to his feet. We stopped the game and returned to our picnic blankets, but I knew something was not quite right. He complained that his head hurt, but not just where he and Mandy had collided, his whole head hurt. We took him home to Mother and he lay quietly on the sofa, downing a couple of fizzing Solpadeines, clutching his forehead. I can still remember every detail of that evening as clear as day: the living-room doors open to the garden behind us, him lying with a cool flannel upon his forehead, the birds singing in the plum trees, Sally, our corgi, sitting comfortingly beside him, Samantha slightly impatient with him. None of us yet understanding that at that moment of collision, a fraction of a second, none of our lives would ever be the same again.

Riad of the Storks, Marrakech

I've come across the letter from Dr H, the consultant clinical oncologist at the hospital (who will remain nameless), addressed to my sister Jean-Marian, who was reluctant to return to nursing after these events.

8 November 1999

Dear Mrs Crate

I was grateful for the opportunity to meet you on Friday. I know how devastating the loss of John is for you and your family. It remains a nightmare for me; it was the worst episode of my whole career, which is now coming to a close. All I can say personally now is how sorry I continue to be for all that has happened.

On Friday I was left wondering whether the meeting in a group really achieved your objective of becoming more comfortable to return to nursing. I can at least reassure you that pharmacy procedures and control of drugs on the ward have been tightened considerably, and that it is now much more likely that rogue or incompetent doctors will be identified more quickly. However, if you would like more information and explanation of the notes I would be only too willing and indeed would welcome the opportunity, of meeting you again on a one-to-one basis. If so, please do not hesitate to contact me.

Best wishes,

[Signed Dr H]

As the only witness – I was actually in the same room, but behind a curtain that had been drawn between John and me – I still marvel that I was not called to the coroner's inquest, nor was I ever written to by any of the protagonists in the misadventure. For some reason, after John died, even though I was the eldest now, and the surviving identical twin, I was excluded from all correspondence and face-to-face meetings. For a long time after Johnny's death I suffered alone and in silence. Dosed up with a concoction of Solpadeine for recurring headaches and my mother's sleeping tablets, I somehow continued my work as an illustrator. I was eventually prescribed Seroxat by a clinical psychologist who diagnosed me as suffering from post-traumatic stress, a drug that I have been unable to wean myself off.

Writing this now under a clear blue Moroccan sky, the events running up to Johnny's death are still seared into my memory. The night after his death my mother came in to see me in my bedroom. I had spent a couple of hours holding the cooling hand of John's dead body, utterly bereft and heartbroken. She and I were now alone in our big house. Mother gave me several sleeping tablets to try to rest my broken mind, but as I eventually fell asleep, I knew that I was willing myself to die.

Thursday 15 and Friday 16 February

Riad of the Storks, Marrakech

At the time of John's death I was an illustrator, constantly busy with complicated briefs from around the world. I worked from my bedroom at an old desk filled to the brim with acrylics, gouache and brushes and a huge architectural-plan chest (drawing cabinet) filled with ancient ephemera, from stamps to maps to banking notes and certificates. I drew and painted my illustrations on my old art-school drawing board, colouring them with fragments of the colourful papers in the plan chest. This method worked, thankfully, and I became well known for my collages, illustrating book covers, album covers and design brochures. I was happy, but not fully content. It was a lonely existence, particularly in the pre-digital time: just me sitting with a blank sheet of watercolour paper, waiting for the phone to ring. Luckily it rang often. After John's death I started working in John's room – it was bigger and brighter, with three large windows looking out over the back garden. John had painted his room white with hints of deep Grecian blue, his personal homage to the island of Paros. All his model soldiers were still out on the shelves next to any Airfix models that had survived the bruising battles of childhood fights, along with seashells and rocks and design books, pressed flowers and terrariums of tropical plants. It was a joyful room filled with a design ethic far beyond his years. Bit by bit I moved my art materials into his room but I always felt like I was trespassing on his space.

During summer I would work late into the night on overdue deadlines and often accidentally fall asleep on his bed. For some reason I would always awake with a jolt at 1.25a.m., confused and disorientated. I told my mother about my midnight awakenings and she told me that this was the time of John's birth, with me following ten minutes later. I would return to my own room and sleep restlessly until I'd hear the first calls of the birds.

Saturday 17 February

Late flight from Marrakech – glorious sunset
over Casablanca – to home

I spent the afternoon cuddling my beloved Ange; nothing quite compares to the cuddling of a loved one. Ange is holding a small white rabbit by its floppy ears. My own grey childhood teddy sits above my mother's living-room cabinet and watches over her while she sits and reads. Johnny's brown bear watches over me from the corner of my bedroom. Johnny's other, special, teddy was called Strawbod, a scraggly and slightly moth-eaten yellow teddy with a worn brown nose and a scarf of light brown wool knitted by Johnny when he was nine or ten. When the question, 'What item would you save if your home was on fire?' is raised, I always immediately answer, 'Well, Strawbod of course.' Ten inches of well-worn teddy bear with a badly knitted scarf and beady little brown eyes. Daft, I know, but to me one of the most important objects on earth.

Sunday 18 February

At Mother's

Ange drove me down to Mother, still frail but uncomplaining. Discussion ranges from El Greco to Alexander McQueen ('Oh, I did love his work at the fashion exhibition at Belsay Hall in 2002') to how moved she was by a tiny drawing of the crucifixion by Rembrandt at the Royal Academy (there are tears in her eyes as she describes it).

Grey teddy sits watching over her, next to a framed black and white photo of curly-haired, baggy-nappied twins, shot in a professional studio. I only know the difference because I've been told so many times: John is playing with a teddy, me with a set of plastic keys. Mother believes grey teddy is John's and the brown one is mine. Maybe she's right and it's me who's got it the wrong way round. It doesn't really matter any more.

The Mews

Today as I was going through Mother's papers I braved the obituaries:

Obituary, Kingston Art College:

It was with great sadness that the school of Graphics and Design learned of the death of John Loftus after three months of illness. John was an outstanding student from 1983–86. He obtained First Class Honours and was employed at Nucleus Design Associates where he quickly became an invaluable member of the design team. He was a superb draughtsman, a fine typographer and filmmaker. He won a Thames (TV) Bursary for Television Graphics in his second year and we have a marvellous visual legacy of his work on film and slide. The funeral took place on 20th November. It is hoped that a memorial tree can be planted in the grounds of Knights Park Centre.

Notice in *The Times* and *The Independent*:

Loftus, John William (1963–1987) such a special person. A wonderful friend, so loved and so much missed. You may not be with us now, but your spirit lives on.

Small card given at John's funeral:

JOHN WILLIAM LOFTUS
31ST OCTOBER 1963 – 11TH NOVEMBER 1987
We seem to give them back to thee, O God, who gavest them first to us. Yet as thou didst not lose them in giving, so we do not lose

them by their return. Not as the world giveth, givest thou, O Lover of souls. What thou givest, thou takest not away, for what is thine is ours also if we are thine. And life is eternal and love is immortal, and death is only an horizon and an horizon is nothing save the limit of our sight.   Fr. Bede Jarrett O. P.

It's ironic that this card was probably given out at the funeral because John was an atheist, and quite vociferous in his arguments against organized religion and the damage it can do. Where I shied away from religious argument, for fear of some divine intervention, he was quite happy berating the Catholic Church particularly, but all religions almost equally. He would have probably preferred a quote from *The Lord of the Rings* or Antoine de Saint-Exupéry's *The Little Prince* or even *Winnie-the-Pooh*.

Tuesday 20 February

Morgan & Mees Hotel, Amsterdam
Shooting seaweed with Bart van Olphen

I've shot with my chum Bart for over two years now. He is a food writer, presenter and conservationist; his big issue is the sustainability of fish in our oceans and he fights for it with passion and great gusto. He's a native of Amsterdam and I'm here with him working on a project called Sea Green Netherlands, to try to get people to eat more seaweed. Many of the trips I've been on with him have been the hardest of my life. They are often extremely dangerous, and have involved slippery decks, rough seas, sinking and decrepit boats, Kalashnikov-waving militia and shark-infested waters. Bart writes about our adventures while I nervously photograph them, and seaweed farming sounds like a breeze in comparison. It's a very bonding experience when you jump back onto dry land from a Bart-organized trip and he says, 'I really thought we were going to die out there.'

Each time I travel with my work I take a few papers with me from my mother's file. It's a strange and eclectic mixture of Samantha's highly decorated illustrative cards, Johnny's postcards from Paros, letters from friends and relatives from after his death. This time Jean-Marian has sent me a small poem she wrote to John after he died:

> When darkening clouds fill
> Skies so grey
> When childhood memories
> Of a now gone day
> Still laugh and cry
> In a far off place
> In my mind
> I still miss you xx

Wednesday 21 and Thursday 22 February

Zeeland, the Netherlands

Today we're off to the south to explore the seaweed of Zeeland. The sea is a soft shade of aqua blue and Toine, our seaweed scientist and surf dude, bravely jumps in. The temperature scale on my phone says $-2°C$ and the sea, where it meets the shore, is frozen into the sand, making faux constructionist patterns that crunch underfoot. My hands are almost frozen to my Leica and the wind blows cruelly from the sea. After an hour or so we can bear it no longer and retreat to the local surf club, Natural High, for hot chocolate.

The cold pain in my hands reminds me of the cruel days of winter at school. John and I went to an all-boys grammar school called Wallington, in Beddington in Surrey. Academically it was great and artistically it was fabulous, thanks to a few talented and passionate artists on its staff. But we found it a cruel and bullying environment when away from the art room. Sportsmen were rewarded and pampered while the more sensitive were often victimized and vilified. John and I hated the sports field and detested the masters that used the pitches as their stalking grounds. We often joked that because we'd had to share certain cells and brawn in our birth we were definitely destined for the weedier teams.

There was zero tolerance of weakness or sporting ineptitude. One master, known unaffectionately as Jock, was particularly nasty. He was in charge of five years of compulsory Scottish sword dancing, a hellish hour of dancing in pairs over two crossed swords, in bare feet to encourage a lack of mistakes, a wrong toe here or a wrong toe there and the pain was sharp and quick. If you turned in the wrong direction he would pull down your shorts and spank your bare arse with the blunt side of the sword, heating the left side if he wanted you to turn left, or the right if it was right, screaming into your face 'Hot side first, hot side first!'

John and I were picked on because we were twins. He called John 'Mark I' and me 'Mark II'. I think he hated everyone, but he hated the weaker, non-sporty kids most of all. After sword dancing we were made to strip in the cloakrooms and run naked across the corridor to the showers, which he would turn up to full heat. The secret was to run as fast as possible through the steaming streams of water – because there was so much steam you could flatten yourself against the tiles behind and avoid a scalding. If you returned dry, Jock would slap your bare arse with a table-tennis bat and forcibly propel you back into the scalding steam of the shower room. Across the corridor you ran, always naked, embarrassed and ashamed, often bumping quite literally into your favourite (female) French teacher.

It was miserable, in the freezing cold, ice or snow, and if you forgot your shorts you were made to play in your underpants. There were no boxes or gum shields, if you fell you bled. The plunge pool afterward was, like the showers, kept ridiculously hot but you had no choice, you plunged or you were pushed. I cried so often. Sometimes our hands would become totally incapacitated by the intense heat straight after the cold and we would, weeping, help each other button our shirts and straighten our ties. An unbuttoned shirt merited more punishment and one felt punished enough.

Yesterday was the first time in a long while that I felt that same pain in my hands and I've shot in sub-zero temperatures on the glaciers of Iceland and the ice floes of Nova Scotia. It's not easy to shoot wearing gloves and the little metal Leica camera soon matches the temperature of the outside air, but at least one can take breaks and run in for a welcoming hot chocolate. That regime at school probably wouldn't be allowed now. There were plenty of parents who believed the experience would be 'good for us' and 'toughen us up', but it didn't work for us.

During our second year at Wallington, John complained about constant stomach pains, particularly on Mondays and Wednesdays. Monday was Latin, Wednesday was Jock. After tests, a psychiatric assessment and a barium meal, John was eventually diagnosed with a peptic ulcer – stress-induced, I am sure.

Eventually we turned to our father for help. He, like us, had gone to an all-boys school, but bullying had not been tolerated there, between boys, or boys and masters. John's peptic ulcer essentially got him off games. I, however, being his identical twin, could hardly claim the same ailment. So Father came up with 'Osgood-Schlatter', a satisfyingly rare inflammation of the knee joint that got me a good four months of library time versus Jock and his cronies time. When the 'Schlatter' was eventually called into question my father kindly wrote to one of these teachers, (a nasty little sadist who liked to scream in your ear 'Run like the shit!' – the first swear word I ever heard). He said, quite simply: 'David will be excused from rugby this Wednesday, and all future Wednesdays, because he is suffering from general malaise.'

It was genius, and the look on Sir's nasty, pinched little face was a picture!

Friday 23 February

Island of Texel, the Netherlands

I've always wanted to visit the islands that hook up from northern Holland into the North Sea. Shooting the seaweed and the people who make seaweed their passion, I see it in a new light. I know, to many, seaweed is just a slippery and slimy plant that fills rock pools at low tide, but to these people it's not just a food source of rare minerals and umami, it's also medicinal, a fertilizer, and quite possibly a future source of fuel.

I do love the Netherlands and its extraordinary man-made landscape. So flat, so ordered, that you can see the sun rise and the sun set on the horizon. When the weather is this beautiful nature provides a haze-like filter to the endless trees. Ice-covered dykes criss-cross the land between the canals with their ubiquitous *Chitty Chitty Bang Bang* windmills everywhere. And the birds. I awoke to hedges filled with tiny birds (coal tits, wrens and robins) and our drive through the countryside passes fields filled with bean geese and colourful Egyptian geese, framing heart shapes with their necks. Also spotted are owls, buzzards, several herons and a pair of flirting great crested grebes. No one in the car shows even the slightest interest in my ornithological sightings, but I list them mentally to tell Mother on Sunday.

Today's shoot was for the British Heart Foundation, photographing portraits of young survivors of chronic heart disease. First a lovely comedienne and her wonderfully moustachioed husband and sidekick, called Short & Curly. Young, funny, utterly charming and inspiring, followed by a shoot with a sixteen-year-old tap dancer called Jayden, three years on and dancing like a young Fred Astaire, after having been found dead by his father and resuscitated with CPR by him. All normal but extraordinary people, amazing stories and a truly inspiring and uplifting day. The British Heart Foundation seem nervous but pleased.

Thinking of the randomness of the tumultuous events that have affected these people reminded me of an event when John and I were Jayden's age. We loved *The Persuaders!* I wanted to be Roger Moore and he wanted to be Tony Curtis. We would sit, side by side, in our pyjamas on a Sunday morning and vow to own their cars, live their lives, and reside in a mews. But I cannot drive. My father was a car enthusiast, racing Astons and Jaguars, but John and I never quite recovered psychologically from an accident we witnessed in Germany.

We'd been driving, as a family, from Grandad Opa's near Toplitsee – the lake where the Nazis hid all their stolen bullion – a joyous trip of sunshine, edelweiss-pressing by John and lazy lake swimming. Father was at the wheel when we were overtaken by a very fast BMW with its boot held closed by a piece of string. Suddenly, simultaneously, there was a flash storm and the boot of the BMW pinged open, launching suitcases and holiday paraphernalia into the windscreens of the following and oncoming traffic. In a blur of seconds that seemed like a slow-motion nightmare, cars and lorries piled into each other. We saw a VW Beetle cartwheeling down the other carriageway, a man in a white shirt crisscrossed with bloody stripes, a lorry careering towards us, two little boys gazing up at the driver in horror, swerving sideways at the last minute, screaming and sliding past us and down the bank. It was our father's skill as a racing driver that saved us, but for many it was the last moment they saw before they passed into never-ending darkness. What struck me, and has never left me, was the lack of control, the sheer lottery of the moment, between life, serious injury, and death. It wasn't a fear of driving that stopped us continuing with lessons, it was the unpredictability of the road and the fact that one person's mistake or careless recklessness could cause such random mayhem and ensuing carnage.

Sunday 25 February

Cheam, Surrey

Took an early cab down to see the mother. She had a small list of 'David-to-dos': buy a few books for her Kindle, pop a few arty books back on the shelf, put fresh bird seed out for the tits. We discussed Simon Barnes of *The Independent* and how he managed to move gracefully between being their cricket correspondent and their birdwatching expert, my grandmother's love of golden-covered Royal Coronation albums, Derek Randall, the then acrobatic and unpredictable England wicketkeeper, and white sugar on freshly buttered bread, to which my mother stood up in her dressing gown and brandished her antique walking stick, impersonating Sir Ian McKellen playing King Lear, naked, at the back of an empty stage. *'Never! Never! Never!'* she roared with Gandalfian splendour. She never ceases to amaze me.

The Mews

The press talks of the 'Beast from the East' arriving today, 'Snow-mageddon' – jeepers, these people talk crap sometimes. London was warned to 'be home by 6p.m'. It's now 10p.m and the sky is clear and black and blue and the stars are bright.

My earliest memories of snow are from when our young family stayed in my Auntie Ailsa's cottage in Frosterley, somewhere in Weardale, County Durham. Ailsa is an enigmatic cousin of my mother, frosty herself and rather fierce. She suffered no fools and ran a charity under the patronage of the Dalai Lama, helping refugees from Tibet. I remember her trying to persuade my elderly mother to join her in a Hercules transport plane to Bosnia during the genocide of 1995. I had to step in and explain that I wasn't sure Mother could even make it up the aircraft ramp, let alone trudge through the refugee camps of Bosnia and Croatia.

Frosterley was Ailsa's bolthole, a tiny terraced Victorian cottage on a hill leading up the wild heather-swept moors. The first snow was at Easter, following two days of warm sun. John and I raced up onto the moors to build our first ever snowman, using flints as eyes, heather as a purple-rinse hairdo and rabbit poo as buttons. We didn't go up into the moors after that day because a small plane crashed and was reported missing and John and I were convinced that it had crashed near to our snowman and we didn't want to be the ones to find the pilots. Frosterley was also the first time we saw an adder, the first and only time I heard our parents argue, and the first time I pooed in the outdoors. Or was it John?

Shooting at the Mews again today – great to be in the same place, at home, to catch up and catch my breath. Last night I dreamt of Frosterley and the crash on the moors. It's hard to believe that somewhere so close to civilization was so wild and dangerous. The dream included a moment with John. In dreams he is always there, alive, but not healthy, his life on hold somehow, semi-transparent, often sick. Sometimes I hear the ornamental cow bell he had beside his bed when he'd come home from hospital, the chime signalling that his headache was too much to bear and, as in my dreams, I would rush to him down the long corridor. In last night's dream the corridor went on and on and on, but I got there eventually to find that his room was the room the two of us shared in Frosterley. John and I would hide under the covers of our bed in the inky darkness of countryside night-times and use our matching torches to form circles of moving light across the walls and ceiling of our little attic room. 'This is the voice of the Mysterons,' we would whisper in our deepest unbroken voices, a line from *Captain Scarlet* indicating baddies were coming to take over your body, scaring ourselves as much as each other.

The bed seemed massive but was probably just a normal double bed, and it had several sheets and blankets and one of those old-school quilts that ultimately became a duvet. All were tucked so tightly that once tucked up for the night one could barely move. We had this funny routine where we would push ourselves to the extremes of the bed to get as much air under the sheets, then we'd spoon each other, on our sides, John in front and me behind and we'd start to cycle, legs going round and round in unison, pretending we were on a bicycle made for two. It was a great way to warm the bed. When older, hot-water bottles were more efficient but less fun. I remember once waking in complete darkness and the covers were so tight I couldn't move. However hard I tried, I couldn't raise my head, whatever way I turned it just seemed to get tighter and tighter and more claustrophobic. Ultimately I panicked and cried out and John stood up in bed, ripping the sheets free. I've not slept under tucked-in sheets since, and upon arrival at a hotel the first thing I do before getting into bed is untuck the sheets at all four corners.

The following Christmas John got a Captain Scarlet uniform, which I was mighty jealous of, although my yellow and brown Native American uniform with red and green feathered headdress did grow on me. What was annoying was that, in fights, he would always kill me with his pistol before I'd even reached for a suckered arrow in my quiver. Ten minutes older, always.

Tuesday 27 February to Friday 2 March

The Mews

After John's death, I found an interesting reluctance in our friends to communicate with me about our suffering. There was a feeling that John was the one that had suffered, not us, and therefore we should get over it and on with normal life. But life was anything but normal. Somehow I was managing to finish briefs, albeit rather tardily, but I can barely remember my social life. Most of John's friends, after an initial period of sympathy, had faded away. Many were designers and occasionally I would pass one in the lobbies of design studios. I came to hate their look of surprise and shock upon seeing me, still at that point wearing one of John's shirts or jumpers, like a sartorial comfort blanket. What followed their shock was a mixture of confusion and fear, followed by a muddle of 'must meet ups', followed by a hasty retreat and eternal silence.

Many of my own friends weren't much better. Peter, my best friend, would do his best to drag me out for a drink or ten. The first time I saw him after John died he met me at Sloane Square station and we wandered up the King's Road to a bar at the Chelsea Drug Store, while he excitedly told me about a Stephen King novel he had been reading on the Tube. 'Listen to this,' he said with relish. He then proceeded to read a passage describing insects creeping into a freshly buried coffin to devour and return the body to the earth. It was vividly, stomach-churningly ghastly and I sat in shock and disbelief that Peter, my dearest of friends, could be so unfeeling. I realize now it was the nervousness of filling quiet with chatter and not intentional insensitivity.

We are still the greatest of friends but that day is seared in my memory for all sorts of terrible reasons. It had started relatively conventionally. I'd shaved with John's electric razor so as not to look in the bathroom mirror. Mother, amazingly, had gone into her surgery to work, and Molly had made me a cheery crumpet breakfast. They knew I didn't want to go into town, but were glad to see me trying. I had tried, it seemed unsuccessfully, to leave my girlfriend Debbie, but she had just ignored me, putting it down to my unstable state of mind. She had called Peter to persuade me to come out and I had thought at least he would cheer along proceedings.

I caught the train up to Victoria and then the Tube. I had a few errands to run before meeting Peter, so out I jumped at Monument station and walked the long tunnel to Bank. It seemed like the whole of London had the same idea and the platform was an ungodly crush, so I let the first train go and wandered right down the platform to the back of the train. As the train slowed I was aware of my reflection in the glass so I bowed my head and waited for the doors to open. I stepped in, keeping my head down, and the door closed behind me. As I raised my head to look up, a suited man in front of me, indeed the only other passenger standing, dropped a sheet of papers and books onto the floor. The windows between carriages were always kept open, the stale wind between stations preferable to the stagnant stale smoke stench of the carriage. There he was. As the swirling papers fluttered to a slow-motion halt it dawned on me that I was facing Dr S, the doctor who had given the fatal injection that had killed Johnny. He looked utterly stunned. Shocked. He opened his mouth, but didn't make a sound. I stood, staring at him, also unable to speak. As the doors opened at the next stop I turned and walked out, leaving him standing in a sea of legal papers bearing my twin brother's name. I looked to the skies and thought Lord! If there is someone up there moving us like chess pieces on a board then I had just heard him say 'checkmate!'

Sunday 4 March

Time to talk about Timothy

Last night I met up at the Colbert with my best chum, Tim Knatchbull, walking there, from the Mews over Albert Bridge and along the King's Road to Sloane Square, buffered by an icy wind and horizontal snow, the creaky crunch underfoot an alien sound to a Londoner when dirty slush is the norm. Arriving slightly early, I wander across the square to peruse the often-ignored fountain at its centre. Completely frozen, this unloved sculpture is now an iced sculptured beauty. Water frozen in mid flow, Venus has regained her looks.

Tim and I sat in our favourite corner, he with the weakest gin & tonic known to man – 'I'd like half a measure of gin and two bottles of tonic'. He instantly chattered fondly of our first meeting back in September 1989, an extraordinary turning point in our lives. In later years I described it thus: 'we talked for hours like long-lost friends, reunited after forever apart, twinship, youth, muddles and mix-ups, shared loves, life, childhood experiences. The fear that it would be a meeting of tears and pain was completely unfounded and instead I found myself laughing like I hadn't laughed in ages. We became very close, very quickly, Tim helped fill the vast chasm that had opened in my life'.

I'd met Dr Elizabeth Bryan in the summer of that year. She was a colleague of my mother's and worked at Queen Charlotte's Hospital, where John and I had been born, as Director of the Multiple Births

Foundation and Vice President of the International Society of Twin Studies. My mother had written to Elizabeth after John died and it was Elizabeth who suggested I meet Tim. He was the twin who had survived the assassination of Lord Mountbatten. We were two men with a terrible sorrow, each born an identical twin, a source of unbridled happiness in childhood; we were never lonely, always a focus of attention. And then in different, tragic and dramatic ways our twins had died.

When Tim was given my phone number it sat on his 'things-to-do' list for almost six months. He'd met a couple of other lone twins and found that he had nothing in common with them, and was worried that there was little that he could offer me. I stalled too, worried for Tim, not wanting to revive ill-feelings for him.

Finally Tim called and we made an agreement to meet in a pub in Knightsbridge, walking distance from his parents' home and from the home in which John and I had lived upon our birth. We arranged to meet for half an hour but ultimately spoke for hours. As Tim said later, 'David put me in touch with feelings that had lain dormant. It wasn't easy to cry in a pub where everyone else was having a good time and throwing blunt instruments at a dart board, but it was as if no one else existed. It was an absolute turning point. I knew that David would be my closest male friend for the rest of my life.'

Years on, married with children, and godfathers to each other's firstborn – me to Amber, Tim to Paros – we are still inseparably close. We used to sign each other's visitors books, and once, out shopping, the manager said to us 'You must be twins.' 'We are,' replied Tim, adding quietly, 'Just not each other's.'

More shooting for the British Heart Foundation. Today we are in Poole and my subjects are a young teacher who had a heart attack as she was about to finish running a marathon, and a young, athletic kite surfer who suffered two heart attacks and a stroke that had stolen his ability to speak. Both lovely, charming, caring and good people who were struck very young with heart disease, while doing the exercise that they loved. Both remind our little team how lucky we are.

> 'It's a dangerous business, Frodo, going out your door.
> You step onto the road, and if you don't keep your feet,
> there's no knowing where you might be swept off to.'
> —J. R. R. TOLKIEN'S, *THE LORD OF THE RINGS*:
> *THE FELLOWSHIP OF THE RING*, 1954

Sitting in Ange's lovely Fifties chair, I think I know what Tolkien means. Too tired and distracted to write too much . . .

Friday 9 March

When John came to from his operation in Intensive Care he took several days to vaguely acclimatize to his surroundings. He floated between sedated and restless sleep and very emotional moments of awakening. He cried a lot. The operation had been enormous and he couldn't understand why he still had a headache, why his vision was slightly wonky and cross-eyed and why the lack of feeling on his right-hand side had not improved. There were no answers but the doctors said that everything should return to a more normal state after a period of rehabilitation and therapy. John wasn't convinced but met the reassurances from those we regarded as experts with his usual calm stoicism. As a right-handed drawer, writer and designer, his greatest fear was the lack of feeling in his right hand. But he had started writing a bit with his left hand, and his speech, though initially slurred, had returned to normal. He was told he might need an operation to correct his line of sight.

I sat beside him for many, many hours holding his right hand, urging him to, 'Squeeze, squeeze as hard as you can.' Bit by bit, little by little, tiny improvements began to happen and his lop-sided face would break into a moment of relative smileyness. Of course fate had other plans and his efforts were in vain, but during my last happy moments with him, opening our birthday presents, I was in awe of how determined he was to do things himself. Each parcel opened represented a small victory, each card read was a step forwards.

Enter Doctor S.

Sunday 11 March

Today's shoot is for the British Heart Foundation. Our subject today was a young girl suffering a syndrome called DiGeorge, a gene disorder, luckily very rare, which causes congenital heart problems. Photographing someone so tiny with a heart disorder that necessitates her having to breathe through a tracheotomy in her windpipe was obviously upsetting for us all. While we were with her we all remained chirpy and upbeat. Her three young sisters played around her while her kind and loving parents watched on. It was hard to imagine the stresses that the young family had been under, but there was so much love and joy in the house that the spirit of the place was infectious and it was only afterwards as we walked back to the station that we communally sobbed and hugged each other. Sometimes ill health just seems like some sort of bizarre reverse lottery in which entry is compulsory and losers are picked at random to spend their life in suffering.

Today is Mother's Day and I feel bad that I have not seen my mother for days. I miss her and our sits at her window watching the jays and the wood pigeons. I shall go to her tomorrow after my shoot, making hay while the sun shines.

Monday 12 and Tuesday 13 March

Cheam, Surrey

Finished my shoot early yesterday so hopped into a taxi and trotted off to see Mama. Subjects of chatter ranged from the hopelessness of book choices at her book club to the Greek gods of mischief, to the unexplained reasons behind missing chromosomes. We sat overlooking the communal garden so were occasionally distracted by the birdlife in the wood that frames its edges. Sitting very close to her she seemed so tiny compared to the doctor I used to see constantly on the run in The Beeches, her body almost impossibly concaved to the point of toppling over. The cancer treatment, which is thankfully just in tablet form, is making her very sleepy and causing very painful joints in her feet and her legs. I was shocked to see how much her circulation had deteriorated – her hands a vivid purple and I assume her feet are much the same, even her nose was blue beneath the little puff of concealer she's tried to hide it with. While we talked she ate her lunch, tiny little cubes of cut-up ham sandwich, one of the few things her stomach still lets her digest. I could see a little wren in the hedgerow below us and felt how similar they seemed. It seems impossible that someone can eat so little and still survive with such spirit.

When I hug her carefully upon taking my leave, I always hold her by the shoulders, partly so I can gauge her weight loss. She is so thin, so skeletal, I can only feel bone through her floaty jumper. As I was leaving I said my usual, 'Love you Mother, watch your feet' mantra. John always used to quote from his favourite series *Hill Street Blues*, where the sergeant would say as the officers all got up after their morning briefing, 'And folks, remember, let's be careful out there.'

Mum looked at her feet and chuckled, 'Trouble is, I spend so long worrying about my feet and not tripping that I'm now worried I'm going to bump my head.' She pronounces 'head' in a remnant of her County Durham accent, 'heed', long and drawn out. So I turned as I walked down the stairs and said, 'Okay dearest Ma, from now on, it's "watch your feet and watch your heed."' And, as always, 'I love you', and then, in memory of John, 'Be careful out there.'

She always watches me while I hop in my taxi and waves until I'm out of sight. Normally she looks rather serious and sad, but this time she was smiling broadly as she waved goodbye. Maybe it was because my taxi driver was also waving, but maybe it was the reminder of John and his love of *Hill Street Blues*.

Wednesday 14 March

The Mews, day ten of shooting in a row

The stress of shooting every day – weekend included – is getting to me and I'm making small mistakes in exposure or focus. After five days of intense concentration I notice that my eyes tire and almost become lazy, and I'm finding it harder to focus on this writing. Occasionally, on thinking about John, I cross my eyes like we used to do at school. It's hard to imagine John's disappointment upon awakening from his operation to find that not only had the feeling in his right-hand side not returned, but that his eyes were crossed and he was suffering from double vision. Such a cruel double blow to a talented right-handed artist and designer.

If I cross my eyes now I get an instant headache, and bad memories of ringing cow bells and lumbar punctures return, pinning me to my chair in a sad and miserable funk. It's extraordinary how, after over half my life, these painful memories are so vivid and clear. Fifteen or so years after John's death I spoke to his girlfriend Samantha at a family party and she told me that she barely remembered the days spent nursing him in hospital. Part of me was envious of her memory lapse, part of me unsure whether it was just good old British stiff upper lip, part of me disappointed that such a shocking and desperate time could be somehow blanked out of her memory. Quite rightly and thankfully, though, she had moved on and married Richard, a kind and thoughtful man, and had children and moved away from London.

As I journey through this process I've thought that I might sit down and chat through memories with John's friends and ex-girlfriends. But I can also see that some should be left quietly to forget, and I think Samantha is one of those people. When she married Richard I understood that a chapter in my life was closing and that she, quite rightly, was moving on with the rest of her life.

I remember little of her wedding, my post-traumatic brain blurring the present and struggling to get me through the day. Samantha had asked me to read a psalm in the church on the day and, after many refusals, I reluctantly agreed to do it. I stood, kissed my mother on the cheek and walked slowly to the front. As I passed the eerily silent front pews, all eyes upon me, I heard a gasp and, slicing the quiet like a knife, a lady exclaimed: 'Oh my God, John has come to the wedding.'

Thursday 15 March

The Mews

A day of shooting stills, filming and editing. In the pre-digital days, the editing process consisted of a bike courier to the lab, a tense wait of a few hours, then a bike home, followed by a couple of hours hunched over a lightbox with a magnifying loupe and a pair of scissors, while carefully cutting out transparencies deemed okay to send to the clients. Now in the digital age it is hours of screen time, something my headache-prone self screams to avoid but cannot. Last night I had to go through all five shooting days of the British Heart Foundation. At a guess, I averaged about 800 shots per subject with two portrait locations per day. I look, I colour balance, I check focus, I check expressions and framing. I might straighten a slightly wonky horizon or vertical, I adjust contrast, saturation and exposure. Each picture or capture, if not deleted, will take five or six minutes before moving on to the next. The total remaining captures are renamed, backed up twice, and then processed to transfer to the client. It's certainly not the fun part of job but it is impossible to avoid. I shoot every day, so it tends to be a night-time chore and an immense strain on the vision.

Last night I edited the British Heart Foundation photos of the sweet and delightful little girl with DiGeorge syndrome. I will certainly never forget her serious little face. Taking someone's portrait is an intensely intimate affair; you witness all of the emotions, frailties, strengths, insecurities and confidences of your subject. I often think it's a one-way ticket; I'm so focused on my subject's eyes and their character that I notice little else. Occasionally upon editing, I notice objects or intrusions in the background that I hadn't noticed through the lens. I'm not someone who alters my images afterwards so my preference is to delete, though in little L's case I deleted very few. On this rare and beautiful shoot it was a two-way experience; I focused on her and her big blue eyes also completely focused on me and my camera, straight at me. She is someone I shall never forget.

Saturday 17 March

The Mews

On 1 January 2015, in Marrakech, I gave Ange a beautiful cloth-bound book of 800 or so blank pages, and vowed to draw in it every day for 365 days. I finished the last illustration on 31 December, in the same spot in Marrakech. Just as when I started this book on 1 January 2018 with the intention of writing every day, and I had no idea whether the project would last a day, a month or a year. I hadn't drawn for years and hadn't written anything except the odd magazine article for a while. My illustrative effort started so tentatively. Upon completion I handed Ange her book, as promised, and she was delighted. During that year she would often quietly ask me, like a parent to a homework-avoiding child, whether I'd 'done my book today'. She does the same now; sometimes a new blank page can look awfully daunting.

Tuesday 20 March

Shooting at the Mews, snow still on the ground. The last time I remember snow remaining for days is probably from our childhood. Dined with Ange at Daphne's in Kensington and ordered my ultimate comfort food, spaghetti vongole.

Twisting my fork to eat my spaghetti takes me back to the time when Johnny perfected his left-handed eating abilities. We were both trying hard to establish our differences and one of my distinguishing habits was that while he was a spaghetti twister using a fork and spoon, I was a spaghetti chopper, slicing my spaghetti into small strands and eating it with a spoon. By that time I had perfected my very own signature spaghetti bolognese, taught by my mother: chopped onions, carrots and celery, good minced beef, button mushrooms, bay and sage, tomato purée and of course spaghetti. I knew John had been practising for weeks as a left-hander, and I didn't believe for a second that he'd been that way inclined for over fifteen years. One night I cooked up my finest spag bol to catch him out. I must have smiled so smugly as he tried to negotiate the spaghetti twist with fork and spoon, an impossible left-handed task to a natural right-handed eater.

I got my comeuppance years later, not long after John died, when Peter, his old boss, took me to his favourite Italian restaurant. He'd invited me in to tell me of his plans to plant a tree in John's memory and name Nucleus' new building John Loftus House. He also asked me whether I would take over John's godfatherly duties to Clio, his newborn daughter. I must have looked awful; I certainly felt terrible. I can remember Peter kindly taking the menu out of my hands, ordering a fine bottle of wine, and telling me that he would order. He ordered spaghetti bolognese. The memories were so vivid that I broke into a hot sweat and had to run to the bathroom to cool myself down. Upon returning to the table, there it was, the long strands of spaghetti coiled into a terrifying and daunting mountain. I was twenty-five years old, there was no way I could ask for a knife to chop it into bite-size pieces. I looked, I watched, I learned. It was the first time I twisted and the last time that that particular difference remained a difference.

The Mews

I'm sitting quietly on our roof terrace, surrounded by a lifetime of special mementos. Broken models of fighting boats, conch shells from the Bahamas, pottery found in Paros, a Tibetan wooden elephant, a Buddha's copper head. It's cold, but I've made a temporary camp in a suntrapped corner, sleeves rolled high, face to the sun like a Galapagos lizard soaking in the rare warmth, eyes closed and deep in thought. Purple crocuses I've planted are barely holding their own, the shock of the springtime snow a rude reminder that the spring sunshine of weeks ago was a globally warmed aberration.

Last night I was at the Saatchi Gallery in Chelsea, performing my newly appointed role as chairman of the judges for the Pink Lady Food Photographer of the Year awards, a global competition for professional and amateur food and travel photographers. I was nervous, the room was filled with the great and good of publishing, those who had achieved, exhibited and commissioned food and travel photography. My job was to introduce them to each other, and then encourage good-natured debate as to which photos deserved to win. Everyone here disagreed, so I did my best, opening with a nervous little speech, trying to get the job done with minimum fuss and falling out.

I sat next to the sweetest chatterbox, a man called Barney, who until last year had been a presenter on the TV show *Blue Peter*. Charming, eloquent and entertaining, I really loved his company. He had just taken a sabbatical after nearly twenty years presenting children's television. His current bliss was to drive his camper van down long coastal highways, chasing electrical storms with his camera kit, a few clothes and little else. He's basically living the old-fashioned 'find yourself' hippy lifestyle, the kind of life that's hard to sustain, but certainly enviable to me. The joy he gets from taking photos, for himself, without a client or commissioner, are the happiest moments of his life.

I wonder whether I will again take photos in the same way. I love my job, I really do, and I am blessed to be sent all over the world shooting and directing and shooting again, but to go somewhere purely to shoot for oneself seems like a distant pleasure.

Yesterday I started planning my ten days in Paros, the island I used to visit with John. This time I'm going back, after over twenty years, with my wife Ange, and my children Paros and Pascale. They will all be seeing the island for the first time. Sitting at my father's old desk in the garage I'm struck, upon opening the drawers, how much the inner darkness still smells of him. Such an evocative smell, a fragrant mixture of wood, ink and leather. Some items in the desk haven't moved in over three years, there feels no need, there is little in there that is practical. It's just stuff. Memories and stuff.

Thursday 22 March

The Mews

Today I continued to shoot through an uncomfortable but not severe migraine, resting on my bed between shots, drinking bottles of water and downing several double Solpadeines. Headaches have terrified me for over half my life and the nature of my job, particularly during intensive periods like this, can be a terrific strain on eyes and head. Alternating right-eye focusing followed by laptop, quickly followed by focusing and back to laptop. I've had two or three major migraines in my life and they have all hospitalized me overnight, so this is a relatively mild one. Like most people, I steer myself to a darkened room, don't look at my phone, close my eyes and shut out everything and everyone. Now I can feel the headache behind my right eye and if I press gently the pain will increase, so I hold my head gently and try hard to meditate. It rarely works but it is all I can do and the shoot must go on.

We all have phobias: the dark, spiders, bats, flying – they are all quite rational really. I used to be frightened of guns, but since I've had them pointed at me I've realized it's not the gun itself but the irrational and unpredictable person holding the gun that scares me. Since being hit on the head with a bullet I've realized that the pain is the same pain. Don't get me wrong, it really bloody hurts, but the pain is manageable.

When John and I were young we feared Ice Ages, Halloween and, as I've said before, brain tumours. Since Johnny was ill I can add lumbar punctures to my list. A lumbar puncture, also known as a spinal tap, is a medical procedure in which a needle is inserted into the spinal canal, most commonly to collect cerebrospinal fluid for diagnostic testing. It can also be used to relieve pressure on the brain. John, in his usual way, accepted them as a necessary evil in his fight against what was happening in his head, but to me they were hideously nasty and almost barbaric. I wouldn't wish a lumbar puncture on my worst enemies. As I lie nursing my feeble excuse for a migraine it is all I can think of; John, lying in the foetal position in my father's pink cotton pyjamas, his lower back exposed to accept this horrifyingly long and thick needle into his spine.

Our childhood prayers, kneeling side by side next to my lower bunk, praying that the Ice Age wouldn't return, and that we wouldn't catch a brain tumour went silently unanswered.

Friday 23 March

It's the headache that will not budge. One of my ambitions through the writing of this book has been to give up the Solpadeine. It's been over twenty-five years of daily doses and I've noticed that they no longer work on me as a painkiller. Paracetamol, codeine and caffeine; I know I shouldn't be taking them every few hours – it's time to stop.

Shooting at the Bluebird restaurant in Chelsea today

Since John died I have found it hard to relate to other identical twins. I have a few chums, including one of my best friends, Peter Hornsey, who is a non-identical, fraternal twin. What is striking in the case of the non-identical twins is their lack of contact with each other in adulthood. Peter and John barely speak; Peter is a corporate lawyer, ultra-fit and slim, bleached spiky hair and a penchant for punk and new wave, while John is a hairy, burly farmer ploughing fields in Lincolnshire. They are like chalk and cheese.

Reflecting on the profound relationship of twins, Jack and Finn Harries often come to mind. They are the identical twin sons of writer Rebecca Frayn and film producer Andy Harries. The first time I met them was as toddlers, soon after I had agreed to be featured in Rebecca's *Cutting Edge* documentary, *Identical Twins*. During the filming I was shot photographing two identical twins, Jane and Emma, two very talented and beautiful designers who collaborated on some amazing design projects. Both girls were lovely; however, whenever I saw them I found myself tongue-tied and uncomfortable and ultimately terribly sad. I knew what it was: I was deeply jealous of their bond with each other and the future they had before them, the future that I had been so tragically denied. We eventually lost contact and I knew that it was my fault, my inability to be lucid in their company, my lone-twin neediness and my sorrowful state.

With Jack and Finn it has been very different, I feel the usual neediness inside me, but I feel that with all of my friends. But the pain of jealousy isn't there. Whereas with Emma and Jane I felt like half a friend, with Jack and Finn I felt a very close bond, even though I'm as old as the sum of both their ages. Like John and me, Jack and Finn had celebrated a youth-long twinship by being each other's best friends, hanging out together, shooting ideas, talking together, in a way that didn't end when they finished school.

Upon leaving, Jack decided to document his gap year, travelling around the world, larking about and sofa-surfing, sharing the videos he made on YouTube under the title of 'Jack's Gap'. Five months in and Finn was introduced to their rapidly growing following, through their dare-do antics and on-camera bonhomie. I watched in awe as their online audience quickly grew from one million to two million and upwards!

I bonded with Jack and Finn over camera advice. Between the two of them they have so much talent and creative and intellectual energy, but feel in a constant state of rush – so much to do in so little time. It's interesting to watch the period they find themselves in now, the ebb and flow of projects, of relationships with each other and others, with girlfriends and their parents.

It reminded me of a time when John and I were at a similar age. Our father, who was in his seventies, had a very minor stroke, so minor he literally laughed it off. But Mother recognized it immediately as a sign of grander problems, so together they decided that we should sit down as a family to discuss all the what-ifs and eventualities if something should ever happen to either or both of them. Father had taken to sorting out his stuff, his albums and family sketchbooks, his ancestral art collection, his father's stamp collection and so forth.

I sat alone on our favourite stair as John argued endlessly with our parents that he didn't need to talk about the what-ifs and wherefores of losing them, that he was happy to pass that mantle over to me. It was the one time that he didn't recognize his ten minutes of life superiority to me. It was the same step that I sat on, all night, alone, as John's body lay in a 'state of rest' next to the family treasures, under the huge oil of Loch Lomond, beside his beloved Steinway.

I feel like I've known Jack and Finn for ages and it seems extraordinary, considering how much they have achieved, that they are not yet at the age at which I lost John. Now they are forging different and separate careers, Jack as a gifted documentary maker and photographer, Finn as an architect in New York. As I see them at this crossroads in their lives, both personally and creatively, I can't help but wonder about the what-ifs. What if John hadn't died? Would we have struggled in a creative partnership like Jack and Finn did, finding solace in a temporary degree of separation, coming together, as they do, on special projects? It's hard to know. John found my creative style limiting and frustrating, although he was always complimentary. Commissions he sent me from Nucleus were definitely meant to test me and push my own boundaries, and though he never saw me forge a career as a photographer, he saw the pictures I processed at home and loved that it was a skill set so different from his own. I had a darkroom at The Beeches and would often spend hours under the house in red-lit darkness developing prints. I would curse him sometimes as he tried to beat my down-the-stairs-in-three-or-four leaps record, causing lumps of plaster to disengage from the ceiling and plop into my cat-litter trays of processing chemicals. I have no memory of him ever joining me down in my den, though our father would often join me to help hang my prints on the laundry rack, much to Molly's chagrin.

John particularly liked my series of Parisian prints, images of our Uncle Pierre in Place de la République, his home there, and images of the Paris Metro, few of which sadly have survived. Occasionally he'd borrow my prints to paint from and on my mother's wall is an almost perfect gouache rendition of eighteenth-century shutters, the view from Pierre's apartment, copied in muted tones from one of my photos, printed under the stairs in my musty darkroom.

I know my friendship with Jack and Finn is probably intensely one-sided, and I am aware yet again of my neediness as the lone twin, worrying unnecessarily if a text or Instagram message isn't noticed or returned. As individuals I am aware that they are as important to me as any other friend is. In fact, they are especially important to me. Ultimately, these special bonds can only be explained through conversation with other identical or lone identicals, but to talk of the death of one's twin to surviving identical twins is almost impossible; the break of that bond is too painful and shocking to describe, too unbelievable to imagine.

Sunday 25 March

Shooting at the Mews on a Sunday for Clarence Court eggs

I saw Mother yesterday, sitting in her corner chair in her dressing gown, holding court. She had been in to the hospital for a scan and her cancerous lumps had not diminished. She's overtired and her legs hurt a lot. She asked me what I thought about stopping the drugs, therefore losing the pain in her legs, but allowing the cancer to grow. Not an easy conversation, but we discussed the pain in her feet and legs versus the pain of a rapidly spreading cancer as opposed to a slowly growing one. She feels that she should 'carry on regardless'. We discussed the misrepresentation of the garden robin, Paros' work placement, the art at Belsay Hall, and migraines and the division between Loftuses who suffer from them and Loftuses who don't. She also gave me a display of two new walking sticks, ergonomically designed to fit her hands and remain standing if she lets go, possibly the daftest thing my medical brethren have brought her, as they fall over on an uneven surface and she has to bend her aching and concave body down to retrieve them, a near impossible task, leaving her frustrated but chuckling.

Day spent shooting Christmas turkeys ridiculously early. Now on a flight to Stockholm, 31,060 feet above the Hook of Holland.

John wasn't a huge fan of flying and as I'm sitting in the cramped and noisy flight, soporifically overheated, I can understand why. Our father Eric loved anything with wheels or wings, the faster the better. The first flight I remember him taking us on was an old turboprop to Jersey to visit a wartime friend who delighted us by removing his false eye over tea, bouncing it on the table, failing to catch it and losing it at the bottom of his swimming pool. I remember John and me being driven around the island, visiting wartime tunnels and bunkers. That trip signalled the first time we learned to swim and the first time we both had a schoolboy crush on the same girl, something that amazingly would never happen again. We both showed her triumphantly that we could hold our breath and swim four or five strokes underwater with a limited amount of coughing and spluttering. She promptly back-flipped into the pool and swam four or five lengths without a ripple, let alone a splutter, so we told her there was an old man's eye at the bottom of the pool and never spoke to her again.

John's first girlfriend was called Liz, a non-identical twin who had an annoying twin brother called John. My first girlfriend was called Jayne and I thought she was the most beautiful girl on earth, far more beautiful than Liz, whom John thought even more beautiful than Jayne. We lost our virginities to Jayne and Liz, probably around the same time, but didn't share the information with each other. However, we did tell our best chum Paul, who then told each of us the other's story. Both were fairly disastrous and underwhelmingly brief! I went out with Jayne for about five years, John with Liz for about four, art college coming along to split us both up with our loved ones, both running to our parents with broken hearts, tears of woe and declarations that there would never be another Jayne or Liz ever, ever.

I barely saw Jayne after she dumped me, though she did come to John's funeral wearing a leather jacket and sporting a fine mohawk. The only thing I recall her saying was 'We should do this more often.' I was sitting on the stairs of The Beeches at the time, a group of my old school friends bantering away with over-enthusiastic bonhomie. I remember feeling utter bleak disbelief, unable to cope with the alcohol-induced post-funeral euphoria and wishing them all gone, away from our home, knowing that my relationship with most of them would never be the same again.

Wednesday 28 March

Flight from Stockholm to London

Yet again I find myself on an overheated flight after an amazing two days shooting with Niklas Ekstedt at his two restaurants in Stockholm: Ekstedt and Tyge & Sessil. After over twenty years of shooting some of the most talented and inspiring people in the world, it's great to spend time with someone so refreshingly inspirational, entertaining and passionate. He's a remarkable chef, a wonderful ambassador for Sweden and now a great friend. It's the fourth time we've worked together and every moment, regardless of tiredness, is a joy. I'm so excited that we are going to shoot two books this year, including a project recording some of the ancient hunting, fishing and cooking techniques of the Sami, the indigenous people of northern Sweden and Norway. I can't wait!

But right now I'm flying home to shoot Prue Leith's book cover. It's a portrait, graphic and modern, with one of my favourite graphic designers, James Verity. So different in style from today's shoot, which was full of bright and cold Stockholm sunshine, pitch-dark interiors, indoor fires of juniper wood, smoking Sami Arctic char and reindeer hearts, fermenting herrings and boiling vats of lingonberries.

Yesterday I snuck back to my bunk for a moment during the shoot to load and back up my images. Finding my eyes heavy, I set my alarm for all of twenty minutes' rest. Just before the bell rang I fell asleep into a dream of eerie and biblical proportions. The sea and the skies were etched like the skies in our old family Bible, grand and thunderous. I could see every line of the drawings, layers of rough waves moving backwards and for-wards and sideways like pantomime seas, though far more menacing and horrific. I sat with John on a filthy, tar-covered beach, the specks of dark oil sticking to our pale bodies like cancerous sores. I knew John was not alive and as the spots of oil merged he began to fade and disappear. I cried and cried but not a tear would come, for what seemed like an eter-nity. I remember telling John how, though in a dream, I could feel the wind in the air and he looked back at me, so sadly, and told me that, once dead, one could no longer feel the wind.

The alarm was ringing as I choked myself awake, leaping up, gasping for air, thwacking my head on the top bunk. Not the most restful of sleeps.

Friday 30 March

The Mews

What happened to the last few days?

Thursday was lovely, surrounded by a great team. So much in a pho-tographer's career relies, in fact lives or dies, on the team around them. We were shooting the cover of the new Prue Leith book, unbelievably her first in twenty-five years. She arrived quietly, but once in the Mews with my team she was smiley, charming to all, and bounding around the studio. James, the designer, had shown me some wonderfully bright geometric designs for the cover so we shot her in a vivid stripey dress with bold orange jewellery, her trademark funkily colourful spectacles, twirling a fork of the brightest green pasta against a summer-sky blue-coloured backdrop. All was jolly, she was happy, the new client was lovely and the sun shone when torrential rain was forecast. What could go wrong?

That evening, Ange and I marked my successful day with a meal at a brasserie we don't normally frequent. There were just two other tables occupied and there was a quiet ominousness about the place. We were in high spirits, however, so rosé was quaffed and dinner ordered.

A few hours later – around 3a.m. – I awoke, much as usual, but this time I felt the room starting to spin, my stomach tight and cramped, shivering with cold and yet my forehead clammy to the touch. I fell asleep briefly and when I awoke with a start I was worse, so I crawled into the bathroom, then fainted upon reaching the relative cool of the toilet bowl. Waking with my lip stuck to the toilet seat I remembered my mother's anti-vomiting mantra: 'If you are still breathing deeply you cannot vomit.' Taking deep breaths, I managed to run a cold tap on my fiery forehead. More deep breaths, then I crawled back to bed. Fitful sleep eventually returned, dreams of endless rooms, hundreds and hundreds of them, all decorated in minute detail with tiny abstract geometric drawings. I awoke again, cold and with painful head and stomach cramps. The world was a-spin and again I crawled to the bathroom. My mantra failed me in my toxic and delirious state and I vomited the entire contents of a very pricey dinner into the toilet bowl until there was nothing left. I felt truly awful.

When Dr S had administered his antibiotic overdose, within seconds John complained of sickness and nausea. I grabbed the nearest bin and held his delicate head, careful not to touch his intrathecal reservoir, which looked like a little upturned medicine cup strapped to the pate of his head. He looked me in the eyes and we both knew something bad had happened, but without the help of the doctor or his colleagues there was only panic in my eyes. He vomited violently, so much for someone who had eaten so little. He kept apologizing, to me and then to the nurses. 'I'm so sorry,' he kept repeating. I just held him as the nurses rushed around me. I called the doctor, but he ignored me, sitting at a desk in a room across the corridor from John's room. I can still see him, head bowed, unmoving, reading a drug box. They never found that drug box and I was never asked to repeat what I saw.

Since that terrible, terrible day, I have not once vomited. Until now.

Poor dear John, vomiting on our birthday, into a wastepaper bin, endlessly apologizing. Little did we know that it was me who should have been apologizing to him; I had let him down at this final moment when he needed me to be his clear and lucid champion. Had Mother or Samantha been present they would have boldly stood their ground and said 'no' to Dr S. I had meekly complied, allowing the unthinkable to unfold.

Afternoon, Saturday 31 March

The Mews

My body still aches, but all else feels stronger. All my plans of writing on board my little Dutch boat – called the *Twee Gezusters* and built in 1921, she's a small reminder of my earlier years living on a houseboat – were scuppered by sickness. I'm hopeful that by Monday I shall feel like the walk to Imperial Wharf, where it is moored. When I was younger that whole area was unchanged since pre-Vietnam days – the huge bulk of Fulham Power Station and long empty skeletons of wharfside warehouses. I'd walk down to the bridge at the end of Lots Road and watch the herons catching fish at low tide, sustained by their ability to see through the thick brown silt of the ebbing and flowing Thames. The most I ever counted there was thirty-six. Like the buildings, most have now gone, though I still see one or two down by the boat, together with their friends the bean and Canada geese, endlessly dive-bombed by their enemies, the black-headed gulls.

John would have loved the boat and maybe that is why I keep it on, much against any sane financial advice. My son Paros sees it as a place of quiet contemplation, as do I. Pascale shares it with friends and they celebrate its uniqueness in a digital world, sharing its books, Polaroids, paints and its vinyl record player. I've contemplated hanging a bucket by the door where, once aboard, one pops one's mobile phone, keeping it free from digital disturbances. At the moment there hang my father's old binoculars, his ancient exposure meter, a most-important bottle opener and the cow bell that John used to ring from his room at the end of the corridor when he was in pain. I never want to hear that bell ring again, ever. Maybe I'll take it to the old boatyard in Naousa in Paros where John used to sit and sketch the old caique fishing boat and hang it there so it can ring silently in the wind, unheard by my tone-deaf ears.

Sunday 1 April

The Mews

As John and I became teenagers we were given the choice to separate into two different classes. Year Two was the beginning of streaming and the 'A' stream was divided into two classes of thirty or so: one for Latin learners and one for German. There was no logic in the directions we took other than a not entirely convincing belief that maybe it was a good time to sit, not only not next to each other for the very first time, but in different classrooms. So John trotted off to Latin, a subject he grew to hate and fear, and me to study German, a language so hopelessly under-used in modern life that the only time I've used it since was during a car accident in my twenties when I found an Austrian lady strapped into a recently tumbled car, in such a state of shock that she couldn't speak her normally fluent English.

This second-year divide was initially painful as we'd never sat next to anyone but each other, but we would still meet at breaks, lunch, assemblies and games. Gradually these meetings became fewer and fewer as we began, tentatively, to make new friends, for the first time as individuals and not as identical twins. Many became friends to both of us, of course, but they were definitely known as John's friend Marek, David's friend Tim, John's friend Steven, David's friend Mark.

It was with a combined sigh of relief that we joined together again to complete our Sixth Form, both taking a foundation diploma in Art and Design, A-Level Art, and A-Level Biology. The foundation was fantastic, a two-year course in everything and anything design related, from woodwork and metalwork to pottery and painting. And it was a hoot to be sitting back next to John. We were on a course where rebellious thought was embraced, artist temperament was nurtured, and a sense of eliteness overcame us. I know that's bad, but at the time it gave us, the un-sporty, sensitive, artistic types, a safe haven against the bullying staff and oppressors. We were a desperate bunch of artistic chumps really, all, except John and me, completely different, all fascinating in our own ways. But it was in those pre-fab outhouses of pottery kilns, workshops and studios that John and me grew, and over the happiest of two years the seeds were planted of who and what we would both become.

Monday 2 April

Shooting on Easter Saturday at the Mews,
Friday's delayed shoot

The relationships of identical twins with each other's friends is often complicated. As I've said, all of John's college friends, including his girl-friend, seemed to drift away from me after John's death. It was, I assume, either my likeness to their fallen comrade or their inability to know what to say to me, and I did understand this, heartbreaking though it was at the time. Quite a few of my own friends also abandoned ship soon after John's death. I know I became a much more needy friend and I think, as often happens in romantic relationships, the needier partner can be pushed away by the more independent one. In my relationship with John he was certainly the more independent and not just because of his ten-minute headstart in the world.

I think it's why, for a long time, I made some terrible friendship choices and spent too much time making an effort where acquaintances probably found me overbearing. I remember organizing a stunning weekend party in an old hunting lodge in Loch Carron on the wild Scottish coast, facing out to the Isle of Skye. I couldn't really afford it but I paid for flights, cabs, enough wine to support a small clan, hired a mad-arse cook, even sent out a diver to catch fresh langoustines and scallops. Celebrating my birthday in such an extravagant fashion, screaming out to all, 'You're my new friends and I'm bloody fine!'

As my clinical psychologist told me weeks later in one of our rare and unsatisfactory meetings, if a patient plonks himself on the couch and answers 'How are you today?' with 'I'm fine', it stands for F.I.N.E. (Fucked up, Insecure, Neurotic and Emotional). I rarely agreed with her, but in this there was more than a grain of truth.

Tuesday 3 April

The Mews

I'm in the Mews listening to 'No Sound but the Wind' by the Editors. Ange is half-asleep beside me; I'm post-bath, wearing my smartest PJs, feeling calm and content. It's taken many years to find these quiet moments of contentment. For such a long time a feeling of guilt would overcome me. 'Why should I be happy when John is dead?' But life, normal life, is not sustainable in a permanent state of mourning, loss and guilt. Of course those feelings can knock me over, like every seventh wave among incoming breakers, but now maybe I just ride them a little better and a little longer. Ange looks so beautiful, gently purring. I always liken her to a mole, gently peeking through a sea of white linen, never letting go of the floppy ears of her little white bunny she cradles next to her overheated cheeks. I adore her and feel lucky to be alive and smiling beside her.

Wednesday 4 April

The Mews to a treehouse in Barcombe, Sussex

Ange has a writing exercise she completes every day at bedtime. She writes down a list of five things – it can be anything – that she feels gratitude for during the day. So Ange, so simple, beautiful and positive. What a great way to end the day. I had such a long shoot today, but I loved it, travelling down to Sussex with one of my best chums, Nick Pope, in his old Land Rover, to shoot the Hunter Gather Cook crew – five wonderfully bonkers and lushly bearded friends, cooking in the Lewes treehouse, foraging and carving and butchering and hunting and pickling and smoking.

So I thought I'd just write a list, in chronological order, of the things that made me happy today, from the moment I awoke spooned into Ange:

The smell of her hair and my milky tea.

The rising moon in a clear blue sky, the mist, a pair of fallow deer, a white windmill in Sussex, hedgerow after hedgerow of yellow primroses and daffodils.

A sign for the Bluebell Railway reminding me of a childhood trip with our father, flowering magnolias.

Nick and his dog BB, baby squirrels nesting in a barrel, the friendly welcomes and hugs from the bearded ones, and the treehouse.

Woodpeckers hammering in the ancient wood, moss-covered ash trees, whittling willow, garlic flowers, snowdrops, a babbling brook and memories of childhood dammings.

A glass of Malbec warmed by the wood oven in a cold afternoon, more rabbits, a murder of crows in the ash trees.

'Forest bathing' appreciation, a round of hugs, laughter and home, to tea and toast and my darling wife.

The day as a list of moments of joy, what a wonderfully positive way to end it.

5 August '84, Parikia, Paros

Dear Mum, hope all is well at home and that the patients are behaving themselves. I'm sitting in the shade of a chapel which looks over the whole town and the sea on the other side. I got quite badly burnt yesterday while walking around the bay and that's why I'm keeping in the shade today. Things have not gone quite to plan so far and I've had to sleep rough in just my bag, I did however have some drawings bought from me and they are being framed and put up on the walls of an Australian yacht. The weather isn't too hot but the sun is terrifically strong and David will be pleased to hear that I haven't seen any jellyfish! I shall try to ring tonight so long as there aren't too many people. All's well though.

John xx

19 August '84, Paros

Dear Mum, just to say that I'm thinking of you at home and am hoping that all is well. Looking at the flowers around me and I think of the garden at 58 – I hope it is looking grand. I look forward to sitting in it having a nice cup of Earl Grey, having a good chin-wag with me mam. I'm with a couple of chaps from Manchester at the moment but shall probably head down to Crete at the end of the week and hopefully a day in Turkey. Have seen Delos, Naxos, Santorini, Antiparos, and of course Paros so far so I haven't been doing too bad. Anyway I shall think of you all having Sunday lunch now!

All my love, John xx

Dear Mum, I hope all is well. Got a job painting signs at the boatyard today. It is only for a few days however. I look forward to seeing David tomorrow and finding him some decent accommodation. This weekend I'm off to Samos to catch another ferry to Patmos. Here I shall stay for a bit to see the great monasteries and to catch a ferry to Ephesus, Turkey, to see the 'Home of Mercy'.

Then I must think about coming home, exhausted, thin and needing a comfy bed and a nice cup of tea. Some rain would even go down a treat as well. I'll send a card from Turkey and Patmos though I expect I'll be home before they arrive.

All my love, John xxx

Saturday 7 April

The Mews, with Ange working beside me

It's funny that my father didn't find love until he was fifty. You'd think that such a perfectly mannered, debonair chap would have been inundated with offers of love, but apparently not. His love of my mother was his 'first love'. He waited, hopeful that one day he would fall in love at first sight, as he eventually did. His heart, like mine, was a big heart, full of love for his wife and then for his newborn identical twins, John and David. Later he suffered seven heart attacks, including a massive one from which my mother revived him on the operating table, after he'd been given up for dead. But I don't believe his big, beautiful heart would have survived the death of John. I now understand the concept of dying from a broken heart. I certainly came close, and my father almost certainly would have done. Luckily the searing pain of a broken relationship is the greatest suffering that many of us will ever experience, particularly in our young lives. And ultimately time does heal most broken hearts.

But not all. There is a syndrome known as Takotsubo cardiomyopathy that affects many whose hearts are broken more violently or tragically. This little-known condition was first coined, as it sounds, in Japan, and named after the native word for an octopus cooking pot, which has a unique shape that resembles the broken left ventricle of a human heart. It's provoked when the heart muscle is suddenly 'stunned', causing the left ventricle to change shape, and is typically prompted by intense emotional or physical stress. It causes some actual visual scarring, akin to a real physical break. When John died and I eventually lay down on my bedroom floor to rest, my heart was broken. Like many before me I willed myself to die. Ultimately what saved me was the sense of panic I felt when my body realized that I was bound for success in my quest for eternal sleep.

Note found on Mum's desk:

Into your hands of love, Oh Lord, I command my dear John
Enfold him in your love and peace, now and forever more.
Amen

Sunday 8 April

Our wonderful nanny Molly Florence Wrigglesworth spent her life caring for other people, her parents, patients in local hospitals and, last but not least, the Loftus family, particularly us twins. When my mother called from hospital and Molly passed the phone to me, just the two of us at the breakfast table that was normally the centre of rowdy teas with all our friends, I knew that, other than Mother, she was the only person

I could be with at that terrible moment. She had known John from the moment of his birth to the moment of his passing, and something broke inside her, inside us both, at that extraordinary moment in time that was shared between dear Molly and I.

Monday 9 April

I left the Mews early last night so that I could wander in a circum-navigation of Battersea Park before nightfall. It was the greyest of a fifty-shades-grey day, shadowless and dull. It's rare to see, but no one was in the park, no dog walkers or joggers, the thick mist of impenetrable drizzle keeping them tucked up at home. What was extraordinary was the verdant vividness amidst the quiet stillness. I stopped occasionally to take photos; newly hatching catkins hanging lankly and sodden, patches of multi-coloured bark and moss peeling from the plane trees. I was struck by how much of the minutiae of the park was alive and bursting with colour and signs of new life.

It was a blissful hour of solitary silence, birdsong and observation of the colourful kaleidoscope of winter's decay and new birth, new life. An uplifting, life-affirming hour, sealed with a perfect lingering hug upon meeting Pascale when I arrived home.

'Drinking is a way of ending the day.'
—ERNEST HEMINGWAY

Tuesday 10 April

The Mews

Since I was unwell ten days ago I seem to have more of a wariness around wine. Not a bad thing, a drop in consumption levels; we're talking five glasses down to three, not ultimately a drying out, more a subtle reduction in pace. Today, yet again, and I'm sure it won't be the last time, I have begun my umpteenth attempt at stopping my constant plink plonk, fizz of the dreaded yet deliciously dissolvable Solps. Thirty years of averaging five a day may keep the headaches at bay but Lord knows what havoc they are playing with my inner workings. At least poor Johnny had a good excuse for his addiction, mine is the after-effects of my other addiction – rosé – even though three or four glasses of it are hardly rock and roll. Like all addictions, the partaking of the ritual begins to have its own beauty, the plink and fizz, delayed into extra time if you add ice, the rim of dried codeine around the lip of the glass that you can taste with a dunk and wipe of the finger, the salty, alkaline first sip, the mild fizzing in the nostrils, the hypnotic bubbling and chalky aftertaste.

When Johnny died my Solps consumption rose from one or two to five or six tablets a day, a soporific duller to the endless waking days. Somehow I found the strength not to drown myself in drink though the temptation was so strong.

I could too easily have gone off the rails but I was saved by the need to look after my mother. She needed me and I needed her, and our bond now is closer than ever. I yearn for her company. I'm very aware that she is in need of a lot of medication; a nasty little pill for her breast cancer, a tiny tipple of whisky for the blood vessels and circulation, some painkillers for the pain in her feet and legs, something to help her sleep, another to help her wake, a tonic here, some vitamins there. With me and my Solpadeine consumption, I recognize it as a sign of depressive behaviour, symbolic of my post-traumatic stress, so I'm trying to grab the issue by the horns and wrestle it away from my daily routine.

Another cutting, this one from *British Medical Journal*, 30 November 1991:

> By Ian Loftus [then tumour doctor at Leicester Royal]:

Sir, the recent prosecution of two junior hospital doctors for manslaughter has attracted much publicity. It is the first time that such charges have arisen relating to the administration of intrathecal drugs, but it is not the first accident of its kind. My elder brother John died as a result of a junior doctor administering a massive intrathecal overdose of gentamicin while receiving treatment for meningitis after neurosurgery.

My family felt great bitterness and anger about the circumstances surrounding his death. We sought a full explanation from the staff and a reassurance that steps would be taken to prevent such a disaster happening again. However, the hospital was unhelpful, uncommunicative and, above all, unresponsive to our distress. Furthermore, the coroner and the General Medical Council appeared unwilling to address our questions about guidelines and procedures for administering potentially dangerous drugs.

It is with great distress that I hear of such accidents, including that in Peterborough (see previous BMA journal), occurring with disturbing regularity, and it seems to me that we should strive to reduce the risks of such events occurring. We must be aware of the terrible consequences that mistakes have on patients, their families and also often the hospital staff. So how can things be improved to reduce the risks of such accidents occurring?

I believe that there should be stricter guidelines and better education of junior staff with regards to administering drugs. More careful labelling of drugs, particularly those for intrathecal administration, and certainly checking of drugs with other members of staff should be standard practice and would certainly help to prevent similar accidents occurring. I am in no position to institute such changes but because of the loss suffered by my family, I feel they should be encouraged.

When accidents do happen, as occasionally they will, we must be able to admit that they are accidents, and not see this as a weakness on our part, for we are all human. We must be able to approach relatives sensitively to offer explanations and reassurances; failure to do so can only add to the misery and despair caused by the loss of a loved one.

I. M. Loftus

Brother Ian is now Professor of Vascular Surgery at St George's Hospital in Tooting. Following the Loftus tradition, my son Paros is now a second-year medical student at St George's and spends his holidays on research projects for the vascular department. My mother retired from general practice a year after John's death, a great loss to her patients who were devoted to her. Upon moving back to the shadow of Hadrian's Wall she voluntarily helped the local hospice to administer injections in the palliative care of people with life-limiting illnesses.

Thursday 12 April

A 6a.m. start, a long day shooting the comings and goings of kitchen theatre at The Wolseley restaurant, followed by an interview with *The*

Telegraph about the writing of this book. It was hard to talk to a stranger, journalist Peter, about the personal nature of the book, while being photographed by a sweet German photographer who, in a strange case of disconsolate chance, was born a triplet, a singleton girl with two identical twin brothers, who both died in childbirth.

Five great things to appreciate today:

Foxes on Albert Bridge.

Admiring Charlie Mackesy's illustrations of a mole, boy and horse.

Pascale telling me she loves me more than I love her.

A jay plucking out weeds from my neighbour's window boxes.

The beauty of photographing the egg of a goose.

Deep breath, tomorrow is another day.

Friday 13 April

John would refuse to leave his bed on Friday the thirteenth, believing that being there was the safest place on earth. Ultimately he was killed in bed, just not his own bed, on our birthday, Halloween, a day we had always felt laden with a fog of gloom and ominousness. So often in our youth we would huddle up as night began to fall, bedroom curtains drawn and overlapped so that no one could see in or out, believing without doubt, that witches would have their evil eye on us, identical twins born on Halloween. At least Friday the thirteenth would never fall on the 31st.

When I saw a clinical psychologist after John's death, I would sit there gazing at the ceiling as she mentally prodded and probed her lone twin lab rat, handing her a cheque at the end, no better for the experience, with a new antidepressant prescription to be binned at the first street corner. What did I gain? A life dependency on Seroxat, the controversial 'selective serotonin reuptake inhibitor' that has so many unpleasant side effects when you're coming off them. Life seems more dangerous than it would have been without them. I got a diagnosis of 'post-traumatic stress disorder' (PTSD) and a 'rare case of scenario syndrome', something years later I can find little about other than its basic description which is 'extreme catastrophic thinking'. In hindsight the diagnosis was wrong. Post-traumatic stress I take on the chin; what was happening with me was not catastrophic thinking but a symptom of extreme anxiety and slipping into depression.

Today the World Press Awards were announced, and, as usual, the pictures are extraordinary. Glimpses often of a terrible world that exists far away from our comfortable lives, images of tragic brutality or suffering. One image particularly moved me, reminding me of a pre-Raphaelite masterpiece. It's an image of two sisters called Djeneta and Ibadeta, lying side by side in a hospital in Horndal in Sweden. Soft-focused and beautiful, the sisters sleep seemingly at peace, but for the tubes running from Djeneta's nose. The sisters are Roma refuges from Kosova who suffer from resignation syndrome, which renders the patient immobile, mute and unable to respond to physical stimuli.

I just pray that the sisters dream beautiful and sweet dreams. The world can seem a vast and cruel world at times.

Saturday 14 April

An extract from *Her*, a memoir by Christa Parravani who, like me, found herself a lone identical twin:

I forgot who I was after Cara died. The power of her memory was so strong that I would see her instead of me. I gazed at myself in the mirror and there she was, her rusty brown eyes, frightened and curious as a doe. I'd smile at myself and see her grinning back.

I learned later that this heartbreaking delusion – that you are looking at your dead twin when really you are looking at yourself – is a common experience among identical twins when one dies. The surviving twin finds it impossible to differentiate their living body from that of their dead twin. They become a breathing memorial for their lost half.

Christa struggles as most of us lone twins do. She, like I, had read that 50 per cent – the equivalent of a toss of a coin – of bereaved identical twins die within two years of their twin's death. Like me she rejected the help of psychiatrists and clinical psychologists and ultimately found help from a friend who had recently suffered the loss of her sister and mother. In my case, as I have already stated, it was my introduction to Tim Knatchbull, my lone twin soulmate.

Sunday 15 April

Flight from London to Stockholm and on to Mariefred

A day of headaches and coughs. My paranoia around headaches is, I think, an acceptable consequence of the events leading to John's death. I can only assume that the headaches that John used to suffer in the years prior to his illness were far stronger than mine. I flew a hideously bumpy, overheated and overwrought flight to Stockholm today, a beautiful view of the curvature of the earth enhancing the sunset but otherwise an ill-tempered and uncomfortable flight.

Upon arrival in Mariefred I snuck a dose of Swedish cough medicine, I assume prescription rather than over the counter as the main ingredient seems to be morphine – for coughs! Still, it should thwack the headache into touch!

Monday 16 April

Mariefred, Sweden

Wasted days, like yesterday, frustrate me. I travelled from the Mews to Mariefred in Sweden, I saw the sun set in a purple sky, but I failed to find inspiration to write.

Today was different. My sleep followed the pattern of the day, frustrated, tetchy, irritable and overheated, but the dawn chorus at 6a.m. beckoned me outside into the chilled air. Mariefred is part of the archipelago, so on water, still partly iced-over, the air so still, bullrushes frozen to attention in the shallows. I walked to the water barefoot, and closed my eyes to the rising sun. Absolute silence and utter bliss, broken in a most welcome way by two Egyptian geese chuckling at me, their early-morning companion, equally barefoot. I so love the way they travel around Europe, almost unnoticed and incognito, beautifully exotic with red eyes and golden-brown tufty plumage, looking like they've just walked out of Tutankhamun's tomb. I thought of Ange and her lists of 'things to be thankful for' and I thought how I'd been up for no more than half an hour and I already had:

A hawthorn bush full of sparrows chirping wildly.

The milky sunrise.

The frozen bulrushes and the freezing-cold water on my almost numb feet, reminding me it's good to be alive.

The slight warmth on my face as I tilt my head towards the rising sun.

The bevy of swans wandering silently on the ice floe.

The quirky, Tim Burton-esque, knobble-ended apple trees, still bearing a few of last autumn's fruit, curved over by the weight of their branches.

The Wes Anderson-esque architecture of the symmetrical yellow-painted timber-frame houses, like a scattering of oversized dolls' houses, behind where I dangle my frozen toes in the brackish water.

And last but not least, Tweedledee and Tweedledum, my newly named Egyptian compadrés, making me wish that I'd brought my breakfast down with me so I could share it with them on the jetty.

Tuesday 17 April

Mariefred, Sweden

I started the day as I did yesterday, with a sole-spiking, pebble-hobbling wander down to the water, this time remembering some cinnamon buns for T-dum and T-dee. I was amazed to see the ice upon the lake had melted and disappeared completely, freeing the odd buckled and warped ghost boat from its icy clutches. I was tempted to board and conquer and claim but the biting cold on my bare feet sent me scuttling painfully home to my studio for tea and knäckebröd.

Wandering with a hand-warming mug to sit under the apple tree in a small triangle of early-morning sunshine, I was catapulted back in time to a distant memory of me and John screaming and charging through the damson and plum trees at The Beeches. I've no idea how it started, but after dinner on balmy summer evenings, John and I would strip down to our little white M&S Y-fronts and tear outside and up the garden path, our corgi Sally in hot pursuit and full bark, screeching at the top of our unbroken voices 'White pants men, white pants men!' In and out of the trees, around the 'shuggy boat' swing and up and down the rockery we would career, 'White pants men, white pants men!'

After a few high-octane minutes our brother Ian and cousin Edward would then tear out of the back door to a chorus of barks and screams, 'White pants men, white pants men!' John, David, Ian, Edward and corgi Sally, in close formation, arms aloft and at full tilt, streaming through the undergrowth, blissfully ignorant of rose-thorn scratches or nettle stings. And then, after a seemingly endless bliss of wheeling and whirling about the garden, we would all clatter into each other, grind to a halt and fall about with uncontrollable laughter as our sister, Jean-Marian, would nervously round the rockery corner, just in her underwear, to be met by four breathless chumps pointing at her and laughing our non-existent socks off, screaming at the top of our pre-pubescent voices, 'Yellow pants woman, yellow pants woman!' Tears before bedtime!

Wednesday 18 April

Last day shooting in Mariefred, a grey as grey day. I made my 6a.m. homage to visit my geese, but they were nowhere to be seen and the *Mary Celeste* had drifted back out to sea.

This morning I was thinking about my father and his friends, Patrick, Derek, Ron and Pierre. Patrick was his brother, Derek his cousin, Ron his best school chum and Pierre his childhood pen pal. To John and I they were all uncles and the best uncles a boy could have. They often dined together at The Beeches and when the ladies retired to the sitting room the chaps would send us to bed, shut the heavy door to the dining room and reminisce, particularly about the war. John and I could never quite understand why we weren't invited to these whisky-drinking, pipe-smoking natters but contented ourselves with listening in from our stairway hiding place, side by side so that the pillars hid us from prying eyes.

Father had spied in Austria at the beginning of the war, before being invalided home, much to his frustration. We overheard talk of German columns spotted and bombed, of the Resistance and the Occupation, of collaborators and friends.

John once asked Father 'What makes a good spy?' He was quiet for a long time and we assumed he wouldn't answer. But then, in his quiet, elegant way, he told us to go up to the library to find our set of Beatrix Potter books. Up we rushed in our pyjamas, collected them up and ran back with them all downstairs, not sure where this was going. 'If you can find Potter's secret messages in the books, then you'll make a good spy.'

Of course we both eagerly read the lot, cover to cover, end to end, and found nothing but tales of Jeremy Fisher, Peter Rabbit and Ptolemy Turtle. 'Was Mrs Tiggy-Winkle code? Was Peter a Nazi? Was Mr McGregor a traitor?' Father, calm as ever, 'No poppets, you're looking in the wrong places, looking within the narrative is far too easy to be spotted by a good spy.' Hours and days were spent poring over Potter's books, until suddenly, 'Eureka!' It was me that spotted the first, John the second, and me the third. Father smiled softly, cleaning his pipe, and returned to reading his *Times*. There were indeed hidden messages in Beatrix Potter's books, but they were not words, they were illustrations, tiny hidden subliminal sketches, a carrot here, a bee there, but hidden, lightly drawn and not where you would expect to find them, little obscure messages to those in the know. Later in life I realized what an excellent plan our father had hatched to get us to read more. We had devoured the complete works in under twenty-four hours and I haven't stopped reading since.

Saturday 21 April

An uneventful flight back from Stockholm to London

Saw Mother today and was greatly concerned at how weak she was. She tottered slowly to the door to greet me, barely walking ten cautious steps before needing a rest. She complained briefly that no one had seen her before reverting to the normal proceedings of 'You know, darling, it's nothing. There are so many worse off than me.'

The second day of summer and the garden is blissfully full of avian chatter, blackbirds full of chirp, the first swallow of spring and coal tits and blue tits. Even a cuckoo announced its treetop presence.

This week I have to travel to Cornwall and back, twice, and to Tel Aviv on a photographic assignment to capture some of the characters around the food of Tel Aviv and Jerusalem, a city I have long wished to visit. Chatting about it with Mother, she told me of walking up the Via Dolorosa in the old city of Jerusalem, believed to be the path that Jesus walked. The Way of Suffering, the Painful Way, the Way of Sorrow, from the Antonia Fortress to the Church of the Holy Sepulchre, home of the 'True Cross', or fragments of it, the cross on which Christ was apparently crucified. She walked the route with an old friend from Cumbria, Winifred, who, as a Quaker, didn't feel she needed to enter the Holy Sepulchre. For me, even as a non-believer, having travelled all the way to the point that so many believe is where Jesus died for mankind, nailed to a simple wooden cross whose base still resides protected for time immemorial, I think I'd want to take a peek. But no, Winifred sat and enjoyed the early-morning sunshine while Mother went in alone.

She told me it was crowded, far too crowded, with overemotional tourists and pilgrims from all over the world. I've seen pilgrims arriving at Santiago de Compostela at the culmination of the Camino de Santiago pilgrimage route and that is only the burial site of St James; this is where

Christ met his fate and the church is a fraction of the size. It was oppressively hot and alarmingly overcrowded but Mother, easily claustrophobic at the best of times, shuffled her way to the front to see the fragment of the cross. She's never told anyone this but when she got near she had the most extraordinary out-of-body experience where she became totally at one with herself, totally unaware of anyone around her, blissfully silent, calmly deaf to the noise, the coughs, the emotional wails of those around her. She described it as being deep within a bubble, aware that she was looking at herself, but that she saw also herself alone, no one else there in the church, deeply, deeply moved, so silent that one would hear a pin drop, and completely unaware of the passage of time. When she eventually decided it was time, she left her silent, peaceful state, her bubble, and walked outside into the bustling heat of the Way of Sorrow. Poor overheated Winifred asked her, 'Where on earth were you all this time?' and for once in Mother's life, she didn't have an answer.

Sunday 22 April

Holy Mackerel – two separate trips to Cornwall this week

Last night I dreamt of the first swallows of spring, and of bad omens and a long confession of sins with The Beeches' local vicar. He was a chap, weirdly, I never trusted. I recall how he sat in our garden next to me, despite the cold and damp, under the purple hazelnut tree where John and I would lie on our blankets as young children, gazing into the sky, and he told me 'John is in a better place . . .'

I asked him if he'd ever met identical twins, and no, he hadn't. Did he know that John had been an argumentative atheist? Well no, he didn't. Had he any experience of heaven, I wondered? Well, no, he hadn't. I got up, turned and walked away. It's strange, but whenever I walked past him as he gardened and trimmed his vicarage hedges I was convinced that he pretended he hadn't seen me.

On the train, delayed and past midnight. Tired!

The confessional with Mother's vicar was brief, and to be honest, fairly accurate.

'Father, I have sinned, I feel I could have prevented my twin's death.'

'Move on, my son, he's in a better place.'

'Father, I once threw a stone into Lake Lucerne, but didn't look as I threw it and it hit the only swan on the lake and killed it.'

'Move on, my son, in England you would have hung for treason, but Switzerland is neutral.'

'Father, John and I tried to invade San Marino.' (We did this once at school.)

'My son, you were caught, and anyway if they weren't Fascist they were Stalinists and therefore bad for the health.'

'Father, we tested a bomb and blew a Fascist's garage door off.'

'My son, I've already told you about the Fascists.'

'Father, I wrote anti-Stalinist graffiti in the Soviet embassy's visitors' book.'

'My son, I've already told you about the Stalinists.'

'Father, so "*merde dans la boîte aux lettres*"?'

'My son, okay too, but not very nice.'

'Father, I stood lookout while our chum Paul nicked the *Dada Manifesto* from the library.'

'My son, how Dadaist of you.'

'Father, I hired a car, a V8 Pontiac, for a week and drove all around the Bahamas, but had not passed my test or had driving lessons, but looked really cool.'

'My son, luckily for all, you drive at the pace of a snail.'

'Father, I hate cats, but I love all other animals.'

'My son, cats are the spawn of the devil like Fascists and Stalinists' . . . and so it went on. John would have enjoyed its recapping over breakfast.

In the pub following a lovely shoot with Nathan Outlaw while Marie, my art director, showed me pictures of her kittens in an attempt to sway me to the dark side. Something about the day made me start wondering again whether the sharing of one's personal journey is actually a wise move.

My dislike and distrust of cats is the polar antithesis of my love of birds and animals. Walking to my breakfast meeting at the Colbert this morning, along Battersea Park and over the Albert Bridge, I saw a tubby tabby cat that looked like it had a mouse in its jaws. So smug and proud, waiting for its owner to show off and say 'Hey, meow, by the way I know you didn't ask, but I've killed for you again.' And the owner will post a cute pic on Instagram of smug tubby tabby, all doe-eyed and innocent, its evil filtered and forgotten. Anyway tubby tabby the evil-eyed little crapper didn't have a little mouse but a baby hedgehog! Miss bloody Tiggy-Winkle! I never forgave our cat Whiskers for its slaughter of five baby blue tits that I had persuaded to nest in my little wooden RSPB nesting box attached to Father's garden shed. It was utter carnage and I can still remember the bereft tweeting of their confused parents as if it was yesterday.

Cats are evil and Whiskers was the Dr Evil of evil. She once shat on my pillow so that my overtired late-night flop onto plumped-up linens became an overnight stay in A&E. I never executed my revenge on Whiskers for tit carnage and Pillowgate or the multitude of bird-killing sins, dragonfly beheadings, butterfly downings and face scratchings, but tubby tabby nearly got my pent-up wrath for killing Miss Tiggy-Winkle. Birds have enough to cope with around the Mews with trees and hedgerows making way for concrete patios and air-conditioning units without the added terror of tubby tabby and his cronies. At least sly Mr Fox will eat whatever he can be half-arsed to catch and not just plonk it down at your feet like a barbaric satanic offering. Several of my cat-loving chums are vegetarians – how warped is that?

Walking to my meeting, trying not to think of the crime I had just witnessed, I was reminded again of how much the inner London dawn chorus has changed. I spotted a coal tit, the odd blackbird trying its best in the newly flowering magnolias, its song ever beautiful, but all is drowned out by the shrieks and caws of the green parakeets that fill the trees and raid their nests. Now these vivid interlopers could probably do with an uninvited visit from tubby tabby if he wasn't so fat and lazy to go high enough to try.

I arrived on time to my early-morning meeting, bumping into several friendly faces as I walked, bathed in early-spring sunshine. My poor friend didn't look well, her left eye inflamed and watery. She's been struggling with problems with it for some time and has been on antibiotics and steroids, had scans, biopsies and now has a cataract, all caused by a nasty infection a few years previously. The cause? Cat shit. A cat-shit parasite is living, unable to be removed, behind her eyeball. It's like a scene from *Alien*, and she doesn't even have a bloody cat! She's an avid gardener and, as all gardeners who don't have cats know, cats will either shit at home in their litter or they'll shit in someone else's backyard. Not in their own – oh no. They'll kill all the birds, voles and hedgehogs but they won't shit in their own backyard. So my poor friend somehow rubbed soil, tainted with cat shit onto her beautiful face and that cat shit contained, as the one on my pillow will have done, a nasty eye-burrowing blindness-inducing parasite that likes to live between your retina and your brain.

Did I say, I don't like cats? I really don't, and neither did John.

Back in Cornwall

Why am I writing this diary? The main reason has to be to improve that terrible 50 per cent statistic, that half of identical twins who lose their twin die within two years. Heads or tails, fifty-fifty, live or die. I'm a success story in the survival department, as is Tim. One other identical lone twin I tried to help, not long after I met Tim, took their own life just before our first meeting date. One less death in the world and the suffering hinterland that exists beyond that death has to be worthwhile. It's not just sharing the manner of his death and confronting the facts and the people involved, it's sharing the intimate secrets, the 'white pants men' and the sock cricket and the prayers before bedtime stuff. I wonder whether I want to share those with one and all. But if one removes the joyous adventures of sharing a life with a genetic copy and instant and inseparable best buddy, you are just left with the trauma.

Beautiful things to shout about today:

Goldfinches in the hedgerows of moss-covered birch. Impossibly verdant greens as a backdrop to their flashes of gold and red. First time I've seen them in years.

A tiny but intense rainbow over Tintagel, King Arthur's Seat.

Bluebells and whitebells among the trees, swept by the constant Cornish winds.

Spotting one of the tiny scars on my face, left by John's fingernail as he held my face too tightly in our cot, unwilling to take his eyes off mine.

Photographing fish at Nathan Outlaw's restaurant. We opened a bag brought in by the local fishermen and inside were two enormous cuttlefish, still alive, pulsing with thick black ink, the brownish mottling changing constantly to try to blend with the black sacks of their capture, their bodies glowing brightly with a lurid greeny-blue iridescence, literally glowing in the darkness, I assume as a last resort in its quest for survival. Amazing.

Tuesday 24 April

Cornwall to London, and back to Cornwall, in one day

This evening I was at the award ceremony for the Pink Lady Food Photographer of the Year awards, which is held every year at the Mall Galleries in London. It is special this year as I am now the chairman of the judges, an honour bestowed on me that I take oh so seriously.

The awards were followed by a gorgeous dinner at The Wolseley with my *Blue Peter* chum Barney, Ange and 'the Ps' (Paros and Pascale). Then a mad rush in a cab back to Paddington to catch the overnight Riviera Sleeper, a wonderfully old-fashioned experience, back down to Port Isaac. I loved the sleeper and found its gentle rocking profoundly comforting, reminding me of stormy nights living on the boats. As I was rocked to sleep I chuckled as I remembered John's wee-wee-in-the-face dare on the Flying Scotsman on our trip to the Orkneys many moons ago.

That trip was memorable for so many reasons. John and I were seventeen going on eighteen and for the first time we ungratefully argued with our parents about not going. 'The Orkneys would be so boring, we don't want to go with Nanna, we want to stay at home with our friends, we don't want to hang out with Ian and Jean-Marian.' I've relooked at photos of the trip and John and I look utterly sullen and miserable during the sea crossing to Kirkwell: two moody young punks, all badges and spikiness, both needing a slap around the back of the head. We must have ruined the build-up to going away.

Of course all was forgotten in the days that passed. They were the longest summer days that we had ever experienced. The sky was rarely ever dark, and when it was the night was filled with Milky Way brightness and a constant firework display of shooting stars. The endless white beaches and aqua seas were filled with the most beautiful cowries, which Father told me were used as money in some countries. We did our utmost to collect them all and it was certainly here that John and I started our obsession with beachcombing. Some of our happiest times together were spent on hands and knees, backs bent and burning as we crawled slowly along the foreshores collecting shells, pebbles and pottery. Often we would finish a day creating a collaged display of our finds in typically competitive manner for Father to judge on content, originality, patterning and display. In the Orkneys a shark tooth or cowry would beat a top shell, which in turn would beat a pink jewel of a clam shell. The holy grail of our searches, which in the Orkneys remained elusive but Padre insisted was worth hunting for – clever Father – was Viking artefacts.

We loved everything about the Orkneys and admitted to our exhausted parents that we had been a pair of miserable gits and ungrateful sods. I'd taken my Olympus Trip with me to the beach a few times and found for the first time that I was really enjoying using it. John continued to sketch. Scapa Flow, where a great aunt had watched as the Nazi fleet was scuppered, the Ring of Brodgar, the Viking settlement at Skara Brae – I clicked away. I shot the most extraordinary sunsets over the stone and took my first portrait, a colour shot of my brother Ian, laughing, head thrown back, sitting on the beach at Skara Brae. I miss that Ian, the little brother with not a care in the world.

Yesterday I came back from Cornwall after another lovely shoot with Nathan, such a great man and chef, so delicate and refined. I also wrote to Jamie Oliver, with whom I've done so much work over the past twenty years. I've been taking stock of where I am professionally and creatively at the moment and Jamie's friendship is very important to me. I feel I've been a big part in creating his global brand, but for various reasons, other than finishing a book on Italian nonnas, we have hardly worked together in the past year or so. In a pre-Paros and Pascale world it would certainly have thrown me, but with my 'Holy Trinity' around me and a host of inspiringly creative projects ahead of me, I feel good, I think!

I flew to Tel Aviv shortly after my return from Cornwall. Spent a fitful night dreaming of John and Orcadian beaches. Among the many bracelets that adorn my wrists, tangled between silver skulls, ebony turtles and Buddhist beads, there are hidden two Orcadian cowries. They'll never make me rich, but their history could not be more special.

I'm travelling alone, on a commission to capture chef Barak Aharoni in Tel Aviv along with his suppliers and local haunts. John warned me in Greece that I would struggle on solo adventures but I feel I have no choice but to break my promise to him. I find the city hard to capture, it doesn't have the immediate beauty and patina of decay that can colour images so atmospherically. Even the old port of Jaffa can feel quite new, the restored buildings hide modern galleries and smart homes. I am struggling to find my mojo.

Saturday 28 April

The Norman Hotel, Tel Aviv

A listless day of many mistakes, I feel tired and as a result clumsy and susceptible to error. I sat for a while watching the sun rise over the White City in Tel Aviv, accompanied by a pair of jackdaws, tilting their heads to me and 'tjacktjackling' at me, watching me with their eyes like black pearls in silver heads.

It's so quiet today in the White City, softly warm and pinkish. I watch as the swallows swoop over the pool taking their tiny sips of water from the surface at speed. I seem to be the only person awake in the City and their company is heartwarming and uplifting. I hope that Father is sitting upon his cloud, smiling gently down as I gain such pleasure from my ornithological companions, a love affair that has lasted over forty years.

Sunday 29 April

Tel Aviv

Finished my shoot with Barak today, visiting his spice supplier in Old Jaffa. Five brothers and their father, Yemeni by origin, proudly running their business through a hard-to-find green tin door, graffitied and faded in the endless sunshine. The smell inside is an extraordinary concoction, a heady mix of herbs and spices. It's such an Aladdin's cave of sacks and boxes it is hard to know where to look.

Back at The Norman Hotel, hot, sweaty and smelling of everything from cinnamon to za'atar, I shower and pack for the journey back to London. I have a thing for traditional men's fragrances and love that an old-school tonic from Jamaica can just smell of limes or a Provençal l'eau-de-vie smell solely of lavender. No mixing with bergamot and juniper, just limes or lavender. I love their smells but I also love their labels, their boxes and typefaces and packaging. Recently I saw a small bottle of 4711 and bought it for my travels, keeping it in the front pocket of my camera bag. To me and to John it's the fragrance of our father. He kept one bottle in his armoire and another on his mantelpiece and the rediscovery of it has been a delight. It still sports the same aqua-gold label and simple aroma and it brings back such evocative memories of Father dressing, shaving and smartening up for Mother's return from surgery.

Sitting on my flight, smelling of 4711, I gaze out of the window. Brief glimpses of Aegean blue and then a break in the haze reveals an island whose outline I vaguely recognize. I switch on the airmap on the seat-back screen and realize it is Naxos in the Cyclades. I can see Thira and Santorini to our west so know that we must be about to fly over Paros. And there she is, haloed by whisky clouds, but clear as day. I can see Parikia, the mountain that son Paros has promised to plant a flag on when we visit in summer. I can see the bay of Nassau and the spot where Johnny's boatyard should still be. I can see the bay of Agios Folkas and the towns of Lefkes with its pottery and Aliki. And then all is gone, shrouded in cloud as if it was never there. I took a photo of the airmap on the screen to commemorate such a special sighting and to distract myself from the tears that were running down my cheeks.

Monday 30 April

Dinner with Ange and Tim, who talked fondly of his time at the Dragon School, mucking about with his twin, Nick. I talked about me and John at St Hilda's preschool. We must have been about four or five, and I cried almost every morning, much like Paros did when he first went to school. I can't think why I cried so much while John always seemed calm and

dandy. Maybe I just wanted to be different. It broke my heart walking Paros to school, seemingly in good spirits until we reached the playground where he would hold tightly onto my hand. At Hill House, when he was a year or two older, he was even worse. The tears streaming down his little face reminded me so much of my own reluctance to leave my father. I'd even hold onto John's hand.

And then our first days at Wallington, standing side by side with John, aged eleven, identical in every way, watching the singletons, almost like a slow-motion dance of young manhood, the sporty types bonding over the thwacking of a football, the bullies asserting themselves in the physical hierarchy of the playground, the nerdy kids fearful and still, always remaining on the periphery. There were a few friendly faces, some boys we knew, but all seemed to be fending for themselves, trying to understand their place in the maelstrom of youth. We were the lucky ones, the only identical twins, the only *twins*, pre-ordained best buddies, watching the theatre before us, the screams and cries and shouts and the utter chaos, watching as if in our own bubble. Leaving Paros at school on his own is, in hindsight, one of the more haunting memories of my life as a father.

Wednesday 2 May

The Mews, shooting Prue Leith

For technical reasons I must return to Israel this weekend. I am determined that if I have to return to Tel Aviv I make it a trip to remember. Last trip I bought Volume 6 of *The Complete Adventures of Tintin*.

> Thomson: 'It's as clear as day to us, eh Thompson?'
> Thompson: 'To be precise: dear as clay. That's my opinion and I'm stuck with it.'

Thompson and Thomson, 'Thompson with a "p" like in philosophy and Thomson without a "p" as in Venezuela'. Probably the first identical twins John and I bonded with. From the moment we were born *Tintin* was part of our life, from Father's loo-time readings and bedtime stories to undercover late-night torchlit sharings. We had our own faves; mine was *The Calculus Affair*, John's was *The Red Sea Sharks*. Thompson and Thomson were a pair of completely inept Scotland Yard detectives, identical, but distinguishable by their heavy moustaches, Thompson's being straight while Thomson's fashionably turned up at the ends. They are experts in pleonasms, their phrases use more words than are necessary to get points across.

Tintin books, like Goscinny and Uderzo's *Asterix* books, were to us as much a part of growing up as banana custard and jam tarts at teatime around the round table. I can't think of any other journal or books that would take so many repeated readings.

Thursday 3 May

The Mews

Day four in a row shooting Prue Leith's book. Like her, the days are filled with character, colour and vivacity, whether she is with us or not.

Later I visit Mother, who sits in her reading chair, pained and frail but, as usual, uncomplaining. In half an hour she talks of the ancient temples she visited outside Jerusalem, her inability to grasp why the critics loved Bernie Gunther, the hero of Philip Kerr's novels, *Blue Peter* badges, bluebirds and love birds, and the Loftus males' obsession with *Tintin* and *Asterix*. Sometimes I can't take my eyes away from Mother's hands. At eighty-seven her skin is so soft and clear with little sun damage. Unlike the Loftus men, her hands and fingers are long, thin and elegant. John's and my hands were different to Mother's and Father's. 'Sausage fingers' we called them, small hands and short, stumpy digits. Occasionally I Instagram black and white images of her hands, always with the tag line 'The hands of my beloved Mama, Dr Loftus, hands that have saved so very many lives, including those of her own husband, daughter and granddaughter.'

As I'm about to leave she rises from her chair and is reluctant for me to go.

'Dear boy, do you remember 4711?' What a strange coincidence! It seems Bernie Gunther wears 4711 and it reminds dear Mother of our father, Eric, and his bottles of eau-de-cologne on the mantelpiece. I chuckle and tell her about the little bottle I've added to my camera bag to remind me of Papa. 'Old fine tweed and 4711, that was the smell of Eric,' she says with tears in her eyes.

Friday 4 May

Flight from London to Tel Aviv

As I left Mother's last night she tentatively handed me a satchel of files. She explained that they were notes and correspondences from the months following John's death, including transcripts of the coroner's court inquest, letters to and from the hospital and the General Medical Council and even John's last bank statements and death certificate. I've not seen any of these before and am slightly startled by their appearance. It seems that my sister Jean-Marian has had them and has decided it's time I saw them. Mother had removed one document which she doesn't want me to read, the surgical notes relating to John's initial operation. I can understand her reluctance, to a layman that operation seemed almost barbaric and John was terrified when it was outlined to him, as I was when it was later described to me.

One letter stands out:

24 November 1987

Copy, Jean Loftus, The Beeches

Dear Peter

Thank you for writing to me. What a disastrous experience we
have had – from beginning to tragic ending.

We have suffered from an appalling lack of communication
among medical, nursing staff, an alarming and distressing absence
of an accessible and caring medical presence, and the anxiety,
as well as that of John, his condition, of having to monitor and
correct his treatment. Having made every effort to ensure that his
intrathecal injections were given correctly – the first time one was
given by the staff, in the absence of Samantha or myself – it was
catastrophic.

My dear courageous, talented and gentle son, so well matched
by his devoted Samantha.

And there the page ends. I think I know why the second page is missing.
My mother's beautiful hands could never, ever, have made such a terrible
and disastrous mistake.

Saturday 5 May

The Norman Hotel, Tel Aviv
29°C

In the Jewish faith, Saturday is Shabbat, the day of rest, running from
Friday sunset to Saturday sunset. So all was very quiet as I climbed to

the rooftop of The Norman to watch the sun rise and the birds soar. My friendly laughing doves were there, chuckling to themselves, and the swallows now outnumbered all others. At one point I spotted an enormous blackbird on a neighbouring art deco façade, and realized afterwards that it was the shadow of a jackdaw passing between the rising sun and the building.

I've always had an obsession with shadows and it even influenced my choice of subject for my degree thesis, the role of the femme fatale in film noir, the chiaroscuro highlighting style of deep and harsh shadows fitting in with my creative bent. For a long time I shot almost exclusively in black and white and almost all of my early-career commissions as an illustrator were black and white.

I couldn't quite believe the moment I first picked up the phone to an illustration job, from the *Radio Times*, to illustrate a *Book at Bedtime* murder mystery on Radio 4. In the play a woman in an old wicker wheelchair is pushed by a stranger to her death and I struggled with the face of the protagonist. John, who was chuffed that I had received my first stab at success, stepped in as he could see I was struggling and, easy as pie, drew her half-turned face for me.

Sunday 6 May

Often when I am abroad I feel the need to be at one with the birds, to fly at their height and speed. I've travelled to Tel Aviv four times in the past year and somehow there is never enough time to relax and explore. So realizing I had a few hours to spare yesterday, I chartered a small Robinson R44 helicopter and a pilot, dragging a semi-reluctant Barak with me. As we met our pilot I remembered my chum Jeff, a most accomplished pilot, saying it wasn't the pilots with cowboy hats and boots and unbuttoned lumberjack shirts you should be worried about but the clean-cut aviator ones with their monogrammed captain's uniforms.

I read the name of our pilot, Meer, on his perfectly creased, monogrammed shirt, as I gazed at our reflections in his unmarked aviators. Meer, of course, turned out to be a great pilot, with thirty years' flying experience, a true gentleman with complete respect for his surroundings, including the bird life that shared our skies.

We headed out, low, over the carob and almond orchards, over the 'green line' where the forests of cypress and olive end and barren rock begins, where the old border with Jordan ends, over the kibbutzim and experimental villages where Arab, Jew, Christian and Muslim all live side by side but on remote hillsides, away from the influences and eyes of the big cities.

I can't explain the excitement I felt, despite my lack of religious belief, as I saw the hills around Jerusalem on the horizon. Jerusalem is one of the oldest cities in the world, the Holy City for Judaism, Christianity and Islam.

So here we were, the walls of Old Jerusalem in our sights, a hundred feet or so above the ground. We gained height as we crossed the outskirts of the city, more for good manners than regulations, Meer pointing out the Tower of David, the Mount of Olives, Temple Mount, the City of David, and the Al-Aqsa Mosque. A hazy light blanketed Jerusalem in an almost ethereal mistiness, the old city appearing almost totally uniform but for the blue and gold of the old mosque's dome. I was glad I had Barak sitting behind me; these moments are so special, so moving, and without John I feel an even greater need than most to share them.

Five minutes later we crossed the outskirts of north Jerusalem and immediately saw the desert, and Bethlehem in the haze to the south of us. We flew very low and fast past Bedouin encampments, past camel trains along the dune crescents, witnessing a landscape historically unchanged for centuries, the Judean desert, dry riverbeds and gorges, wadis and dunes, almost naked of vegetation and empty of all but the odd shepherd and his goats. Low and fast, beneath the level of the highest dunes, Meer cleverly suddenly tipped us over the edge of the desert. dropping us down thousands of feet to the banks of the Dead Sea, 400 metres below sea level and the lowest point on dry land. The temperature scale in the helicopter rose quickly, from 20°C to nearly 40°C.

I often wonder if John would have loved to fly as much as me.

Our drop from the desert thousands of feet to the lowest point on earth will remain with me as one of the Great Wonders of my life. A seminal moment, dropping into the abyss, forever etched upon my memory. All in a two-hour period. Unforgettable and extraordinary.

Monday 7 and Tuesday 8 May

The Mews, shooting Prue Leith's recipes

A simple day of simple shoots, relaxing in its way after Tel Aviv, uneventful and calm. A few weeks ago I did an interview with the *Telegraph* and it was published today, introducing the idea of the book and the demons I am confronting.

Start of the article in the *Telegraph*, written by
Peter Stanford, 8 May 2018:

'I didn't kill John, but I was part of the process that killed him, and I live with that every day.' David Loftus says this very calmly, but his words still make the room stand still.

Ange went into hospital on Wednesday for an operation on her wrist, which meant taking the cab over to Parkside in Wimbledon Common.

Being beside the Common made me feel terribly gloomy, remembering the late cab journeys I took to sit by Johnny's bedside.

Ange's arm had been opened up, ligaments unmangled and reattached, pinned together, stitched and plastered, leaving her in pain and gasping for oxygen. I sat with her for the first couple of hours, adjusting the tubes in her nose, watching her oxygen levels return to normal and her blood pressure settle, before returning for a restless sleep at the Mews.

Friday 11 May

Back in Lewes in Sussex for another day shooting with the bearded brothers of Hunter Gather Cook in their treehouse in the forest. Barney from *Blue Peter* joined me as observer, assistant and sidekick. Earlier in the week he had surprised me with a letter from Peter Purves, one of the *Blue Peter* presenters of our youth, talking about badges and twinhood.

Today's shoot was all about rabbits and pigeons. Photographing the how-tos of skinning and gutting the rabbits and deer is both fascinating and repulsive, but as both had been hung, relatively bloodless. I've shot in a halal butchers in New York and the deserts of Arizona with the Navajo and have had to photograph the throats of sheep and goats being cut while the animals are either held up by chains or held to the ground. All are seared on my memory as moments of horror and barbarity that I wish I had never witnessed. As a photographer of every stage of the food chain, it's important to report every link in that chain, but occasionally it's hard not to want to look away. In Wyoming I photographed the capture of the young cattle out on the Prairie, as tough an environment as I have been in. I saw the young cowboys lassoing the young bucks, slicing off their testicles with a pair of pliers and a quick spray of disinfectant. Then the poor calf has the ignominy of watching on while the cowboys drop their freshly chopped-off ballies into a pan, fry them in oil, and down them as a 'prairie oyster' with a beer and a cheer.

The bearded brothers spent the day goading and teasing each other, slapping each other's arses with wet, rolled tea towels and attempting to set fire to each other's beards with sparks from their firelighters. Between frolic and misbehaviour and shots of gin flavoured with their own mixture of foraged botanicals, they managed to cook up an array of surprisingly delicate, ethical, sustainable and hearty, tasty plates of food. It's fabulous to watch, an education for the palate.

Sunday 13 May

A morning with Mother in Cheam. She has made the tough decision to have her breast cancer removed in an operation this coming Friday. She has taken advice from the hospital, the tipping point in her decision being that if they remove the lump then she can come off the chemo drugs that are causing so much pain in her legs. Do I trust their judgement? No, I do not, but Ian and Jean-Marian believe it's the right thing to do. Bitter experience, of course, dictates the opposite.

When Johnny was in the oncology unit he was housed in a small ward of three young men. All three died, but what was particularly tragic about the chap in the next bed was that he had come to there specifically because his company, an American conglomerate, had insisted he, as part of his insurance policy, have what they called an 'executive profiling', a sort of all-over body and mind check to see if you had any underlying medical anomalies. He came out with a relatively clean bill of health, except for a genetic propensity towards a certain type of cancer. He entered hospital cancer-free, for a blood-cleansing technique too complicated to remember and hootingly expensive, in the hope that his vague chance of a future cancer would become vaguer still. It was essentially akin to a type of chemo and it made him terribly sick. A virile, bright and gregarious young man reduced to a vomiting wreck within days of admission, he never recovered and died soon after John. I remember Mother telling me that it was a scandal that he was ever there in the first place.

Tuesday 15 May

The Mews

Yesterday was the last day of shooting Prue Leith's book at the Mews. What a delightful project it's been, the joy of working with a small, hardworking and dedicated team. Today I'm doing a shoot today for Fischer's restaurant in Marylebone High Street.

At Wallington, John and I were occasionally bullied for being twins, any difference from the norm making you a target for the eagle-eyed bully. The main offender was an older boy we nicknamed Tufty after his spiky mullet haircut. I could never take Bruce Foxton of the Jam seriously as a musician, purely because he had exactly the same haircut. Tufty was smaller than us, but had a gang of three others who were as thick as thieves, and as thick as pig poop. He was a horrible little racist who would ambush us on our way home from school and steal our pocket money and scare the crap out of us. We hated him so much.

Wednesday 16 May

Old Basing, near Basingstoke

Today was a day of cowboys, vintage Austin Sevens and MGs, loud rock music, fire and smoke and more bearded boys and pretty girls, doing a shoot for the hat-makers and whiskey brewers, Stetson. I don't shoot a great deal of fashion these days and sometimes when I do it reminds me why I fell out of love with that world, but not today. It was exciting, fun and at times it was roll-around-on-the-ground funny.

I was thinking deep into last night, Ange still in great pain and sleeping restlessly beside me, about the bullied boy of yesterday. It's so hard, as the bullied, to stand up to a bully, and even harder to admit to others that you are being bullied.

Thursday 17 May

So lovely to see red kites flying over Old Basing yesterday. Such beautiful birds of prey, endlessly soaring, reddish brown, with particularly dynamic forked tails, they were hunted to extinction in the UK, killed not for their meat but because they were believed to be vermin. The location for the shoot was an old garage, stuffed to the gills with old MGs, Austin Sevens and collections of number plates, petrol cans, gas station signage and car parts. It was beautifully madcap, next to fields and an old mill. It was like a little slice of *Chitty Chitty Bang Bang*.

Friday 18 May

Shooting in Ramsbottom, half an hour out from Manchester for a foodie client, Kyla, who tells me that it rains every day here. Today, though, is beautiful, with warm sunshine and a gentle, cooling breeze. My grandmother on my mother's side would count 'up north' as above Hadrian's Wall, as far as her spiritual home in the Orkneys. My mother and Molly's 'up north' would be Northumberland, County Durham, Cumbria and the Lake District. My 'up north' would be anywhere north of Manchester, the Peak District, the Yorkshire Moors and the Pennines. For my father it would have been anywhere north of Barnet where he was born. Until he met my mother he had spent his whole life heading south, to Surrey, to his flat in Knightsbridge, and anywhere warm and cultural south of the English Channel.

The landscape around Manchester, Leeds and the Midlands is an area unknown and unexplored by me, but every time I go it reminds me of what I am missing illustratively and photographically. Always rushing to a shoot or back to catch a train, I often desperately want to stop the car. There are so many beautiful old factories with their towering brick chimney stacks, derelict and silent and now smokeless, framed among the weirs and mills and hillsides of the moors. I realize now that as a young family we had skipped this 'up north' in favour of holidays in the Lake District, Cumbria and Northumberland, my mother showing us, but also my father, the places and people she loved so much.

I have such fond memories of walking with my family up the River Eden in Cumbria and hearing the first curlews of spring, swimming in Talkin Tarn in the freezing peaty water, and climbing Hadrian's Wall and exploring its hillside forts looking for Roman coins, convinced that the centurions would have flung them asunder like confetti. I remember us walking the length of Lake Windermere and Derwentwater, hearing tales of Sir Malcolm Campbell and *Swallows and Amazons,* of exploring Beatrix Potter's house, and Tarn End house where Mother lived as a junior doctor. Of visiting Naworth Castle where she lived in her ancient tower when she first met our father and cycling across the causeway to explore the upturned boats that had been turned centuries earlier into fishermen's huts on the Isle of Lindisfarne. John and me sipping surreptitiously from my father's glass of mead, made by the islands monks, climbing over the bracken-rich moors in search of a downed aircraft, and swimming with adders in the freezing pools of nights so dark that the whole universe seemed illuminated.

It's the end of Mental Health Awareness Week and the day of the Royal wedding between Prince Harry and Meghan Markle. It's gloriously sunny, Paros and Pascale are revising and I'm shooting for *Observer* magazine – a cover for their *Food Monthly*. I have more editing to do than I've ever had before, the part of my job I most dislike. On top of this, my Aunt Josephine has been rushed into hospital for an operation. Mother is apparently restless and sore after her tumour removal, and Ange is in pain, her bandaging is too tight and the pin holding her wrist, thumb and broken ligament is painful at best. The ladies are weathering a perfect storm of pain.

Mother just told me over the phone that I suffer from hypnotic dreams, the vivid images that come to us in the spaces between sleeping and waking. But why? I know they can be a sign of depression. There is too much that we do not know about the brain and its workings, about stress and depression, about mental illness and the nature of grief.

Sunday 20 May

Flying late to Stockholm after a gloriously sleepy Sunday

Visited Mother. The operation on her tumour was deemed a success so hopefully she can come off the drugs that are causing her so much pain, though she still has to wait for various tests to be carried out. She was weak and exhausted, but otherwise on good form, wearing a rather glamorous kimono with Japanese scenes in shades of gold and bronze. The operation, though complex to you or me, was relatively everyday to the surgeon and anaesthetist, who kept Mother awake during the whole operation, presumably to their regret as apparently she chatted throughout – I think as much to remind them that she was still compos mentis and therefore 'aware'! Behind what she described as a 'rather nice, calming linen tablecloth', the surgeon removed a 'walnut-sized' tumour from her breast and part of her sternum, 'a slice' apparently, then checked her lymph glands for signs of cancer and sewed her back up. Mother, being Mother, requested to see the offending tumour and the lady surgeon dutifully held it up for inspection. Somehow I expected it to be brown or black and evil, but apparently not, it was more like a small pale kidney or, apparently, a testicle.

Doctors always do make the worst patients, and Mother was probably overcompensating. I bet the surgeon has never before conducted an operation where the patient discussed with her the paintings of Corot and their soothing effect on the walls of a patient's room. Mother was, as usual, uncomplaining and calm, as John always was. She had coped well with being back in hospital as a patient, but there was no way that she wanted to be kept in, so she was home again in time for tea and biscuits.

Once I was back at home Paros and Pascale came over for a hug and we planned a little more for our Parosian adventures. I could feel my own excitement rising as I described to them the Cycladic architecture, the beaches at Aliki and the octopus hanging outside the restaurants of Naousa.

Venus has been so bright in the London sky the last few evenings, it seems to be growing.

Monday 21 May

Story Hotel, Stockholm

I'm back in Stockholm shooting for a cookbook called *Happy Food 2* and spending a fabulous day working with Niklas Ekstedt, who is always so inspiring: he only cooks on an open fire, caveman style, or using pickling and marinating. He is nothing short of a genius, reminding me how lucky I am to work with people like him, who make my life so easy by presenting their wares so beautifully I am but the recorder of their talents.

John never visited Stockholm but he would have thrived here. Childhood holidays got us as far as Denmark and a day trip to Helsingborg from the castle in Helsingor. We stayed with Elizabeth, one of our au pairs, in Copenhagen, learned to cycle fixies before they were hip, and fell in love with numerous Scandinavian girls, none of whom we had the courage to talk to.

Sitting now in a jetty in the city centre, water surrounding me in the early-evening sunshine, all that I can see would have been 'right up his Strasse' as he would say.

Tuesday 22 May

Stockholm

I'll never tire of Stockholm in the summer. I take a walk before work, sit quietly and ponder, and read and write in the early evening. Yesterday was to the gardens of Rosendals, the achingly beautiful park in Kingsholmen, the King's Island. Today I walked over the Strömbron bridge, past the grand Palace and the changing of the guard, along the water to the Old Town.

Wednesday 23 May

Stockholm

I wonder how many weeks of my life I have spent staring into water, from rain-filled quarries and pools in Orkney to Scandinavian ports; from

Old Father Thames, ice-filled Newfoundland seas, Lakeland tarns and Bahamian lagoons to Cycladian deep, blue oceans. Hours, weeks, maybe months, staring, regardless of the weather, my poor retinas scorched from gazing at the bright white sparkle of a twinkling ocean in the midday sun. Sunbathing, water gazing and star watching, combined with beachcombing. These are the four chances of mindful me-time when I can rest, focus on little and clear all dramas, when I can lose myself for hours of vacant thought.

As children, John and I would always insist on being beside water. We put it down to our very distant Nelson ancestry, because it sounded cool. Long walks in the Lake District were rejected, unless the paths were next to a babbling brook and ended either in the source of the brook or a hilltop tarn. Best of all would be around a lake, or up a brook via multiple pools and waterfalls, and if there were no pools, then damming the brook for hours to make pools, then up to a tarn and a swim around the tarn. Oh, and the water had to be clear, not peaty and dark. Our main source of walking information was our father's collection of *Wainwright's Pictorial Guides to the Lakeland Fells*, a fell wanderer's companion of handwritten and illustrated guides, meticulously written and drawn, a page a day, for over thirteen years.

Thursday 24 May

Last day shooting with Niklas Ekstedt

A list of countryside activities according to two young twins:

1. Find rivers or brooks, preferably babbling, clear not peaty, with pools of crystal water in which to bathe.
2. If no pools exist create pools with vigorous damming.

3. Later destroy the damn dam with large rocks, singing the theme tune of *The Dam Busters* at top of unbroken voices, under the mistaken belief that we are returning the fragile eco-system to its former glory.

4. Look for fishes, frogs and snakes, for observation only. (We despised fishing.)

5. Read Wordsworth, Arthur Ransome, Kenneth Grahame and Wainwright and absolutely nothing else.

6. See how long one can stand under waterfalls, which were always freezing so record remained about three seconds.

7. Take an airbed up and float from source to mouth. This was discussed for years and never tried but remains up there on the bucket list.

8. Muck about in a coracle. Hilarious round boat that just goes round and round.

9. See a pike. A pike to us was like a shark is to the *Jaws* generation thanks to the mishaps of Jeremy Fisher.

10. Pretend to be Mole and Ratty – I always had to be Ratty, annoyingly. Father was Badger to us, but sadly we never told him.

Friday 25 May

The Mews

Day of printing in the studio, editing, and catching up. The flight last night was delayed, spoiling my early-evening views of the archipelago of the city, which is always a glorious way to start a flight home. From 28,000 miles a big, fat, red Japanese sun reappeared over the horizon, impossibly blue, the archipelago's lagoons just catching its reflection enough to satisfy my hungry eyes.

The Mews

On a lovely walk with Ange through Battersea Park last night to the Battersea Power Station, we discovered the most amazing twisted and gnarly tree, a type of willow maybe, that formed a speckled sunlit canopy over us as we explored the peaceful and dark glade underneath. It was a magical Singing-Ringing kind of tree that seemed to demand respectful silence under its twisted bows.

Today has been a quiet day of printing for a small exhibition and restaurant pop-up with our chums from The Norman in Tel Aviv, reading on the sun deck and rest. I dozed for a while in the baking sun, but awoke restless and disturbed by a dream in which I was being bullied by someone on a work shoot. I realize that bullying slightly obsesses my waking and sleeping moments. I guess it's not just having been bullied as a child, as twins, and even as an adult, but also because it's the bullying in adulthood that contributed to my weakness in the minutes leading up to the moment of John's overdose. Was I afraid to tell the doctor 'no'? Yes I was. Was I afraid of him? Yes I was, and John was too. Both of us were weak when it came to physical and mental pressure from others, but that was the moment when I could have protected him, and I didn't. Sometimes I think all John's friends disappeared into the woodwork because they too believed that I should and could have protected him from death.

Sunday 27 May

The Mews
8 o'clock after a night of 50,000 lightning bolts

There is a painting called *Sunbaker* by Max Dupain that always reminds me of John. It's such a simple and striking image, a young man lying on the sand, beads of water on his bronzed skin, midday sun so that the shadows are dark and deep. The bather's head is resting upon his arm as he lies flat on his stomach in the sand. I can't think how many times I observed John just this way, from near and afar, lying on the Parosian sands in the baking midday sun. In the last couple of years before his death he had converted a pair of our father's green-striped cotton pyjamas into a pair of long shorts to wear on the beach; they must have been awfully sweaty!

He'd often fall asleep in sun (wearing the pyjamas probably helped), whereas I would read, both oiled in our Factor 4 lotion, carelessly hatless and sunglasses-free. Thinking back on those long summer days, his sleeping beside me always makes me feel terribly sad. I can see him now, lying on his side, fiendishly brown-skinned, his head cradled in his arms, wearing his hippy cotton friendship bracelets around his wrists and ankles, sleeping silently, the gentle sound of the waves and the wind through the casuarina trees, his three-day-old *Independent* newspaper as a pillow to his slumber.

It reminds me of my favourite Hemingway quote from *For Whom the Bell Tolls,* 1940:

> I had an inheritance from my father, it was
>   the moon and the sun.
> And though I roam all over the world, the
>   spending of it is never done.

Monday 28 May

The Mews

Storms asunder, and so much thunder. Visited Mother at home this morning. On a scrappy piece of paper on her desk, among the trove of poems, lists, musings, book-club critiques and curiosities, there are several lines of writing, aimed at me, for me, but unsigned and left for me to see. The paragraph reads so:

> As a nation we are becoming more vocal in expressing personal grief, sharing it and commemorating it. The grief of a bereaved twin is an experience no one else can share, or comprehend, except by another bereaved twin. David's loss was profound, compounded by what we perceived as a lack of care in John's treatment. I felt hopeless to cope with his grief, my own, and that of John's other brother and sister. I read an article in the *Telegraph* about Dr Elizabeth Bryan, who cared for multiple-birth situations and bereavement. I wrote to her, and as was her nature, she actually took the trouble to phone straight back. David tells the rest of that story. She was a wonderful person and the link she set up for David, with another twin, was life-changing. The need continues, thirty years on. I hope expressing this in the book will be of some comfort.

But there can be no end.

Tuesday 29 May

Stormy night, lightning and thunder

Shooting with a crazy early start at Fortnum & Mason after a late last night of framing prints in preparation for an exhibition of images of Tel Aviv, Jerusalem and the Dead Sea for a pop-up restaurant at Carousel in Marylebone.

As I gaze out of the windows at Fortnum's today, a huge red disk, enormous and bright, is being painted in the forecourt of the Royal Academy, adding a glow to an otherwise grey and oppressive day.

Morning, Sunday 3 June

Sitting on a little roof terrace after an overnight stay at Shoreditch House, hot sunshine over the brutalist landscape of supposedly groovy East London. Deciding to end the day on another 'out of comfort zone' experience, Ange and I watched The National play at Victoria Park, long enough to sing along to 'My Girl', which was our first dance song at our wedding in Marrakech, before fleeing the drunken throng for an overnight pampering and breakfast of Shoreditch fare on our sun-baked terrace – coconut yoghurt, chia, avocado, pressed celery, beets, kale and nuts, every trendy food stuff was covered bar turmeric, and I'm sure that was available in a mocha latte from somewhere. We were hip for twelve hours, but I find the severely brutal architecture with its achingly hip graffiti and filth, plus the literally thousands of pissed and stoned youth too much to bear, and I yearn for home. Trying to hail a cab in Hackney last night Ange turned to one hipster, aware that we might be stepping into his hailing patch and asked him, 'I'm sorry, were you trying to hail that cab?'

'Oh no, but thank you, I was hailing a prostitute.'

Monday 4 June

The Mews
Mother's birthday – eighty-eight years young today

Today I received a letter from Naomi, John's 'post-Liz', 'pre-Samantha' crush.

Dear David

Memories of John

I first met John in September 1982 when we both started at
Kingston. Our friendship was an immediate and easy one and
continued until his death. Along with Sam [Connolly] we became
inseparable – just enjoying each other's company, being part of
a vibrant time in youth culture and relishing being able to study
something that we all loved. We were actually all quite 'swotty'
about our work – none more so than John, who would work all
hours, but always had his finger on the pulse.

He was a true gentleman in all senses of the word – kind,
empathetic and quietly softly spoken. I never knew him to get
really angry. He was intelligent, fun and funny, with an infectious
passion for so much – art, music, travel, film, clothes. His laugh
was a very distinctive hiccupping chuckle, eyes screwed tight, head
thrown back and shoulders heaving up and down. He would often
draw me little cards – cheer-you-up pictures, just-saying-hello
sketches – the precursor to text messages!

John was incredibly popular with both sexes, as well as his
tutors. He was a skilled draughtsman and the bright star of
our year. I remember an assignment he completed about the
Sir John Soane Museum. It was meticulously researched and
drawn – exquisite drawings of Greek sculptures and classical
portraits – showing his love of all things Greek!

He was a bit of a style icon too. This would have been before
The Smiths, and their take on 50s style. John's look was preppy-
meets-Greek-fisherman – classic cable jumpers, slim jeans turned
up (always with a tanned ankle and anklet showing). Fabric shoes,
woven bracelets and a floppy quiff with short back and sides. We

thought he looked amazing. He could be incredibly debonair too, at my twenty-first he wore a dinner jacket with a woven bowtie, and he loved to dress up when Sam and I would put on one of our dinner parties. He always had a great tan, even throughout the winter. The only time I saw him look pale was when he was ill, he had migraines quite frequently and would go as white as a sheet. I have always wondered if they were a precursor to the tumour.

John loved music. Bronski Beat's 'Small Town Boy' was the one song that would always have John up on the dance floor and he had the Jimmy Somerville moves down to a T. Other favourites were Fun Boy Three, Ben Watts, even Elton John's 'Too Low for Zero' and strangely even the soundtrack to *Cats*! It was John who introduced me to the soundtrack from the obscure film, *Bilitis* – he absolutely adored this.

The last time I saw John was after his operation. He was sitting in bed, bandage around his head, bright and cheerful, considering what he had been through. We hadn't seen each other for a while and I suppose, what with the gravity of his operation, we got into quite a deep conversation. He told me he'd been thinking of the past and then said something which I never really understood,

'I always thought if things had been different, Naomi, we might have got to know each other better.' These were the last words he said to me.

Rarely a week goes past when I don't think of John, which is proof of the indelible impact he had on my and so many other lives. The church I go to is at the top of Copse Hill, so he is often in my thoughts on a Sunday – chuckling away in that indomitable way he had.

Naomi Lowe

I was so moved by Naomi's account of her time with John, and his last words to her. I sat for a while calming myself in a lavender bath. It never works for me, but I try. I cried for a little while. So much in the letter to reread and to allow to sink in.

Last night I dreamt of Cubs, as in the Baden-Powell precursor to Scouts. John and I were members of 'Brown Six' for a couple of years and hated every living second there. I remember quoting Baden-Powell's diary to Father many years later, 'Lay up all day. Read "Mein Kampf". A wonderful book, with good ideas on education, health, propaganda, organization etc, and ideas that Hitler does not practise himself.'

I asked Mother today why on earth we ever became Cubs, but she can't remember. She was so busy being a mother of four youngsters, wife and cook to a retired, dodgy-hearted husband, and a full-time doctor. I suggested it was so she could listen to *The Archers Omnibus* in peace. She chuckled and changed the subject as the tallest jay I ever saw launched a solo mission to devour the complete nutty contents of two bird trays and a hanging basket. In thirty frantic ornithological minutes we saw jays, wood pigeons, a wren, two robins, several coal tits, a pair of blue tits and one solitary sparrow.

Leaving my mother post-cuppa, cuddle and chatter, I decided to walk for a while. So much was on my mind. I walked down into Cheam Village and headed north-east, towards Carshalton Ponds, the River Wandle and Beddington, home of our old school Wallington. It was an ominously close and grey morning. North points towards the hospital, south to the cemetery, I'll save those for a truly rainy day.

Initially all was very suburban, as remembered. Many of the grander houses have become flats, the cinema where Father and I watched *Diva*, and John and I saw our first X-rated movie, the first *Alien*, was now a nightclub called Wonderland promising 'Anarchy Tuesday' and, rather oddly, 'Skint Friday'. The village hall where I played with my first band, Last Hurrah, was now a mosque. Rather upsettingly, Mr Redings, the second-hand bookshop where my father bought all of my old photography books, and where John and I really started our book collections, was but a derelict shell, neglected and, it seems by the pile of waterlogged 'For Sale' signs, unwanted.

A group of girls from St Philomena's was picking wild flowers from the rubble around the shell, and it made me smile to see that the nuns still insisted on the most hideous brown uniform with long skirt and what we, as boys, always called 'poo brown' socks – to make them less attractive to us at the boys' school. It worked, we always chased the girls from Wallington Girls', or the richer girls from Sutton High or Nonsuch. Walking past the school and round towards Carshalton Ponds it struck me how everywhere felt greyer, slightly drabber and dingier than I remembered it. I broke off to walk along the Wandle, past the 'tallest plane tree in Britain'. The Wandle was dank and foul, clogged with weeds and rushes, the irises, yellow and purple, distracting me from an overwhelming feeling of neglect and decay. As I walked to the waterside I realized that the sadness that I felt was actually tinged with an anger that the Ponds, and the river, had died. The children playing by the river had empty nets; they looked as disappointed and confused as I felt. I said to their father, 'This was once full of sticklebacks, pike, frogs and tadpoles.' 'When was that mate?' he replied . . . 'Well, forty years ago . . .'

There's a scene, an old Super 8 movie, of John and I in enormous baggy pants over our nappies, wild curly hair and smiling faces, feeding the geese and ducks beside a bridge over the Wandle, overlooking the church, my grandmother's old home and the pub. If you wait for a while, till there's a gap in the traffic, and you blur your eyes and close your ears, you can almost see how it once was, but looking down into the water, where brother Ian once nearly drowned, where we fished for sticklebacks and studied the herons, there is nothing. No rocks, no weed, no rushes, no life. I was going to follow the Wandle into Beddington to see more of where we learned to dam and to swim and climb, but passing the unbearably neglected Watermill, unkempt, covered in nettles, a tell-tale shopping trolley wedged into its ancient blade, I changed direction and headed north, to Carshalton station and home.

Wednesday 6 and Thursday 7 June

I'm shooting Gennaro's new book in Walthamstow after a dawn shoot at The Wolseley. So good to spend two days shooting with him – such a kind soul, always inspiring, always a hoot and the pictures are full of life and colour. As a father of young non-identical twins, who are incredibly close, he always speaks kindly and softly of John, sensitively and gently, holding on to the back of my hand firmly in a fatherly way. These are tender moments, rare among many of my good friends and contempo-raries and they give me strength.

Friday 8 June

Cardiff. Train from Paddington

Arrived late and walked to my hotel in Cardiff. The walk is dark, bleakly rainy, and the atmosphere outside the late-night bars feels dangerous and tense and close.

'The journey changes you, it should change you. It leaves marks on your memory, on your consciousness, on your heart, and on your body. You take something with you. Hopefully you leave something good behind.'
—ANTHONY BOURDAIN, *NO RESERVATIONS*, 2007

Anthony Bourdain hanged himself today, in France. He was a complicated man whom I met a couple of times, in his mellower, later days rather than his wilder younger days, though he still drank us under the table. I had the oddest night ever with him and his girlfriend Asia, who had a knife and fork tattoo on her neck, in Miami. Jamie Oliver, Danny DeVito and Mario Batali were also there. Speeding through the late-night streets of Miami high on tequila and zero sleep, we bonded over our love of walking barefoot, regardless of temperature or terrain. Jamie had to appear the following morning on *Good Morning America*, streaming live from Miami Beach, and we were so late in that night I forced Jamie to have an hour's sleep, ran him a bath, ironed his trousers and ran him down to the beach, hungover as hell, with Diane Sawyer, who was then the main presenter, saying live to the whole of America, 'Here comes Jamie, and who's his friend in his pyjamas, he just has to be English'.

We joined her later for a 'hair of the dog'. I photographed a cover for the *Independent on Sunday* of a slightly green-around-the-gills-looking Jamie, surrounded by leggy cheerleaders on rollerskates on the art deco boulevard. Jamie decided he wanted sushi so I took him to the Shore Club, which a friend, Andrew, had designed. We walked into Nobu, which was closed, but unbelievably, it was that kind of weekend, Nobu himself walked in and, even though he'd literally jumped off a jet-ski in a break in filming, broke into his own kitchen and made us the most extraordinary sashimi. I saw Anthony once more, years later in New York and we laughed over meeting, as we did, on South Beach, and how nervous he had been because he'd previously said so many bad things about Jamie. I told him I thought he'd handled it well, blaming his demons rather than himself, and we sat in the bar at Soho House in the Meatpacking District drinking wine. Barefoot.

The dreams that include John, I hold onto and cherish. The nightmares continue to haunt me years after I have them. Monday's was more a dream, but with a constant threat of menace that never really appeared. We were trudging up to Cub Camp on Box Hill in Surrey. I remember it so clearly; John and I must have been about ten or eleven and it was our first time camping, first time away from home. The experience was so ghastly that it often seeps insidiously into my night-time wanderings.

The walk up to the camp at Box Hill seemed endless. Our Brown Six walked together, led by our Sixers, and our Seconder brought up the rear. There must have been thirty boys in total, mostly away for the first time, all with blisters from newly purchased walking boots from Millets, tiny shoulders rubbed sore by heavy canvas rucksacks filled with Cub stuff. The Sixers were our team leaders and they were teenagers, who in my opinion, should have known that this whole set-up was no one's idea of fun.

John and I shared an old grey canvas tent with our Sixer, a chap I'll call Christopher Robin. Now, this Christopher Robin didn't want to play with Pooh, Piglet and Tigger, he wanted to kill them all, and bring them home to show us. Christopher was a big chap, bigger than both of us put together, and he spent most of the night terrifying us with stories of the mad axeman that roamed Box Hill at night, but said we would be okay as he'd armed himself with his mother's kitchen knife and a squirrel-killing slingshot. On our first night in our leaky tent he told us that he needed hugging because he'd just seen a strange man hidden behind a tree next to the Box Hill Long Drop, the remote corrugated-iron dunny hidden behind a tree next to the forest, and the only place where one could take a solitary dump.

And so progressed a lifetime of dreams, for us both, of desperately needing a poop, but being unable to find a place to go. Now, an older teenage boy needing a hug from two ten-year-olds in their matching pyjamas seemed innocent enough at the time but when he asked us to stroke the erection protruding from his novelty underpants, we politely asked Akela for a rapid tent transfer. No such luck, John and I were forced to trudge back to Christopher Robin's fiefdom, also aware that he knew that we had dobbed him in. He was contrite and tearful, and would we forgive him with hug . . . ? No we wouldn't do that, so a long night stand-off, or sit-off, occurred, where two damp and fully clothed Cubs sat in a puddle at the back of the tent, and a sweaty teen in Superman Y-fronts sat blocking the only exit, weeping occasionally, angry and belligerent the next.

At about 3a.m. according to Timex, the two now absolutely busting for a pee Cubs were given a 'final ultimatum', or catch-22. We could either pee in a bottle, which he would hold and watch, or, horrifically, we could whip his arse with the leather pouch from his sling shot as hard as we could. We watched through hands over our eyes as he removed said Ys and pointed his large, hairless arse towards us. I was so desperate and ashamed I just took the slingshot from him and thwacked him hard across the bare bottom, making a satisfying welt across both cheeks.

'Not hard enough.' I couldn't believe what was happening. This moment, whenever John and I, rarely, spoke of it was known only to us as 'Christopher Robin is saying his prayers'. So he tucked his nut sack like a couple of billiard balls and a baby hedgehog between his legs and spread his butt cheeks as wide as possible, and shouted 'Hit me!'

I did, as hard as I could, right on his tightly squeezed nuts. He let out a groan, a horrible silent but violent fart, and collapsed into a quivering heap as John and I rushed past him and out to freedom, a pee, and eternal shame.

The abuse, and abuse it most certainly was, Akela, ended that day. Christopher Robin had tried to spoon us in the night but we kicked him off us, walking boots from Millets are tough and now we knew his predilections we weren't just aiming for the balls.

The following day all the adults were off somewhere in the woods so the Sixers divided us into two teams and we made camps either side of a babbling brook. All the Sixers were on the same side and we could see Christopher Robin laughing and joking with his Cubby cronies. John knew that one thing he could always ask me is, 'Can you hit that with a ball or a stone?' and I could, regardless of distance, within reason. One shot, one hit. He asked me to aim a mud bomb the twenty or thirty metres over the brook, into the fire they were sitting around, toasting marshmallows.

Desperate for revenge, I did as I was ordered by my elder and wiser half and lobbed a fairly hard mud bomb up into the forest canopy. Fifteen little scruffy faces, like the cast of *Lord of the Flies*, watched its slow-motion trajectory up into the leaves and down, landing with a direct hit into the middle of the fire, showering the Sixers with embers, molten marshmallows and scalding hot chocolate. A roar went up from us, but immediately we were silenced as a cloud of rocks, stones, sticks and mud was violently launched back at us. Hiding under logs and behind trees, it seemed to go on for an eternity. Several had been hit, blood had been shed, and all fifteen of us were in tears. I knew I couldn't face it any longer, and that the next night was now surely going to be worse for John and me. John tearfully turned to me and handed me a nasty-looking piece of flint, like a Stone Age axe-head, black, crystalline, sharp-edged and nasty.

Christopher Robin was in such a violent fervour that even though it was autumn and cold and damp, he had removed his top and was bellowing like a chubby Tarzan, animalistic and feral. As he bent down by the stream to arm himself with more rocks, I ran round to the edge of the trees and launched John's flint into the foliage. It came down with a sickening thud and a muted scream and the forest was silent like the world had stopped spinning. Christopher Robin lay face down in the mud, an almighty bruise already forming in the middle of his shoulder blade.

The fifteen innocents ran straight back to camp and John and I back to our tent to await the inevitable fallout. After an hour or so one of the adults came squeezing into our tent. It seemed that our Sixer was sick, injured quite badly in a terrible accident and was now in an ambulance on his way to hospital, and no, he wouldn't be coming back.

'Akela! We did our best!' We hated Cubs.

Sunday 10 June

Home at the Mews

I've decided on a last-minute experiment with my chum Hak, my partner in crime at Hak's, a barber shop in Chelsea. As I've mentioned before, shaving has become, to me, as avoidable as the dentist. Looking in the mirror is kept to a minimum. Since shaving John in hospital I've used an electric (sorry, Father). Set at no. 1 or 2, one can shave without a mirror and feel stubble length with one's fingers. Today I went for my monthly hair trim, short back and sides, long on top. It's wonderfully old school, run by Hak and his girlfriend Lou who gently massages my neck, gives me the sweetest manicure and pep talk while Hak works his charming magic on my barnet. Today he suggested the full monty and I went for it: massages, cleanses, hot towels and a cut-throat razor, warm, loving and as gentle as ever, an hour and a half of unadulterated pampering. They know me and my aversion to mirrors, and carefully presented me with my own clear-skinned self, shining and polished, staring back at me. I was dumbfounded really. I barely recognized myself, and I left the barber shop quietly and sadly, over a sun-soaked Albert Bridge and home.

Later, sitting on the roof terrace in the afternoon sunshine, I received a reply from Hak following my thankful text, it being my first full shave in twenty-five years: 'Oh God bless, that's so special. My dear friend honestly I'm telling you from the heart. I honestly felt there was something heartfelt when I was shaving you David. I felt very calm, joyful and you may find this crazy but a voice whispered in my ear to shave you David. I felt something that I can't describe, only to say that it was beautiful. I'm feeling that this is what John wanted. Thank you sincerely for allowing me to do so.'

Monday 11 June

Shooting at The Wolseley. At breakfast with the owner Jeremy King

'Identical twins are ideal lab specimens for studying the difference between learned and inherited traits since they come from the womb preloaded with matching genetic operating systems. Any meaningful differences or personalities are likely to have been acquired, not innate.'
—JEFFREY KLUGER, *THE SIBLING EFFECT*, 2011

These were the same sentiments that Josef Mengele had, the German Schutzstaffel officer and physician at Auschwitz, his 'medical' facility perhaps one of the most horrifying places that the Holocaust produced. The Angel of Death was a fully indoctrinated Nazi eugenicist whose first job at the camp was dividing incoming shipments of innocents into those who should work and those who should be immediately gassed. His research at the medical institute was the study of the influence of heredity on various physical traits using identical twins. Mengele used hundreds of pairs of identical twins, injecting one twin with mysterious substances and monitoring the illness that ensued. He would often apply limb clamps on one child to induce gangrene, inject painful dyes directly into the eyes, and experiment with spinal taps. When one twin died he would kill the lone twin with a chloroform injection directly into the heart and dissect both twins for comparison, often several sets of identical twins at a time. Mengele would often stitch pairs of twins together by their backs or gouge out the eyes of twins with different coloured irises.

Mengele was never arrested by the American conquerors, but somehow slipped off quietly to Brazil, Paraguay and Argentina where he was able to lead a relatively charmed life before dying of a stroke while taking a swim in the Atlantic. Who said justice comes to those who wait?

Tuesday 12 June

Dinner at Colbert with old school chum Guy

At the Mews with the lovely Meera Sodha, my first time shooting with her since Mumbai. She brought me a gift of a little golden Ganesha, god of 'making things happen'. He's now sitting next to Strawbod in the 'Cabinet of Curiosities' where I write.

Wednesday 13 June

Bath Priory Hotel shoot

I love dawn train rides, particularly those heading west out of Paddington.

The dawn train to Bath on a softly warm morning like today belts out of London and into open fields, far quicker than if you travel north, south or east. The countryside is sublimely green and misty. I saw startled deer, red kites, buzzards and herons, particularly along the canal. For some reason 'The Poppies in the Fields' by The Teardrop Explodes kept playing along in my head and, as if on cue, we were tearing through wheat fields speckled with bright red poppies, the flowers of remembrance. Thinking of the Flanders in Belgium and my father as a boy listening to the roar of the guns from across the Channel while he played with Patrick in their Kent garden, I reread several times some of my favourite poems.

Five beautiful sights today:

Stag standing in a misty field and our eyes locking.

Red kites soaring only thirty minutes out of London.

Endless fields of hogweed or cow parsnip at dawn, poisonous but beautiful.

Looking at the pictures of photographer David Douglas Duncan, who died yesterday aged 102 having survived Korea and Vietnam, his smiling portrait of Picasso in his rocking chair, bare-chested in his studio always makes me smile contagiously.

Hundreds of blue dragonflies, metallic, iridescent, mating in heart-shaped couplings in the bullrushes at Bath Priory.

Friday 15 June

Shooting at the Mews, with hip young guns Sonder & Tell

Yesterday I was looking at a list of meanings of the word 'truth'. There were eleven in total and they started:

1. Being in accordance with the actual state or conditions, conforming to reality as fact, not false

2. Real, genuine, authentic

3. Sincere, not deceitful

4. Firm in allegiance, loyal, faithful, steadfast . . . (and so on)

These definitions have haunted me all night and I have slept very little. We live with not much that can be guaranteed as truth, particularly in politics, media and society. It's become easy to lie or be dishonest and untrue. Initially I was only thinking of 'truth' in the case of John's death. The failure to admit the truth was the difference between John surviving and dying. I think that the whole dictionary list of definitions, one to eleven, was broken. I suppose the ultimate question is why? Not why the injection, which was an avoidable and careless mistake made by a young doctor under pressure, not deliberate, but avoidable. The difference between two similar words, 'intravenous' and 'intrathecal', why hide the mistake? I dreamt that I was dying last night and John was holding my hand watching me. I told him not to shave me, that he would regret it in later life, but he tried anyway, and couldn't connect the razor with my skin. He said it was because I was fading, visually, as I was dying and he could barely see me. I tried to call out but he could no longer hear me, and I cried and cried, like a child. He turned to my father and said, 'Papa, he has gone now.' I woke choking, it was 1.25a.m., the time of our birth.

Saturday 16 June

Lies and mistruths, and being 'economical with the truth'; it seems so easy for so many and I wonder if it has always been so.

I made a rare mistake this week that resulted in a double booking and we had to let down a new client. Ange made the call, both of us deciding honesty is the best policy, that we'd admit the mistake, apologize pro-fusely and rearrange. The call was met with hostility, accusation of lying and a stream of vitriolic emails. Of course if I'd said I was sick and couldn't make the shoot there would have been sympathy, frustration, yes, but little damage done except that I would have lied. To be accused of being dishonest really hurt. The client I did shoot with, hemp producers, plus home economist Rosie Scott, and two young and exciting talented branders called Sonder & Tell, were an absolute delight. The product is healthy, sustainable and ethically fabulous, so ultimately the right choice was made, including telling the truth in the first place.

Sunday 17 June

Pascale has finished her A-Levels and Paros is about to start second-year medical school exams. It's Father's Day, and a trip with Ange down to see Mother in Cheam.

Mother looked so beautiful, almost ethereal. She'd managed to sort out some old dresses and was looking almost Jean-Marie-like, standing at the top of the stairs to welcome us. Of course the glamorous attire and bonhomie hides pains and worries, so many people to miss on Father's Day, her own father, my father and her firstborn.

The pain from the chemo has mysteriously returned to her legs, and she'd been in to see the doctor in the week. As expected, even though mother had persuaded the surgeon to remove part of her chest wall, more tissue than necessary and most of her breast, there is still some suspect 'material'. Of course my bright-as-a-button mother knows the side effects of the treatment suggested, including broken ribs, collapsed chest wall, an inability to talk or to swallow and possible brain damage. It's like the radiotherapy version of a machine gun. Quite rightly she's decided to allow nature's unnatural mischief to take its own course. I'm not sure whether Mother would survive any of the above side effects.

Lovely sight of a small jay in Mother's seed feeder.

I realize that there is a drawer in my old desk at the boat that I must at some point tackle. It contains a pile of John's old postcards, photos, reminder notes and love letters, all stuffed in the top right-hand drawer to be sorted 'on a day when I feel strong enough'.

Mother said today that she rarely dreams of John and I together but often as individuals, but she dreamt last night of John and I squabbling over who would wear our father's blue suit at Jean-Marian's wedding. Of course, in real life John did; he was, after all, walking Jean-Marian down the aisle in the absence of padre, and of course ten minutes' difference being an eternity to an identical twin.

Monday 18 June

New day, new week, a beautifully sunny day. So many edits to do, so many prints to do, meetings to attend, the odd crisis to sort. Paros' exams start this afternoon and he turns twenty-one this week. Twenty-one years, where did they go?

Tuesday 19 June

A day of shooting restaurants, first an early breakfast shoot at Colbert, then off to Scully St James's of Mayfair, a restaurant of funky ideas and fermented fish and pickled vegetables.

So much going on at the moment. I feel I need to stop, take a few deep breaths and quietly reflect on my next steps. Knowing my daughter Pascale had just finished her A-Levels, I popped over to see her on my

way home for a cuddle. She looked so relaxed, so stunningly beautiful that I shot a few photographs of her at the front door, freshly painted light blue. It matched her eyes and her newly bleached hair.

Wednesday 20 and Thursday 21 June

(Very) early morning flight in the fog from Heathrow to Hamburg to help my chum Bart to launch his *Bart's Fish Tales* book in Germany.

Alarmed during the night to receive a text from Ange who in the early evening had a second operation on her poorly arm to remove some metal pins from her ligaments. It seemed she had been left too long in Recovery and her drip of saline had run dry, forming a vacuum, and blood was seeping back from her veins to the empty saline bag. She had fallen asleep, unattended, from the lateness of the hour, the painkillers and the anaesthetic. Not exactly the time for me to be in Hamburg. I get up at 4a.m. and catch the early flight back to London, cancelling my shoot, and headed home to hug the patient patient.

Dinner at Colbert with Paros and Tim to celebrate twenty-one years to the day that Tim and Izzy were engaged, midsummer's day, the longest of the year, and Paros' twenty-first birthday eve. Tim was on one of his 'sort-out-the-problems-of-the-world' kind of moods, keen to fix the National Health Service in one restaurant sitting, with a little advice from our mid-revision, overtired and slightly shell-shocked son and Tim's godson, Paros.

IT FEELS A LOT
LIKE SUMMER

Friday 22 June

A glorious day, warm sunshine and a cloudless deep blue sky over old London town. It's funny that soon after Mother and I discussed how certain birds have disappeared from the Big Smoke they reappear. Two beautiful little bullfinches in full song, probably the first time I've seen them in London in over twenty years, although they look far too small and hardly their bullish old selves. Now we need to see yellow hammers, green finches, the humble sparrows, more wagtails, goldcrests and long-tailed tits. My spirits were high as I walked down Piccadilly, past the huge red disc I now know is by Anish Kapoor, so bright against the deep blue sky, skuddled with the trails of high-flying aircraft.

Saturday 23 June

The Mews

Dinner of octopus and rosé with Ange at Daphne's. Paros turned twenty-one yesterday. A quiet celebration and a haircut and beard trim for him at Hak's on the King's Road, exam revision holding any more raucous celebrations at bay.

Worried that I hadn't really spoken to Mother for a few days, I jumped in a cab down to Cheam. I found her in good spirits, though she's finding London's heat rather oppressive. Her limbs ache a little less and though she worries about her mobility she is childishly stubborn with regards to her treatment, which I love. The hospital have written to her with appointments which she has deliberately missed, so they've written again outlining the treatment they'd like to perform. As expected, it's the radiotherapy machine-gunning with all its side effects – almost inevitable, at Mother's age and with her osteoporosis. Mother smiles calmly at me across the table, 'You know, darling, it would be just like that poor dear chap in the bed next to John, I'd be admitted, but I wouldn't be coming out.'

I topped up Mother's bird feeders and pottered through a few odd jobs she had saved for me, chattering about Kettle's Yard art gallery in Cambridgeshire. The Pre-Raphaelites, the Bloomsbury Set and their house in Charleston, Lee Miller, Farley Farm and Roland Penrose and the British Surrealists. I tentatively asked her again why I hadn't been called to give evidence as the only witness to John's death, but I know it's because she believed me too fragile to take the inevitably hostile grilling from the hospital and the General Medical Council. She talked briefly about how recently a family has taken a coroner, whom they felt had mistreated them, to task, and for the first time in history managed to have him removed from duty. Coroners always saw themselves as untouchable, and indeed were treated as such and above the law. I so wish I had been stronger at the time, and I've always felt that the coroner was someone I'd like to meet one day, just to ask him: 'Why?' We weren't litigious or looking for some sort of revenge, we just wanted admission, clarity and truth.

Monday 25 and Tuesday 26 June

Flying to Amsterdam. Today is hot, 30°C in London

Arrived late last night into Amsterdam, relieved to find that the city is 15 degrees cooler than London. Checked into an über-cool downtown hotel. The wall boasted a huge mural of a chap swallow-diving from a high board with the words 'dive in' pointing at a plump and over-duveted bed, so I did as the wall told me.

Shooting with lovely Bart and his team today. In the evening there is a long (with rosé to soften the blow) meeting with stylists and publisher to discuss an ambitious project to recreate Salvador Dalí's Cadaqués-based cookbook using present-day artists.

Wednesday 27 June

Taxiing out on the runway at Schiphol airport with its vast green spaces and long canals running alongside the runways, I'm always amazed, with all of the jet-fuel smells and the racket of the engines, how much wildlife one sees from the window. From where I sit I can see miles of open countryside, canals, dykes and windmills, so why oh why, as a bunny, would you choose to live between several active runways? It's obviously not just bunnies judging by the number of kestrels. I remember once spotting an alligator chasing a rat at Miami-Dade airport and a rat chasing a mouse at Nassau.

On the flight, I've been reflecting on the last few days, shooting and editing, shooting and editing. When I was at Mother's on Sunday I asked her if I could borrow her photo albums from her upstairs library with a promise to take them, one by one, decade by decade, repair them and study them, and then return to swap for the next.

'If a day goes by without me doing something related to photography, it's as though I've neglected something essential to my existence, as though I had forgotten to wake up.'
—RICHARD AVEDON

Friday 29 June

Loneliness is a feeling different from 'being alone'. One can be alone and completely at peace, but you can feel lonely even when surrounded by people. When John died I was in a relationship with Debbie, I had my mother, my siblings and my friends, but overnight I became in my mind the loneliest man on earth, and my illustrations were but a brief, distracted world that I could crawl into before the suffering would overcome me. As a young man, in a large and empty house with an empty drawing board, overwhelmed by intense sorrow and guilt, in hindsight it seems amazing that I survived the first year or so, but survive I did and, though my relationship with Debbie was far from perfect, I do have to thank her for her perseverance. She was beautiful, loyal and stubborn. I find it hard now to remember much of the post-trauma period but I know that she cared greatly, dragging me out to socialize, to go to see friends, to return to the Lakes and to Greece.

I asked Debbie recently what it was like to come over to see me and she described walking into a room with me as 'like walking into a sea of treacle'. The loneliness of those years was never-ending, a waking and sleeping nightmare, and though I feel it so much less now, it still sneaks up on me sometimes, regardless of the number of people who surround me.

Today was a lonely day, even though surrounded by lovely people. A cab picked me up at 5.30a.m. to drive me to Jamie Oliver's house in

Essex, a misty start to the clearest of blue-skied days. Jamie and I hadn't shot together since finishing the *Jamie Cooks Italy* book last summer, and it feels like an age ago. Though Jamie loves to work with a skeleton team, he is invariably surrounded with a huge team of art directors, food assistants, hair and make-up, stylists and TV production people. With all of Jamie's books we try to come up with something new, something unseen, knowing that whatever we do will inevitably be copied the world over. This new book is slightly different as we had started it, but stopped it in favour of a more mass-appeal project, several years earlier. There isn't the time to reshoot, though as the photographer I feel strongly that I would do it all differently now, six years on.

Enormous pressure to perform, a seriously painful back, a tight budget and a twelve-hour shoot ahead of me created an almost unbearable tension within me.

Ultimately it was a long, hot, hard day, with some beautiful and inspiring food, glorious scenery in the fields and gardens of Saffron Walden, and hundreds of photos taken. We were surrounded by black swans and their cygnets, tufted ducks and their ducklings, peacocks and woodpeckers. But it was also a day of being surrounded by people, some of whom I know very well, but feeling utterly and desperately alone.

Morning, Saturday 30 June

Five beautiful moments to bring back from yesterday:

A mother taking her five ducklings for their first swim.

The ripples in the sun-soaked cornfields reminding me of a dream on the night John died.

A small muntjac deer suddenly exposed in the corn by the wind.

Obsessively filming the reflections of Jamie's small stream on the underside of the leaf canopy of his beech trees.

Returning home to my darling wife, tucked up and sleepy.

Sunday 1 July

Shooting at the Mews with Clarence Court eggs, and what
has become known on Instagram as #teamegg

Another stunning cloudless day in London.

It's a long day with so much beauty to capture: the eggs of Burford Browns and Longford Blues, pheasants and geese, quails and ducks, shooting them with the natural elements of their diet from corn to wheat to cornflowers and daisies. Every eggshell is different in colour, gradation and inky dappling, each one uniquely beautiful and mysteriously fascinating. I shoot them against some organic, almost volcanic, glazed pottery and the combinations of eggshells, abstract glazes, feathers and wild flowers are painterly and rewarding. I love every minute.

Normally at the Mews I just plug my music into the system and play through various playlists; a mixture of indie, electronic, choral, classical, abstract Icelandic music and film scores. Today I suggested Pip, our talented young food stylist, pop on one of her playlists as I sat quietly in the corner, mentally making a list of Johnny-related things to do before we leave for Paros in six evenings' time.

Just as I was making my promises to John, a song on Pip's playlist took me immediately back to a summer's day at The Beeches, sitting on one of John's bright Greek rugs among his terrariums and yucca plants and design books. John had just bought an album that he insisted was the best of the best, *The Affectionate Punch*, by a young band from Dundee called The Associates. Their singer Billy MacKenzie, John quite rightly described as 'having the voice of an angel'. John played me their song 'Party Fears Two', a song about two girls his brother had seen gatecrashing a party – he had admired them for trying to kick the door down in stiletto heels. The song ends with three cups smashing and Billy spitting out his chewing gum. He may have sung angelic pop, but he was a punk at heart.

I can't think how much I've missed those moments of sitting around John's small turntable, each trying to 'out-discover' each other with a new band, each quietly in unspoken agreement but fiercely in denial of the merits of each other's choices. He'd hit me with The Communards and Jimmy Somerville and I'd hit him back with, ironically, 'Johnny Come Home' by the Fine Young Cannibals. If I had a penny for every time I'd walk into his room and find one of my discoveries stuck on his turntable, the needle still quietly scratching away, or vice versa, one of his on my player, I'd be a wealthy chap.

Tuesday 3 July

Pascale's 'prom' or graduation tonight, I promise to behave.

Wednesday 4 July

Independence Day

Shooting for *MasterChef*; two days of short films and stills in the warmest London since the Eighties. (It's 30°C today.)

Pascale's graduation last night. She looked stunning, black lacy dress from a shopping trip with Ange the night before, bright red lips and freshly painted nails. The girls arrived, all gangly and bare-skinned in the

warm early-evening light, the boys, nervous and gawky in comparison in black tie, shirt tails sticking out beneath ill-fitting jackets. Parents in their Sunday best, probably, like me, slightly delirious in the realization that somehow they'd managed to scrape together the money, term by term, to pay for their education. It was lovely to witness the overemotional greetings and farewells and promises made, scores settled, champagne quaffed. So bye bye school, you've cost me a small fortune, educated my children well and introduced them to some fabulous friends for life.

Friday 6 July

First day off in ages and another 30°C in London, hot and sticky and stinky. It's the last morning before our trip to Paros so there's much packing and repacking and texting between over-anxious kids and parents. Escaping the Mews, I take a taxi down to Cheam. Poor Mother is wilting in the heat, her arms are bare, as is her neck, and I know how much she hates a bare neck. We spend a little time poring over old photos of John and me with Mr Frank and Uncle Almond in Canada. She talks to me about the notion of dying younger, but with dignity, as opposed to dying old and without. Today would have been the end of her first week of cancer treatment at the hospital and here she sits, talking over old albums, remembering happy times, glamorous years, listening to the blackbirds' songs, as opposed to lying riddled with tubes and needles in a hospital side room.

'Darling David, I do believe that if I'd gone in, as wished, on Monday, I wouldn't be alive today.' She remembers the last time she was rushed to hospital in an ambulance, having been accidentally knocked over by her carelessly driving neighbour and left bleeding in the street with concussion, her neighbour completely oblivious, a geriatric-on-geriatric hit and run. In Accident and Emergency at St Helier Hospital she was cared for by a young orderly who, very carefully, washed her, brushed her hair and cleaned her teeth, much like I used to do for John. Mother believes that this small act of kindness changed her experience of being hospitalized profoundly and should be the norm in the NHS, that gentleness and kindness can be used in a way that will help a patient forget the more awful, traumatic or painful experiences.

* * *

Now I'm on an Aegean Airways flight to Athens with Ange and Pascale either side of me, Codie, Pascale's friend, Timmy, a friend of Paros, and Paros next to him. Such a strange mixture of emotions: fear, sorrow, trepidation, excitement, worry; I'm a human yo-yo of feelings. I posted a lovely photo on my Instagram just before our late-night take-off, a picture of my tanned and multi-ringed hand holding two photos, me and John, as brown as a berry, sitting on the whitewashed wall of the church at Agios Fokas, the other of John with Samantha in the town square in Parikia port. He's wearing the green-striped pair of shorts converted from a pair of our father's old cotton pyjamas. There's another photo I didn't post, of John, Samantha and I sitting together on a monastery wall near Naousa where we'd met, much to our mutual embarrassment, wearing matching checked cotton shorts, deck shoes and German military vests, which were all the rage then. Even our bracelets were identical.

Saturday 7 July

First day in Aliki, Paros
Early morning in Athens, connecting to Paros

So it begins, my odyssey back to the island of our youth, our teenage years and our twenties. We start with a pre-dawn take-off in an old Bombardier, the Olympic Airlines logo refreshingly unchanged, landing as the sun rises, big and orange in the Aegean haze to welcome us home from home, tired and weary overnight travellers.

Our beautiful villa, above the fishing village of Aliki, is utterly gorgeous and perfect, washed white and deep-sea blue, adorned as it should be with pink bougainvillea, a Parosian idyll surrounded by succulents and olive trees and fields of drying thyme and oregano plants. A small marble-edged and aromatic path leads to an azure sea, a colour that only Greece seems to get exactly the right shade of blue, and a pebbly and rocky cove, perfect and empty, welcoming my Ps and their chums to a refreshing early-morning dip. Their excitement has overruled their tiredness and I watch them with teary-eyed delight as they elegantly disappear beneath the surface with a style and ease that John and I never accomplished, however hard we tried.

The house is beyond expectation, acres of marble surfaces, amphora, ancient Greek doors made into creaky old tables piled high with photography books, old maps of Paros and Naxos and Ios, the walls smooth and curvaceous, as if sculpted from plaster of Paris, so many quiet places to choose from to reflect and to try to assimilate my complex and misty-eyed emotions. I list my aims for our seven-day journey, in some order:

1. Find our old landlady, Jane, if she still lives here.
2. Watch the sunset from John's favourite church above the Parikia port.
3. Find two new doves for Ange.
4. Sit, read, write at Agios Fokas.
5. Draw the boatyard at Naousa and visit the monastery by the sea.
6. See what's on at Cine Rex cinema.
7. Buy a copy of *The Independent* and peruse the cricket scores.

8. Read *My Family and Other Animals* while the cicadas creak and the lizards scatter and the carpenter beetles buzz around my tired and confused head.

> 'Not what we have, but what we enjoy constitutes
> our abundance.'
> — EPICURUS

Sunday 8 July

Parikia, Paros

I didn't really have any idea how I would react to visiting Parikia again after so many years, but I wasn't at all prepared for the emotional intensity as I walked up the narrow, freshly white-washed streets towards 'Jane's Rooms' in the hope of finding John and my lovely landlady. We'd parked beside the ancient Church of a Thousand Doors and walked through the main square, up the path of Lochagou Kourtim. The bakery was still there with the finest spinach pies in Greece, the Cine Rex posters were up and all seemed unchanged, *The Independent* shop was gone and most of the old traditional neighbourhood shops had become rather chi-chi linen and pottery boutiques, but just as pretty, and if anything, so chic that it almost didn't feel touristy and almost distracts me from my mission. Though the Yria pottery with its octopus plates and pottery doves brought me crashing back to earth. Turning right past the Frankish Castle made from ancient Grecian columns laid on their sides, a haven for snow-white doves, the road curling past tiny homes, where the old black-clad widows used to sit, constantly nagging John and I to let them sew up our torn jeans and Siouxsie Sioux t-shirts, though sadly thirty years on they are all no longer, their stone steps empty and silent. The emotions conjured by this street overwhelmed me.

I tried to point out my window, my balcony, John's window, but I could barely get the words out. The old sail store where our friend Peter used to sleep with the cockroaches, too tight to pay rent, had a 'For Sale' sign on the light green-painted shutters and 'Jane's Rooms', though still with a sign, are shuttered up and look like they've been closed for a while. A local lady, probably the daughter of one of the widows in black, chunters in broken English that Jane now lives in Krios and no longer rents the rooms, but on asking for her number she catches me by surprise by yelling the name of Jane's fisherman husband, 'Agiris! Agiris!'

Telling everyone to wait by the church in Agios Konstantinos, which tops the hill of Kastro and was a favourite spot of mine and John's to watch the sun setting over the Aegean Sea, I tentatively wander into one of the rooms literally built into the 4000BC ruins of the old castle, rooms that Jane used to call, accompanied by a hearty laugh, 'the honeymoon suite' as they had their own 'zesto nero' (Greek for hot running water, a veritable luxury in the Kastro).

And there he was, sitting on an old ouzo crate, in the cool and dark, covered head to toe in thick marble dust, hands covered in nicks and cuts and bits of plaster, hair matted and grey. Agiris, the older fisherman, building a new shower unit even though seemingly he could barely stand. In the dark he looked at me, framed and backlit by the doorway in the setting sun.

'I can't see you, but I know you,' he said, 'You are the twin.' Barely able to hold myself together I stumbled over to him. His thick and gravelly Greek accent and broken English hadn't changed, but the strong and athletic fisherman and captain was no longer. Hidden under the cloud of dust was an old man, broken and unwell. He told me it was nerves, damaged somehow, I didn't really understand, but I could tell that he was not a well man. I held him firmly by his shoulder, listening to his broken smoker's drawl as he remembered the twins who came to visit every summer.

Promising to tell Jane I was here, he continued his work and I walked up the last few ancient steps to the church, bathed in a deep orange light. Paros, Pascale, Ange and friends were sitting in a line, under the chapel's arches, unchanged for centuries, much as John and I did every night, every day, for weeks on end, summer after summer. It was a quite extraordinary moment, towards the end of a beautiful but mentally bruising day, memories ganging up at times to embellish and remind me of the beauty of our shared youth.

And the sun set behind the rocks at Parikia port, as it did every night, and will do for ever more, unchanged, making way for a clear and star-filled sky.

Evening

The first full day in the villa is one of leisurely swims in the clear waters of the stony beach below the house, fringed with aloe vera, casuarina trees and flowering thyme bushes, the smells so evocative of precious decades. The Ps and their friends seem instantly at one with the Parosian ways, swimming, sunbathing, reading, drinking and laughing like a pack of hyenas. Paros and Timmy seem particularly keen to explore and have planned trips out to various marble mines, potteries and ouzerias. Dinner is taken at Taverna il Balcone in the tiny fishing port of Aliki; fresh octopus, herrings and swordfish heads hang drying in the setting sun. It's a sublime evening, perched over the clear water peppered with black sea urchins, family and friends tucking into anchovies, calamari, octopus tentacles, swordfish steaks, feta and rosé, waxy potatoes and gigantes beans.

Lazy morning absorbing the smells and sounds around the villa with a breakfast of peaches and apricots, yoghurt and honey, fresh coffee and almonds, listening to Paros plan his Parosian adventures. His top destinations include visiting the Valley of the Butterflies, one of the few places on Paros I'd never been. It reminded me of the wonderful 'donkey man' as John used to call him. He used to walk all the way from the port of Parakia to our little beach at Agios Fokas, knowing he'd find us, but only us, lying there, to bring us a beautifully chilled watermelon. We called his donkey Kalá – Greek for 'how are you?' – and he treated his humble mule more as a pet than a working beast of burden. He was a man of few words, tanned like old leather, and he and Kalá had the habit of turning up anywhere and everywhere – sunset ouzos at the Rendezvous Bar, breakfast spanakopita at the village bakery, he'd always be there with the same one word: 'butterfliesonmydonkey, butterfliesonmydonkey.' Years and years of the same, 'butterfliesonmydonkey'. We never said yes, knowing that The Valley of the Butterflies was at least 10 kilometres from the outskirts of town and a tough and rocky path up. But he never stopped asking. The last time I saw him, twenty-five years ago, he said something else, for the first time ever; he clapped his hand on my shoulder, gave me a rare broad smile and said, 'Maybe tomorrow.'

Ange and I tootled off in the morning after a peachy breakfast to find a small bay I remembered to the north of Aliki. John and I had never been to the Caribbean before, but he had insisted that he believed the water to be 'Bahamian' in colour. I remembered it being a long rocky stumble heading east from Aliki beach towards Faraggas, and there it was, as remembered, less of a stumble as paths had been built and, rather sadly, dry stone walls had come down, but wild garlic flowers grew everywhere among the sea lavender and huge rocks of fawn marble, the water as crystal clear as in my many dreams and memories. Several Richard Long-esque cairns now dotted the marbled shore, I assume to mark the spot where fellow intrepid cove searchers had also 'found the spot', like old-school geotags balanced impossibly against the offshore breeze.

Upon return to the villa, the girls were snorkelling off their tiny beach, which they had declared their own, scattering the shore with their towels, straw hats, Kafka novels and tomes of Greek poetry. Paros and Timmy disappeared on one of their adventures, walking the Byzantine trail to Lefkes, Timmy slathered in 50+, Paros dressed like an Indian Twenty20 cricketer, and with no sunscreen, looking more like a Greek fisherman by the hour. The multi-coloured and multi-cultured outfit was probably wise, in hindsight, as part of the trail included a climb down into one of the ancient marble quarries with only the torches of their phones to light their path, though I think – quote my son – 'the finest cold beer ever consumed' outside the belfry of the church of Agia Triada is probably their own addition to the walk. Paros, the son, did describe Lefkes as one of the 'most beautiful villages he'd ever been to', which made me smile contentedly. They even visited the old pottery of Yria, where John and I had bought our doves of blue.

The evening, Parikia town

Paros, the boy, so often in his early years called 'the boy Paros', I can't remember why, is laid out beside me, defeated by a Herculean breakfast of apricots, ham, crusty bread, olives and yoghurt.

I'm trying hard to assimilate long dormant feelings with the pressure to write 'in the moment', but finding it increasingly difficult. A great part of me yearns to lie beside the water and to fall asleep, salt drying on my skin, eyelids closed to the glare of sun, following the tiny collagen floaters in the darkness that I find so strangely comforting, knowing that three of the four people I love most in the world are by my side. A long sleep in the land of dreamy dreams.

Last night I met Jane again, for the first time in twenty-five years, at the port, a port that has grown considerably in those years. There she was, my Shirley Valentine, leaning against the old windmill that marks the meeting point of road and sea, pedestrian and sailor, a pink flower in her hair in case I didn't recognize her after a quarter of a century. She needn't have worried, at just over seventy now she was as gorgeous as ever, her deep black, almost Grecian hair now a mixture of grey and blonde. She was smaller, slimmer and a little unsteady on the feet, but just as wonderfully bonkers, her laugh so hearty and merry that the years passed in a flash and she was still our bold and brassy seaside landlady, though so much more Greek than English now.

Conversation was easy and Ange and the Ps and their friends all loved her and her gently teasing manner. I'd forgotten how much she ribbed me about being the less perfect twin, the scruffier dresser, the one with the wilder friends and less stable girlfriends. Our friend Peter had been particularly singled out as the butt of her jokery, and he was once again, to much hilarity, from his drachma-stuffed but never opened wallet to his refusal to pay for a room, which meant sleeping in the fishing nets and smelling like an old kipper. Smeragda, her ancient mother-in-law force-feeding him raki and prawn brains and threatening to beat him like she tenderized the octopuses on the rocks. Jane's memory was as sharp as a steel trap, chatting about John and Samantha, nights at the Rendezvous with John's favourite barman George and at the Cine Rex watching *The Big Blue* and *Cinema Paradiso.* It was so lovely to see her and I felt none of the overwhelming sadness I have had on previous evenings. We returned to our fragrant garden, freshly watered and smelling of rosemary and basil, to watch the Milky Way, the shooting stars and Venus rising.

I wonder sometimes if one lived somewhere like Paros, and threw open the shutters to the blissful battering of the senses daily, would one shout from the rafters every day, 'Damn it's good to be alive!' or would one become somehow used to it. I believe I could seat myself at my bedroom window here, staring out at the ever-altering shimmer of the darkest blue Aegean, and be pretty contented for the rest of my days. It's hard to describe the difference being here to being elsewhere in words, when one has been day by day using illustrations and then photos to explain oneself. Yesterday I took a few photos on my old Leica in black and white, and some infra-reds on my phone, and it's still so unmistakably Greece, the seas are black with pin pricks of over-exposed white stars and spangles, much like last night's sky, the architecture and clouds impossibly bright and white, the pines and cypress, casuarina and olive, juniper and pistachio also unmistakably Parian or Cycladian.

Pascale's reading of Kafka, Timmy's of Solzhenitsyn and Paros's endless medical textbooks do not ideal holiday reads make, though I can also remember lying under the casuarinas at Agios Fokas sleepily reading Camus' *A Happy Death*, nursing my ouzo hangover and hopeful of the 'clip clop' of Kalá's doleful hooves. I can remember contemplating 'a happy death' as I read the book, the rarity in life that one can die content, happy and well.

Sadly we don't choose when we die, generally, unless it's through some violent self-inflicted wound, and even if we could choose, how would we know the moment at which to pull the plug and to die a happy death? I so understand my Mother's 'Do Not Resuscitate' notice on the necklace around her neck. Nowadays, as happened when John died, there is the immediate rush for the defibrillators and life-support mechanics. John was already on life support and his life was ebbing slowly away, but there was still the demand to try to revive him until my Mother had to hold them back. Did he die a happy death? Absolutely not, he felt wronged and robbed, confused and deeply, deeply traumatized though he rarely showed it except in the occasionally tear-filled breakdown, mainly with me, maybe because he was looking at the healthy 'him'.

I still occasionally catch myself in my mid-night half-sleep, saying a prayer for John and for Papa. A hypocritical semi-conscious prayer to a God that I don't believe in, that didn't answer us in our hour of need or the needs of so many others, where I ask him to look after father and son and to protect my loved ones and keep them from ill health and its evil consequences, and to protect me from disease and cancers, knowing that it would be highly unlikely that I, like my Mother now, would accept treatment. I would rather die an early and happy death than find myself in a situation where I am no longer rational enough to make that decision for myself.

I draw myself back to the moment and list what is stunning before my Cycladian window:

The isles of Antiparos, a soft arid cut-out on the horizon, visible in the early morn before it vanishes in the haze, the *Mary Celeste* of islands.

The white, bulbous lines of the Cycladian houses, as if moulded from thick marzipan and icing, smooth and curvaceous and solid.

The flash of aqua blue in the dark Aegean, of Panteronisia, a little slice of Bahamian blue between a tiny cluster of unknown islands peppered, or should it be salted, with small white yachts and caiques moored for a day of picnicking and diving.

The bougainvillea, a riot of iridescent pink fronds, like huge fingers of a dazzling beast in a Ray Harryhausen *Jason and the Argonauts* movie, wafting in the morning breeze.

The bees, busy as ever, not fooled by the fake promises of the bougainvillea, instead concentrating their buzzy business on the flowering thyme and rosemary and oregano.

Wednesday 11 July

It's interesting how hard I find it to write while for once I have time to sit and do just that. I am so overcome by the emotional impact of each small step on this trip that the further I walk the harder I am falling.

Yesterday, Tuesday, was Naousa on the north coast of Paros and, even now, sitting at one of the cool marble tables in our villa's garden, listening to the hum of the honeybees, I find it hard to put words to my feelings. I took my old Leica with me yesterday and Ange commented that it was the first time she'd seen me shooting for pleasure rather than just work.

I've come down to the small pebbly cove to watch Paros and Timmy 'tombstoning' from the marble rocks into the deep blue sea to snorkel their merry way around the bay. I love listening to their banter and tomfoolery, carried by the wind. Reverting as we all do, to the unself-consciousness of excitable children, two little boys playing and mucking about. As I look out at them now, post mid-jump photo, I'm aware that I have, in the desk on the boat, an almost identical photo of John and me, with Peter H, at the same age, twenty-one or twenty-two, wearing snorkels, pretending to synchronized swim, like hieroglyphics in the sea at Agios Fokas. Thirty years and a generation apart, but still up to the same innocently daft mischief. It's easy to forget the sheer simple joy of sitting here, on a rock, feet in the cooling, clear water, the only other sounds the waves on the shore and the wind in the pines. Paros has brought me two simple spoils from the blue yonder, a seagull skull and a green and yellow anemone, which I shall add to the Cabinet of Curiosities when home.

After an early-morning cold glass of white wine we drove the windy stony road to the boatyard at Noausa and the monastery of St John Detis in Ormos Ay Ioannou. The youth all headed to cool off in the sea as Ange came with me to wander slowly through the propped-up hulks of old caiques and fishing vessels. The boatyard seemed unchanged in thirty years, as I picked my way through the rusting paint-peeled remnants of past berthings in their oily piles, wondering whether the carpenters and repairers ever cleared anything away, making it the most photo-genic and sketchable place to be. I tried to visualize the illustrations that remained of John's; there's one above my desk, on the boat, and I think I managed to find an angle to shoot an identical photo on the old Leica. As far as my memory is concerned it could be the same spot, and even the same boats. John would sit by the monastery, until now I hadn't realized it was called St John, which towers on a rock above the boatyard, then sit in Naousa port selling his sketches to fund his summer stay. It's a sadly haunting place, beautifully neglected, brightly painted woodwork of deep blues and oranges among the paint-stripped carcases of mari-time workmanship.

We negotiated our way through the detritus to St John Detis, 'detis' meaning to 'make well', although poor St John, who gave shelter to passing fishermen in distress, was beheaded for his troubles. We climbed up the rocks that the monastery seems to grow out of, blending itself seamlessly with its surroundings, a low dry stone wall between it and the old boatyard. It's an idyllic spot and Ange and I dived into the water to cool down and cleanse ourselves after the dustbowl surrounding the boats. You can stand on the roof, next to the dome with its white cross, painted blue so that the white cross appears to be floating against the sea and the sky, and look out over the bay at the boatyard and Naousa beyond. All from here seems virtually unchanged.

Dinner is back in Aliki at our new favourite spot, Taverna il Balcone, set upon a beautiful stone jetty that juts out into the sea, allowing us to sit close enough to the water to feed our bread to the fishes and watch the promenaders strut their stuff. Parian rosé is drunk while tucking into chicory and gigantes beans, octopus tentacles and fresh tuna as the sun sets, turning the still water from an inky, silvery, pink-stained blue to black as the sky begins to show off its Milky Way. I do love it here, surrounded by those I love.

Thursday 12 July

Agios Fokas, sitting with a Parian rosé at sunset

Yesterday was hard, but not as hard as the day before, and not as hard as today was. I realized that Wednesday was also Tim and Izzy's wedding anniversary and, as each other's best man, we like to remember it. Today he sent me a small portion of his best man's speech.

> I always longed for David to find a soulmate. And then one day Ange arrived. And I hoped and prayed that they would give full rein to their intense and moving love. They have done that, and we – all of us at the wedding today – are their proud witnesses, their greatest supporters and their lifelong companions and journeymen.
>
> I speak for many people when I say thank you for your love, and I wish you all the love and luck in the world, as Mr and Mrs Loftus.

Ange and I dropped the girls in to Parikia and drove up a dusty track through sparkly new-builds, past the beaches that Peter and I used to trudge past, having jumped on the little caique from the port. The new track sadly veers from the path we used to take, studded with molten wax candles used to light the path to Agios Fokas, the acres of oregano and thyme plants now dotted with holiday villas. Agios Fokas and its environs were happily untouched though, its running lighthouse and the beach between its rocky headland and the church just the same, still empty, still a secret to a few, not loved by those that like a sandy beach due to its 'ticker tape' seaweed piled up on the beach, but when tried, like a perfect mattress beneath a wicker beach mat.

I so clearly remember the day Johnny showed me this beach. He was brown as a berry, his little linen knapsack containing his sketchbook and pencils and something I hadn't seen before, but nowadays you see everywhere, a cotton kit for making woven friendship bracelets which he would wear around his ankles and sell to hippy travellers doing the island-hopping trail. He was so proud of everything 'new' and discovered alone, without his younger twin. I wandered around the old chapel. Traditionally Greek Orthodox chapels are kept unlocked, but times have changed so I tried the door expecting it to be closed, but no, the heavy wooden door creaked open, letting me enter the cool and dark, lit by its tiny yellow stained-glass windows and a single candle. I lit a couple of tall tapered beeswax candles for Father and Johnny, sat for a few minutes, the silence only broken by the waves and the constant scratching in the pines of the cicadas. Even the tiniest chapel is a beautifully cool and calm place to sit, surrounded by the Byzantine icons, black and white photos, wooden altar pieces and candles burning. The tiny chapel of Agios Fokas will always have a special place in my heart.

Leaving the darkened cool of the chapel, we hung our bag in the wind-swept pines and clambered over the beach for a swim. Even the rocks and weeds underneath seemed strangely familiar. If ever there had been a 'Johnny's beach' this surely was the one and only. Swimming in the chilling water, looking back at the chapel with its broken wall of pines, our wicker bag hanging and the ticker tape of seaweed blowing in circles in the breeze, the only thing missing in the picture was him. I know that as I sit in my dotage one day this will be the moment most reminiscent of him.

Evening
Lefkes village

Paros and Timmy have been harping on about going back to Lefkes so we drive up the mountainous roads to watch the sunset and have dinner. The satnav in our crappy Nissan Micra decides to send us the 'scenic route' up through the mountains on a dirt track, an experience I love, but the boys don't, howling occasionally in fear at the steep drops either side as we climb higher and higher through the vineyards and olive groves and flowering oregano all backlit by the setting sun.

I let the boys lead us through the narrow streets up to the church of Agia Triada, loving the way they show us the village as if I've never been, insisting we climb down the steps of the cemetery, where widows in black tend the white marble tombs, to a pine-fringed plateau to look out at the view towards Naxos, the hills all around us edged with derelict windmills, and then back up to their favourite bar, joyous that the bar owner recognizes them, to order 'the finest cold beer ever consumed' and a cold white Meltemi wine for me, along with a round of stuffed vine leaves and anchovies.

The boy Paros is such a sensitive soul and he mentions the moment I saw him jumping from the rock in our bay into the sea and tells me that as he jumped and saw me on the shore taking his picture silhouetted against the setting sun, he was aware of the memories in me that that moment would conjure. And he was right, I have an almost identical photo of Johnny, in those pyjama shorts, jumping off a rock in Agios Fokas. As I look now at the silhouette of him on my phone it could so easily be Johnny, same wild hair, knees tucked in for maximum splash, same deep tan and little tummy from too many gigantes and Mythos. It's a truly memorable and beautiful evening, so lovely to spend time with Ange and the boys in such a sublime setting.

Friday 13 July

Aliki

I spend the day today trying to collect my thoughts, coping with repeated nightmares through the night, mostly medical and hospital related, and many featuring Mother and John. I'm very aware that I haven't fulfilled my list, but Cine Rex is showing a violent movie and I am becoming increasingly sensitive to violence, so Cine Rex can wait.

Ange and I decide to walk and talk and wander along the coastal path sharing the smells of limes, pines, juniper, and the company of wagtails and a pair of bullfinches. Ange is so supportive of this journey I am taking and walks with her good left arm placed between my shoulders as she calmly questions me about John and his island. We lunch at our usual spot, octopus and chilled Meltimi wine.

The evening meal is a hoot, the boys make meatballs with the local olive oil and herbs from the garden, and chicken souvlaki following a starter of watermelon wrapped in local ham and sprinkled with feta and oregano, all washed down with a lot of laughter and a few bottles of the local rosé and ouzo. As the sun goes down and the sky over Naxos and Sikinos turns an impossibly vibrant gradation of orange to deepest blue, we are joined by three bats making the most of the bugs in their hour of feeding.

Last day in Paros

We have last-day blues; the week seems to have gone so quickly, as holidays always seem to, so we wake early, skip breakfast and all six of us trot down to the sea. The water is chilly and refreshing and we all agree a return to Aliki is a must.

I march Paros and Pascale round the church to the jetty we used to dive from and tell them the story of the place, the church, 'meloni, meloni, butterfliesonmydonkey' man and Kalá the donkey, the metal charms in the chapel and the oregano-scented path lit with candles. I show them where John and I lay on our ticker-tape seaweed mattresses and green-lined wicker beach mats. I show them where we snorkelled and swam and mucked about with our unsynchronized swimming, and then I tell them what I had seen out in the water two days earlier, the perfect Parian scene of the bag hanging in the dusty pines, the chapel, the rocks and the jetty and that the only thing missing in that picture was Johnny. I think they understood the intensity of my feelings for the place.

Ange buys me a small white dove from Yria's pottery shop. Carved out of snow-white clay, it fits perfectly in my hand.

The main street is still as beautiful as I remember, the bougainvillea-covered chapels, ancient fountains, every flagstone rinsed in fresh whitewash, every olive tree and plant, their trunks painted white to head height. It's a dazzlingly gorgeous and romantic sight. Paros and Timmy at one point stop at a small t-shirt printers to print Paros a 'Paros' t-shirt and as I stand in the door waiting for them I realize I am standing opposite the cinematically stunning barber shop, perfectly preserved. The barber who used to cut John's and my hair, a German who settled post-war, a man so lovely that even the Greek islanders adopted him as their own, is now long gone, but peering through his windows I see his portrait framed beside the razors and soaps, preserved by his daughters. Once a week we would come to him for a short back and sides, reading our cricket scores and crosswords in *The Independent*, followed by an ouzo in the Pirate bar, which is still there, next door. Reading our books, Johnny his Tolkien, me my Zola, before taking them to the bookswap store in a small square set off from the seafront, to swap it for some other book to try to impress passers-by.

I snapped a few shots of the corner, realizing that it still remains one of the most beautiful spots I know and we strolled around to the sea-front to eat lunch and natter. As the others ordered, I excused myself and walked a few blocks up the seafront to an atmospheric little ouzeria called Meltemi, the wind of the islands. I'd been told that George, the old owner of the Rendezvous, where John, Peter and I took our sundowners, now owned the place and I nervously popped in to enquire about him. Sadly he wasn't there, but the three Greek ladies working there bright-ened as I entered and told them my story. Very quickly George was at the end of a crackly line. It was hard to talk, his English was never great and my Greek is far worse, but we remembered old times and promised to meet upon my return. His voice was so lovely to hear, deep, smoker's Greek, full of depth and character, taking me straight back to our first meetings, our many drunken nights, downing tequila slammers together, and the time I came back to Paros alone, telling him that John was here no longer.

Back at the restaurant we ate stuffed vine leaves, courgette fritters, fried Greek pancetta and crispy calamari and then lovely Jane arrived for farewell drinks and photographs, Ange taking a lovely black and white of us both laughing, me kissing the side of her head. As I walked her back to the cab rank to take her home, and us to pick up the car and the girls to get to the airport we said our farewells, with hugs and kisses and promises to return soon, see a movie together at Cine Rex, to photograph her copy of Johnny's *Lord of the Rings* and maybe, just maybe, to create a little version of home on the island, a home away from home.

Sunday 15 July

Back home, there's a stunning crescent new moon above the Chelsea rooftops this evening. It's rare to see the moon so low in the West.

Six items I brought back from Paros:

1. A small, light blue ceramic head of Aphrodite on a little chalky plinth, a present from Pascale.
2. A heart-shaped chalky stone, reddish in colour, found by Paros on the beach at Aliki, 'Papa, it can replace your broken one.'
3. The skull of a seagull, most of its neck vertebrae attached, found while Paros was snorkelling off the bay.
4. A tiny white dove from the Yria pottery shop in Parikia, from Ange.
5. A small, vividly verdant green anemone, again, beachcombed by the boy Paros.
6. About forty photos, in black and white, of Naousa, the boat-yard, Agios Fokas and a laughing Jane. All timeless.

Monday 16 July

30°C, a hot and sticky Mews. Crescent moon, pink sky

A complicated day. I pay a visit to look at what is in the top drawer of my old desk on the boat and there are two cards in a bright red envelope that thwack me straight in the heart.

Postcard, postmarked Paros:

Dear David

First of all, love to all the family and hope you are well. I am
sitting outside of a café in Athens, we have just been out to get me
some sandals. Athens is Fab! – lots of ancient Greece and all that.
Yugoslavian countryside was unbelievable (should have been one
of 100 great railways series). We travelled (your eye on the map
of Europe) from Belgrade to Bar on the coast (near the border
with Albania). People however were really unfriendly, with a few
exceptions. We picked up an American cyclist on the Belgrade
platform and he stayed with us (Jeff) for a while. England is his last
country in a 6-month cycle tour. The Belgrade railways however
lost his bike, I think he's sending his panniers to our house so look
after them! Off to Paros (see map again) tomorrow and shall send
another card,

Love John

I found this postcard, depicting a very Loftus-esque photo of an urn
in a window, marking John's first-ever trip to the island of Paros, in
the top drawer. I think he was with his then girlfriend Liz, and a friend
Robin. The boy he met, the American, was called Jeff, and his panniers
did arrive a few weeks later, followed a month later by a bronzed and
windswept Jeff, who stayed for a few weeks, forming a lasting bond with
Molly which continued up to her death.

The Mews
30°C again, clear blue skies

Sitting in the window seat at the Mews trying to brave my way through the handfuls of paper I've removed from the top drawer. There are a few items too upsetting for words. Most heartbreaking is the last birthday card that John gave me on the bed, the day he was killed. So simple, so sweet. The effort in writing every letter, crossed vision and right hand not yet showing improvement, so trying to teach himself left-handed writing, is painfully obvious.

'Dear David. Love Johny x, I. O. U, 1 prezzie.'

Johnny spelt with one 'n', every letter very wobbly and laboured, it's such a painful reminder of the physio he had already started, to regain the use of his right side. I had forgotten that the card might be at the boat and I find it hard to explain the depth of my sadness as I read it now, so very fragile, heartbreaking beyond belief, stirring so many god-awful memories of his suffering. The last time he wrote, the last day he smiled, the last day he drank, stood, walked, our last birthday, all simple actions we take for granted.

Wednesday 18 July

The Mews

Letter, in a red envelope, marked 'David, open when alone, Mum', found in the top drawer at the boat, and unopened until now.

28 December 1987

Dearest David

I find the enclosed a comfort. Only read it, if, and when you feel
ready. And if you don't like it tear it up. The first part is from a
poem Beverley sent, from the Sacred Heart Monastery, Hales
Corner, in Canada. All love, Mom.

But loving brings anguish, and the deeper the love, the
greater the sense of desolation at the loss – so we need time
too, to grieve – and we all, including dear John, surely deserve
that.

Dearest David, Dearest John

Safely Home

I am home in heaven dear ones,
I am now at peace for ever.
Then you must not grieve so sorely,
For I love you dearly still.
Try to look beyond earth shadows,
Pray to trust our Father's will.

There is work still awaiting you,
So you must not idly stand.
Do it now while life remaineth,
You shall rest in Jesus' hand.

Stopping by Woods on a Snowy Evening

The woods are lovely,
dark and deep,
But I have promises to keep
And miles to go before I sleep.

Robert Frost

* * *

A tiny angel, handmade, attached to a card, Christmas '87:

Christmas just doesn't seem the same but I know that Johnny is in our hearts and if he were here he would be enjoying himself. So think of him with a smile. Try not to think of the gaps he has left us but of those he filled while he was alive.

If you shut your eyes, you can see him smiling and will always be able to. Here is your very own guardian angel, her name is Joanna. Keep her safe and she will help you,

All my love Wamfi [Samantha Connolly]

Thursday 19 July

Shooting at The Wolseley

Possibly hungover, having consumed a nasty combination of sake, white wine, rosé and Solpadeine, in no particular order, and the Solps should have finished the binge as opposed to preceding it. I tend to drink every day, but only in the evening (Paros – the island, not the boy – was an exception to the rule), and almost exclusively rosé (Paros was again an exception, discovering that I have rekindled a love affair with ouzo and mastika). I started, at 8a.m. today, at The Wolseley with an oyster washed down with a swig of Guinness and champagne (having just shot the dish, not ordered), patting myself firmly on the back for not hurling it back up onto the set, and, momentarily, I felt like I was floating upon a soft cloud, a euphoric moment noticeable for its brevity, two minutes at most, to be replaced by an imaginary roadside drill operating at full volume inside my skull.

When John and I were little boys we used to sit at the breakfast table, post-afternoon tea of crumpets and jam, drawing Numskulls inside imaginary heads. The Numskulls were a cartoon strip in a comic called *The Beezer,* which we were allowed to read on condition that we also read *Look and Learn.* The Numskulls were tiny people who lived inside a man operating different parts of his head: Brainy (controlling the brain), Blinky (the eyes), Nosey (the nose), Luggy (the ears) and Alf and Fred (who controlled the mouth). We would sit there for hours on end drawing increasingly complicated versions of the inner workings of the head with ant-sized Numskulls operating extraordinary contraptions and machines and cogs, pulleys and bellows. These would combine our love of all our comics, including *Look and Learn*, but also our father's favourite of the day, W. Heath Robinson (illustrator of the absurdly complex solutions to simple tasks).

Friday 20 July

London
The heatwave continues. Shooting the Principal Hotel

I've been going through the photograph album of our shared birth and babyhood. The hurting, crushing sorrow of it and the oh so confusing oddness of not being able to tell us apart. Sometimes Papa has inked on the back of the photo 'John' or 'David', and every time I guess which is which I get it wrong. As we get older it's often memories of clothing worn that allows me the ability to know J from D, and D from J. At six or seven years old I went through an orange phase and look like a young Hare Krishna, next to Johnny's all-light-blue ensemble, like a pair of hippy Joe 90s. Forget telling the difference when it's corduroy dungarees and matching Swiss mountain jumpers and pudding-bowl haircuts. It gets easier 'in costume' as John is almost always Captain Scarlet and I am a Native American in full headdress and suckered bow and arrows.

Saturday 21 July

The Mews

Pascale left this morning on a two-week interrailing journey taking in Amsterdam, Berlin, Prague and Budapest. Oh the worry of it! She's arrived, with one of her best chums Marina, at her first stop, safe and sound. No writing today, too many hours of editing pictures in front of a laptop do a headache make! Another hot and close day.

Sunday 22 July

The Mews

The album begins with two pictures, black and white, inscribed by Mother 'Honeymoon Cruise – Pegasus, Greece, Yugoslavia, Greece, three months after wedding. 1962.'

Father is wearing perfectly creased Oxford bags, leather brogues, smart shirt and a jumper with a silk scarf around his neck. His hair perfectly slicked back, he is being handed a necklace by the captain of the

ship. Everyone is smiling, including a smartly dressed Mother in the background. After a couple of mysteriously blank pages there are a few colour images of their wedding at Carlisle Cathedral two months earlier, Mother, Father, Mother's parents and my cousins Susan and Michael, Uncle Almond's children, as page boy and bridesmaid, and the Dean of Carlisle. The photographer seems to have been keen on Padre's Aston Martin as some of the pictures show the car in sharp focus, bride and groom soft.

The next few pages jump to our birth, two identical little fat babies, squished into rather grand sitting-room chairs, wearing what can only be described as mini wedding dresses (were they expecting girls maybe?). Unsurprisingly, both of us are decidedly unsmiley and grumpily stern in our looks.

On the back of one of them Mother has written, 'John and David 1963–4, little fat dumplings. Too much food! But happy, only a few months.' Hilarious! The photo is next to a very smiley older picture of Mother and Father in the living room of their apartment in Queen's Gate Place in Kensington. Mother smiling broadly at the camera while Father looks at her admiringly.

Occasionally we're out on our pram walks in Kensington Gardens – or in our high chairs or in our carry-cots on the balustraded balcony overlooking Queen's Gate Mews, always staring straight at the camera, unsmiling and unblinking, hair growing by the month into rather elegant quiffs, like curlers has been used down a centre parting.

One of my all-time faves, a photo of John and me sitting on a picnic blanket, our mother between us, is wonderful as it's the first shot that just screams of joyousness, shot at The Beeches. Mother looks stunning between her firstborns, whoever is who, one of us laughing heartily while the other grins, the long garden behind us, the plum tree blurred in the grainy distance. We seemed always through baby years to toddler years to be dressed in identikit combos of elaborate lace dresses, bloomers, gargantuan nappy holders of Victorian design, or woollen tights beneath Aran jumpers in winter, archaic little leather sandals, coloured shirts or cardigans, always buttoned up to the neck, always smart next to our even smarter parents. Even on beaches our Father seems to be wearing a suit and brogues, always grinning from ear to ear with pride.

I know it's hard to believe but my earliest memories go back to that flat in Queen Gate, to the balcony, and to John and I bouncing up and down as toddlers on the sofas in these pictures. There are some photos that follow of a rather glamorous party in Kent with my Uncle Patrick and Aunt Josephine and here I have my first memories of bonding with the cousins Sarah and Edward, also my first of many memories of wetting my pants in public, something that took me far too long to grow out of, becoming an almost daily occurrence at nursery school. (I was offered by Mother a prize for not wetting my pants, but have no memory of actually winning one!)

There's actually a photo a few pages on of John and I in corduroy shorts and little matelot shirts, standing at the French windows at The Beeches, and the only way I can tell it's David on John's left is the tell-tale darker patch spreading upwards and outwards from the crotch area.

Two last images that strike me are one of us both pushing old-school wooden horses up Beeches Avenue with our lovely old artist godfather, Mr Frank, smiling good-heartedly down at us. Then one, inscribed as ever by Mother, at the front door of The Beeches, '1st day at Nursery, 3 years and very young.' White shirts buttoned to the top, with matching jumpers, cord shorts, white socks and leather closed-toe sandals, both holding our favourite toy cars, our little Bugs Bunny front teeth poking over our bottom lips as we both try to grin through our fear of our first day at school, restlessly standing side by side in front of a pipe-smoking Papa.

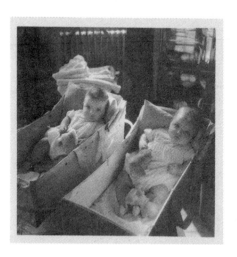

Monday 23 July

Such a sticky and muggy day yesterday, a walking-in-hot-treacle kind of day, an off-kilter, unsettling kind of day. I dozed twice, once in the sun and once lying on our bed in front of the fan, dreaming haunting, disturbed dreams, to match the disturbed nature of the day, the sort of day that people erupt inexplicably into violence, the day when ants come from nowhere and take flight in swarms.

No shoot today so I whizzed down to see Mother who has been finding this heatwave rather hard to bear. We discussed memory, particularly the sharing of memories with John at such early stages in our life that our baby memories exist against the odds, and that I find dates so hard to remember whereas events are crystal-clear. Mother then reminded me that yesterday, the day I was studying the photos of her marriage to Father, was not only their wedding anniversary but the anniversary of Father's passing away. It saddened me that I had been so wrapped up in my own dramas that the dates had passed without acknowledgement, without sending a note to her. None of the family had, and she had had to sit, alone, with her thoughts and memories, while sweltering in her under-ventilated flat.

Tuesday 24 July

The boat, Imperial Wharf
Forecast 32°C

'Un ange passe'– a French expression for an 'awkward pause in conversation,' as an angel passes by.

I was thinking of this as I wandered over Albert Bridge in the early-morning sunshine. I felt the tell-tale brush of cool air as a plane flew between me and the sun's persistent solar beating. I watched the shadow skit up the Thames, over the boat, westwards, like a huge falling angel, the sun so low that I could barely hear the plane's engines at that point, I could only hear the bells ringing at Chelsea Old Church, a campanologist's calling over the swirling rising tide as I follow the shadow boatward.

I constantly question my sanity with regard to owning a boat in Chelsea, that is until I come and sit on it. The calm I feel now as I write about angels and shadows, with the dark and swirling tide bringing in clumps of kelp from the Estuary, surrounded by tall and statuesque herons angling the muddy pools, bean geese and their goslings hassling me chirpily for a share of my muesli, the gentle breeze that always seems to follow the tides like the air is being dragged along with the flow, cooling the stickiness in the air, makes it all worthwhile again.

* * *

I'm acutely aware of my setback, at the moment, mentally, since Paros the island. I'm seeing my doctor tomorrow but I'm fairly sure the hyper-activity increase in my head, the headaches and the nightmares in every sleeping moment are not just to do with London's heatwave, but a return of some of my symptoms of PTSD.

Wednesday 25 July and Thursday 26 July

London
Meetings, editing and Rachel Khoo's cookbook launch

32°C in London does not a comfortable night's sleep make. Sticky and close, trying to sleep to the sound of a noisy fan, retro and cool, but not cooling, just mildly circulating overheated and still air, polluted and heavy. Wildfires in Mati near Athens have killed many this week in scenes of biblical, apocalyptic ghastliness, young mothers and their children, unbearably, found huddling in their scores, together, embraced in their moment of death. I read tonight that twin nine-year-olds, Vassily and Sofia, are missing. Human tragedy and suffering that no one can possibly comprehend. I feel sad, terribly sad, and angry too; having no obvious outlet for that anger, I stew and overthink and stress.

Friday 27 July

London
Blood moon, 32°C

Back at Jamie's studio today for the first shoot with him in ages. It was great to hang out together, creating some beautiful magazine covers, with the added delight that he brought my godson Buddy to work with him, the sweetest of sweet boys. I taught him to say 'Things haven't been so sticky since sticky the stick insect got stuck on a sticky bun' (from *Blackadder*).

Storm clouds are gathering at the boat, set to break this heatwave with thunder and lightning. Before I shut the boat up, I just check the top drawer and stuck at the back I find an old invitation to an exhibition I had called 'Two'. I'm not surprised I can't remember the illustration, I was probably then at about my lowest ebb.

The introduction is written by Johnny's boss, Peter Matthews:

It was at the Kingston Degree show of 1986 that I first came across the brothers Loftus. John's show was the most startlingly original, most carefully considered and meticulously presented I have ever seen. I, like most other designers present, would have gladly given my eye teeth for him to join my team. As it happened all that was required was the occasional large glass of decent wine. But as I soon found out I was doubly lucky, for as well as being a staggeringly talented designer, John was to become a very close friend too.

Through John, David and I became firm friends and I quickly came to realize the strength of influence each had on each other's work and personality. How twin brothers can be so exceptionally gifted and so damned nice at the same time I'll never really understand.

But life's bitter irony was to strike us all a cruel blow. John suddenly fell desperately ill. Throughout his awful suffering up until his untimely death, his humour, his bravery and David's devotion to him shone through the horror of it all.

This exhibition, 2½ years later, is a celebration of their unique, sensitive and much imitated talent. It is proof, in my heart at least, that David ensures that John's talent and influences lives on.

Saturday 28 July

The Mews

I didn't leave the Mews today, I sat on our little roof terrace on and off in the sunshine. The temperature has blissfully dropped and the breeze is gusty and refreshing after so many close and sticky days. I doze, I read, I think, I try not to think. I read to take my mind off my thoughts. All is quiet.

Sunday 29 July

The Mews

Sitting now on a dark and gloomy Sunday, the back of the heatwave broken with lightning and flash floods, in my Cabinet of Curiosities room, surrounded by piles of papers from the General Medical Council, coroners' verdicts, solicitors' statements, grovelling letters and scraps of papers bearing notes and scribbles, the word that seems to stand out most, bold and strong, is 'deceased'. I hadn't until now realized that deceased meant 'recently died'. Whenever I'm asked 'Where is John?', I have replied 'Deceased' as it somehow felt gentler than 'He died', or indeed 'He was killed'. If you look up the definition of the word, I'd be okay in the States where 'deceased' just means 'dead'; I prefer the 'depart from life' or 'no longer with us' descriptions. One book suggested, 'asleep, at peace, at rest, departed and gone'. Whereas another suggested, 'When someone is deceased, they are dead – not dying or even just about to die. They are dead.' I guess it all boils down to one thing in the end: they are no more.

How wonderful is death

Death, and his brother sleep!
One, pale as yonder waning moon
With lips of lurid blue;
The other, rosy as the morn
When throned on ocean's wave
It blushes o'er the world;
Yet both so passing wonderful!

Percy Bysshe Shelley

Monday 30 July

A painting on acetate overlaid upon a drawing of a bright sun depicting abstract bright yellow sunbeams, dated 23 May 1988, and found in the top drawer of the boat:

'A little ray of sunshine to say that Johnny is proud of you, with all my love – Wamfi.'

Dearest Ange, my darling wife, who worries about me, has this week written to Dr S, whom she has located living on the continent. I didn't read the letter, but it has been posted. Who knows how he will react?

Tuesday 31 July

Shooting Jamie Oliver for a new campaign

Last night, sitting in the bath, I was thinking about the way my and Johnny's careers might have converged, meandered or diversified. We'd both always hoped for a career in art, after flirting with helicopter pilot and politician for a while. Architecture was an option for a while; John loved Mondrian and we were both introduced to the work of Richard Rogers by our father. He had surprisingly progressive admiration for modern architecture and design and an architecture path seemed a more stable way to tread. In our fifth year at Wallington Mother sent John and I to stay with 'Uncle' Brian Onions. Anne, his wife, was one of her distant cousins, and Brian was a bigwig at ICI. With hindsight, I wonder if we were sent away, up to Middlesbrough, to see how 'real people' worked, and jeepers it was certainly an eye-opener. John and I both loved Brian; a gentler man is rare indeed. He took us under his northern wings and showed us around the foundries and labs of ICI Wilton, but only after he'd made us smarten up and remove all of our poncey London punk-band badges and bracelets.

Secretly we both hated it and it put us both off architecture for years. The architecture side was so mathematical and technical, the plant so cold and bleak and distant, but we didn't want to let old Uncle Brian down so we stoically bore with it. Unused to being sent away from home, John and I behaved impeccably, keeping our badges by our bedside and only re-pinning them onto our lapels when we were safely on the train southbound, any ideas of architecture as a career replaced by dreams of snorkelling coral reefs and living on a boat.

Wednesday 1 August

Today I'm looking at album no. 2 from my mother's collection, mostly shot in black and white, square format so on Father's Yashica camera.

The album covers just a couple of years in time, trips around the country visiting family and friends. There is a beauty of John and me, with our matching spades, eating finger sandwiches, sheltering from the wind, perched on a picnic blanket upon the step of a huge wooden coastal groyne, then another of John or I sitting on an old leather hamper with metal clasps, proper china teacups and biscuit tins. We're dressed in cream corduroy shorts, white socks and woolly jumpers. Father Eric is smiling in every photo, so smartly dressed, as are we, even on the beach or in country streams, as are Uncles Derek and Patrick. Smart family Loftus.

There are some lovely images from the early years at The Beeches, playing in the garden under the plum tree, John and I riding our large wooden steam train, made by Mr Frank (we called it 'Billy'), or being pushed alarmingly high in the 'shuggy boat' swing by Uncle Pierre. One photo shows Mother looking rather fragile, tending to Ian on a see-saw in the garden. He was such an intense and difficult child and would often drive Mother to murderous thoughts, but in this picture she is holding his little hand, and she looks so thin and breakable. On the back she has written, 'Out of hospital – Guillain–Barré – took years to fully recover, still after-effects in legs from angiogram, I think.' I had forgotten that Mother had been ill, somehow, as ever, working her way through it even though she was almost on her knees. I remember now, discussing it with John at the time. We were used to Father and his dodgy ticker, but Mother was the glue that held us all together, kept us all well and on track, feeding our stomachs and our brains, and she had somehow been struck seriously ill with this rare, and to us worryingly complicated, autoimmune disorder which can lead to paralysis. It was genuinely terrifying at the time but has somehow been lost in the fog of other sickness memories.

Otherwise it's a happy album of beaches and Christmases, John and me in identikit Aran jumpers and cord dungarees, or full-on onesies, so ahead of our time, in the snow at The Beeches, on a rare white Christmas. It's funny where I can tell the difference between us by a memory: a christening where I remember falling and cutting my knee, so I've got a handkerchief wrapped around my grazes, or remembering my trunks had a little buckle on the waistband. In one I think it's me, aged about seven, but it's John, it's written on the back, wearing my Native American costume, something I wouldn't have allowed.

Our first Airfix models, our first transistor radios, our sister's first dolls' house, walking along Hadrian's Wall with my first binoculars by my side, another tell-tale marker that 'that one' is me, skimming stones as ever, learning to swim in frozen Lakeland rivers, lined up photos of four skinny children in misfitting swimmers. So many happy memories abound.

First day of the first Test against India this summer, going to read about it tomorrow in *The Independent*, for old time's sake.

Thursday 2 August

27°C at 9p.m.

Tonight Jamie, Gennaro and me launched Jamie's new Italian book with an octopus feast for influential bloggers in his studio. To cap a busy day we also launched a new year of the Pink Lady Food Photographer of the Year awards, with me named chairman for my second year. Things are feeling back to normal.

Friday 3 August

The Beaumont Hotel, Mayfair
32°C

Ange had left a present on my desk last night when I got in from the book launch. It's a 1975 copy of *The Beezer Annual*. We'd have been eight. I don't remember the comic stories, they're unfunny and slightly inappropriate now, but the 'factual and historical' stories, very *Look and Learn*, I remember every detail of – John and I would study the detail of each drawing for hours. There's one on Hadrian's Wall, one on a kestrel called Chalk and very dubious one on a gun called Mons, which makes me think that the cartoonists and writers of *The Beezer* were having their own laugh, 'Oh let's slip in a story about "Mons" this year, let's call the Martians "Gobblers", who eat wood, and put in lots of stories about spanking, bullying "toffs" and calling everyone Fatso or Fatty.' Editor replies, 'We'd better then give the little buggers some facts about Hadrian's Wall.'

It's bizarrely over 90 degrees in old London Town today, far too hot and sticky, 'a sticky wicket' as John used to say. India have just bowled out England for a second-innings lead of 194 and are 46–3 in the chase in a very tight first Test. (I write this for Johnny.) John would have loved this weather, sitting in the garden at The Beeches after work, tweaking his Monkey bike or lazing on a blanket, his face, like a Parosian lizard, pointed upwards and outwards at the sun. It was a Loftus thing, not a strip-down-to-the-swimmers kind of tanning, more a roll-up-the-sleeves-and-the-turn-ups-shoes-off-face-to-the-sun kind of tanning. In the tanning stakes he always won, he tanned faster, never seemed to burn, always got the tell-tale black crease between forearm and bicep before me, hair bleaching in the sunshine a little quicker than mine, tan lasting longer than mine.

My demons are rosé, Solpadeines and tanning. The trouble is that tanning is a Johnny legacy, like drawing, like Paros, like *Lord of the Rings*, like bracelets, and there aren't that many legacies to hold on to.

Saturday 4 August

Morning

Visited Mother this morning, the 32°C heat in London is draining her, but she's bright and breezy as soon as she has opened the door and put the kettle on. I was early enough to catch her listing her cranial nerves, one by one – a daily exercise to prove her medical-student mind is still firing on all cylinders – while checking *The Times* obituary columns to see if any of her learned colleagues have popped from this mortal coil, as they are, with age, increasingly likely to do.

This week Paros passed all of his exams with flying colours. I'm so very, very proud of him and I am certain he will make a wonderful doctor. My

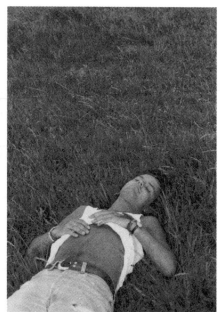

brother Ian's own department, the Vascular, has had its own problems, with his surgical partner accused and then losing his job over allegations of bullying, again between departments. But the one thing that both Ian and Paros have, that sets them apart from the rest, is their extraordinary empathy, and it's a relief to see, in my small world of Mother, Ian and Paros, that empathy still means something.

Today I told Mother that Ange has found 'Professor S'. She almost spat out her tea when she heard that Dr S had made professor, 'Prof of what?!' she exclaimed. Talking later of the coroner, she says to me, 'To them it was just another day, bantering and making jokes with all of the lawyers, immune to the suffering of those around him.' I asked Mother again, 'Why was I not called?' But there is no answer really, and we'll certainly never get an answer from him now.

I started writing on the boat today. A pair of herons, elegant and still, watch me as I write, and, dear Johnny, England has just snatched victory in a very closely fought first Test against India in Mumbai-esque temperatures.

Sunday 5 August

Morning at the boat
28°C

'Naxos is a bit of a slut, while Paros is all gold
and white like one of her once famous marbles.
If Naxos is a vivid parrot, then Paros is a
white dove.'
—LAURENCE DURRELL, *THE GREEK ISLANDS*, 1978

Yesterday, I took the little white pottery bird from Yria down to Mother's and left it beside her corner chair to watch over her. She held it in her hands for ages, appreciating and stroking its soft, white chalkiness.

Now I'm sitting on the boat with my beloved Ange, the only sound the trickle of water of the ebbing tide beneath the hull. No herons today, but plenty of mallards ducking and a-dabbling, uptails all, and a pair of cormorants fishing in the murky depths of Old Father Thames. Today is the anniversary of our first kiss, seven years ago, at the bottom of Dean Street in Soho. She's lying beside me, reading one of my Charlie Parker thrillers, on a pink leather Moroccan pouffe, shielding her face from the hot sun in a paperback-shaped shadow.

I'd admired Ange from afar for many years, always secretly fancied her when occasionally we crossed paths on projects when she worked for Jamie's Foundation. Always smiling is how I think of her, one of those big, beaming, unforgettable smiles. When you're on the receiving end of one of them, your day, however dull or frustrating, immediately brightens and feels just fine.

Today we are lunching at Casa Manolo on jamón ibérico and cold Albariño and salty anchovies and olives. We met here an hour before we were 'officially' wed at Chelsea Town Hall.

Once Jamie had furnished me with her number it took me a few weeks before I'd worked out what and how to text and why and where to meet and what to say, honestly believing I had no chance. Although we'd been separated for over eight years, I was still married to Debbie, and was a full-time father to Paros and Pascale. I had begun to feel impossibly undate-worthy.

After a lot of false starts, I eventually got a date with Ange, and we met at the lovely Quo Vadis on a balmy summer's evening, 5 August 2011. It was such a delightful evening, so relaxed and chirpy and talkative and jolly. We ate little, drank buckets of rosé and all was dandy, but I got the impression that she was totally unaware of my feelings towards her and, though she'd begun to understand that I was single, I thought there was absolutely no way in hell this gorgeous girl was going to want to share a snog with a broken and bashed old fart like me.

I told her a bit about life, marriage, the Ps and I falteringly told her about John – she tells me now that the way I told her was as if I was telling the story for the first time, there was so much hesitant emotion in my voice. An hour or so later, waiting for our black cabs at the bottom of Dean Street I braved a hug and a gentle kiss, surprised and relieved and oh, so over-excited to see her head turn towards mine for the first of an eternal number of kisses on the lips. Our fate was sealed, sealed with a loving kiss.

Wednesday 8 August

Shooting in Old Basing

On a three-day shoot with Christian (DJ BBQ), T-bone Chops (Chris) and Forage Sussex (Dave) in T-bone's parents' garden in Old Basing, a man's world of old smokers, vintage Austin Sevens and hand-forged axes.

Thursday 9 August

Old Basing

Third day shooting the madcap antics of the BBQ boys, black and white images of them standing on an old scimitar or a steampunk smoker playing two-headed bass guitars or wielding axes or live lobsters to heavy rock music and the distant crackle of thunder. Their world is a fiery one of smoke and brimstone and fire and skulls and blackened metal and noise and all rather wonderful for being so far from my own world.

Ange and I visited Mother. She barely moved from her corner chair, looking more and more like a Beatrix Potter character. On seeing us she was chirpy and bright, inspecting Ange's wrist injury with 'oohs' and 'ahhs' and recommendations of lotions and potions.

I've been looking at some of Johnny's drawings, fascinated by the delicacy of his hand, his use of perspective, and, what was hardest for me to emulate, his use of colour. I've been scrabbling around in the garage at the Mews and I've found a few drawings and watercolours he made in Florida when he was holidaying there with Liz. They were staying with my godfather in the Florida Keys. He was a designer of space rockets who had become so socially afraid that he had begun to live on a yacht moored offshore from his family home.

When John returned home he refurnished his bedroom in the style of the Keys, hitting Habitat for a clapperboard-style desk and deckchairs to replace his old Victorian armchair, which he dumped on me, painting his room in a Breton palette of blues and whites, with yucca and avocado plants. His bedroom became a hub of creativity, light and bright, filled with easels and paints, books and drawings, pictures by Mondrian and Caulfield, colourful and graphic as opposed to my darker, more music-driven, gig poster-graphic style.

I was the dark to his light, the yin to his yang; where his room was filled with daylight and lit with Marie-style spotlights, mine was permanently shaded, gloomily lit with deep red darkroom lights, lava lamps and fairy lights; where his brightly painted shelves held framed Warhol prints, model cars, boats and soldiers, neat and ordered, mine held collections of skulls and fossils, wartime ephemera, half-torn Joy Division and Rip Rig + Panic posters. Where he had books on the art of Tolkien, the architecture of Rogers and Foster and the sculptures of Goldsworthy and Moore, I had the linocuts of Revolution in France and Spain, the album covers of Jamie Reid for the Sex Pistols, Dada, and the sado-masochistic works of Alan Jones and Adam and the Ants.

We were always terrified of dentists, mainly because of our treatment at the hands of the dentist of our teens, Mrs B, who lied every time about how long she'd have to use the drill, and laughed her toothless (worry-ingly so) laugh every time you lashed out screaming in pain. After John died I found a new dentist, having avoided them for decades. Quentin is a specialist in dealing with those who fear dentists more than anything else. Like me. In the early days of my treatment he went through the process of fitting a crown, talking me through the moulding, telling me that the chap who moulds the crown is an ex-pottery student from the Royal College, soothing me into the drilling and injecting moments with me believing that we're actually embarking on more of an art project than a piece of serious dentistry. It was Quentin who suggested carving an icon into the tooth, 'Like a boat or a camera icon,' he suggested, 'or something to do with John?' That's why I have a carving of a yin and yang in my first molar, bottom right-hand side.

Sunday 12 August

The Glorious Twelfth

At the Mews I have a room I call 'the Garage' as it once housed my assistant Rosie's decrepit Mini, my Alaskan canoe and a 1950s cable car stolen from Verbier by my chums for my birthday. It's actually the stable, where the shire horses for the local brewery were kept, big imposing wooden doors at one end, our washroom at the other, and twenty years of photographic bumph in between. Behind the printer are several large portfolio cases, A1 in size, dusty and battered, zips rusted and broken, stuffed where they can be unseen and forgotten.

Until today. These were the folios our parents bought us when we'd finished our post-O-Level summer holidays in the Orkneys, so large for two teenage twins that you can see the scrapes along their bases where they would catch on the ground on our walk to and from school. I popped one of our wedding playlists on the iPod and started to disentangle the mess of bulging and broken folios, releasing a billow of dust.

It's only the first sleeve and immediately I seemed to lose the feeling in my legs, plonking myself clumsily on the floor, disorientated by what I had found. Extraordinarily, at the same time, my phone pinged through the speakers, the first message from Samantha since I told her I'd started writing my 'diary'. Oh, how I wailed, a sobbing mess of a man, lying spread-eagled on the cold-chill garage floor surrounded by papers and photos and all the collected crap of a career I've had without him. Utterly, utterly desolate and heartbroken, tears flowing freely and uncontrollably wailing like a kicked dog.

It was the simplest of messages, accompanied by a photograph, insignificant to anyone else, a picture of a tiny scrap of paper, the back of an envelope, written in fountain-pen ink, blotchy and scrappy, the ink seeping and smudged and as if written by a child. It just reads 'I found your pen'. Though barely legible, you can see the strain and patience it must have taken to write it, next to little experimental curls and strokes, practising his handiwork, together with a note from Samantha that reads, 'The last words John wrote.' 'I found your pen', enough to send me hurtling back to that last week of horror at the hospital. I curl myself into a weeping ball, the shape we were in the womb, the spooned shape of our babyhood, the shape I'd find him, sleeping and curled in his bed at the hospital, the shape I resort to in the corner of my bed, face to the wall, when I try to find peace among the turmoil, somehow believing that the smaller one can make oneself the less it will hurt.

Monday 13 August

The Mews

Shooting at the Mews for a cancer charity with a chef who has been fighting thyroid cancer.

It took a huge effort and an hour-long hug from Ange to heave myself out of my curled-up ball of sadness. God, it's amazing how something as benign as four words can send you spiralling to the depths of despair. I can't say whether it was the fact that it was the last message from John to his beloved Samantha or the wonkiness and spider-like erraticness of his type or the banality of the message. As the message pinged through the speaker I had just pulled out an A2 piece of card, a hand-painted poster for Merlin the magician, made when John was seventeen or so, and the first time he had experimented with a technique both of us used in his designs and my illustrations. Type was our thing, not the standard typefaces of art college like Times Roman, but scripted type, hand-painted, inked or drawn. Our technique was to take words of letters and repeatedly inscribe them on paper, carefully, carelessly, slowly or hurriedly, scraping and scratching the paper, causing splatters or pools of ink, smudges and mistakes, but using fine pens, often Rotring pens which were so fine but had a habit of catching in the paper if you were, deliberately, careless. We'd then blow these up on a copier, tear them up, paint over them in coloured gouache paint, then shrink them down again, thus creating our own typefaces, unique to us, legible of course, but somehow both antiquated and modern at the same time.

On the Merlin poster, the type is just that, enlarged, ragged letters: The Magic of Merlin by Philip Pullman (I had no idea that John knew of Philip Pullman), mixed with finely drawn portraits of a Gandalfian Merlin, like frames from a contact sheet mixed with highly enlarged letters of magical symbolism. How he knew that Pullman would write such magical books that would mean so much to Ange and me I do not know.

Often we'd create huge intense backgrounds of colour with chalk or gouache. John was better at graduating colour with it than me, so I'd use chalk and still do if I need uniquely colourful backgrounds for my photos. We'd then finely mottle them with splatters, cut them into strips, and rework the pieces like an overlapping jigsaw, creating a sort of constructivist textured background. When John made his Merlin poster I had illustrated an imaginary stage set for *On the Waterfront*. Again – though the technique was similar, intense colour, dissected typography, collaged images, overworking and layered, splattered and distressed, yet perfectly golden in ratio – they were so different in their final interpretation, his light and animated, almost cartoonish really, whereas mine was so dark and gloomy, dingy dockland walls and peeling posters. When our parents saw our Foundation Show at Wallington, same age as Pascale is now, eighteen, I remember our mother looking at me, rather concerned, 'Darling, why is it you have to make everything so terribly dark?'

Ultimately, as I became well known as an illustrator I used that same style, same technique, to illustrate book covers, magazine covers, ads, record covers and wine labels, but absorbing John's more refined and lighter approach, I learned to write script in multiple styles, studying illuminated manuscript and ancient styles of calligraphy while John became successful at Nucleus using those same techniques in a much more commercial and graphic way. His style was so ahead of its time, to constantly invent, by hand, your own typefaces rather than just choose them from the Bumper Book of Everyday Typography.

Tuesday 14 August

Charity shoot at the Mews

Sitting in the Cabinet of Curiosities listening to Talk Talk, one of the few bands both of us were allowed to love in equal measures. Simultaneously, my makeshift desk is scattered with snapshots and papers, ephemera of our shared lives, the pictures spanning twenty-five years. John and me, topless and arm in arm, skinny and bronzed, long hair soaked, both laughing hysterically as we play in a swimming pool, Niagara Falls, aged fourteen. God we were happy on that trip. John and me at The Beeches, September 1975, in uniform, nervous smiles, first day at Wallington Grammar. Me, alone, far too brown, wearing shorts and a punk jacket, hair slicked and moody, underneath the arches at sunset in Parikia town, aged about twenty-three. The last is John, in black and white, shot on my favourite sepia film, close up and handsomely moody, aged twenty-four, in the garden at The Beeches. I remember taking the shot on my old Nikon, one balmy evening. He had decided to dismantle Lofty, his Monkey bike, to clean its elements and put it back together. I was just so happy that it was off the road for a few days. It's so hard to believe that this beautiful boy was less than a year from dying.

Thursday 16 August

Shooting at The Wolseley, after breakfast at Colbert with Tim

A rare, endlessly grey and rainy day in London; how we have become used to the long and balmy summer days. The day started with breakfast with Tim in our favourite quiet corner of the Colbert. Over old-school tea and toast, Tim explains that he has 'hit a wall' and plans to take some time out, something I had deep down expected since his dear mother died, as he is now the sole survivor of that terrible day in Ireland, as well as the sole surviving twin. We hugged outside in the rain for a while and I watched him as he walked slowly down towards Sloane Square station knowing that I wouldn't see him for a month or two, and that sometimes we just have to accept that, though we have so often propped each other up through stormy times and though we are so in tune with the complexities of each other's grief, it's too much to expect of the other to be the whole cure. We're just an important part of the process of curing.

It's a dark day, a gloomy day. It was at exactly this point last year that the idea of this book came to me, to write down my memories of John, my love letter to him, marking what was the thirtieth year I had lived without him. It was a while before I fully made up my mind to do it and I would be lying if I said I hadn't considered stopping, downing pen, on an almost weekly basis. Sometimes it's just all too bloody painful and mind-numbingly, chest-crunchingly, sad. This morning, I thought of my father, standing on the station platform at Carshalton Beeches station, looking up at his firstborn twins, waving his bowler hat at our school caps, that proud smile on his face. I thought of Mother, staggering on the stairs at The Beeches, admitting to herself that Guillain–Barré syndrome could no longer be ignored. I thought of sitting on the bend in the staircase, waiting for Mother to return from John's brain scan. And then I thought of us both, he with Samantha, me with a new girlfriend to introduce for his approval, on a sunny day in Richmond Park, surrounded by his new friends from work, and his boss, Peter; a picnic with wine and laughter, followed by a cricket match.

I thought of John, colliding with his friend Mandy, trying to catch a high-flying ball, watching the ball and not the impending thwack of head against head. And it was then that I realized that it had been now, the second week in August, thirty-one years ago, that on a beautiful summer's day in Richmond Park, that unbearable chain of events had begun.

Catch-up day at the Mews, flying to Scotland

Flew out of City airport to Aberdeen and drove with Ange through the darkness to Douneside House.

Beautiful moments of the day, with my beloved Ange:

Pistachio porridge with local honey for breakfast, post-lovemaking.

A circular walk, along the brook that runs through the estate, beneath giant canopies of gunnera, up onto a pathway, raised upon ancient stones, along endless avenues of beech trees, known as 'the beech belt', close together the trees for a perfect 'infinity' path, Tolkien-esque and atmospheric, leading to nowhere. It runs along steep fields of corn, long due for harvest, wafting gently in the gusting wind, the shadows of clouds scudding hastily along the rippling crops.

Memories of dreams of John.

Bullfinches, Mother's long-lost favourites, in the hedgerows fringed with violently pink fireweed, or willowherb.

The dark and peaty River Dee, wide and free, flowing beneath the old stone bridge at Aboyne. Threatening clouds fail to darken a bright and breezy day. I spot a trout in the ripples.

The marriage of Andy and Foxy, two old chums of Ange, to the sound of a young boy on the bagpipes. A great deal of wine, laughter, Scottish dancing and merriment. Yes Jock, the dancing reminded me of you and if there is indeed a hell I imagine you might be there, dancing over hot swords, the devil crying 'Hot side first! Hot side first!'

Sunday 19 August

Flying home to London with Ange, tired and happy

Apparently today is celebrated as National Aviation Day, commemorating the birth of aviation; it's actually the birth date of Orville Wright, which must have annoyed Wilbur.

Monday 20 August

At the Mews, a day of editing

Tim, my mate Jeff and I are very much 'The Three Musketeers'. I tried to speak today to Jeff, but he was high above Arizona in his helicopter with his doors off so all I could hear was the clatter of the rotors and the violent gush of the wind. From flying loops through rainbows, snow storms and hurricanes, low over lakes and oceans, buzzing beaches and waves, through the middle of forests and cities over waterfalls and mountains, we've shared some extraordinary travels and adventures together as pairs or as a threesome. We are all godparents to each other's firstborn children, and are more like brothers than friends, Tim was Jeff's best man, Tim mine, and me Tim's and it was Jeff who read the Antoine de Saint-Exupéry passage at our wedding in Marrakech.

> 'Tout pour un et un pour tous.'
> —ALEXANDRE DUMAS, *THE THREE*
> *MUSKETEERS*, 1844

Tonight I cooked a risotto using dried porcini and hazelnuts. I made it up as I went along, as I always do when on rare occasions I make supper. I don't enjoy the process but feel that I must have absorbed so much

culinary knowledge over the years that it's a great test of that know-how to concoct something hopefully special for Ange. I've been trying to remember if I ever saw John cook, but I don't think I can. Living at home, Mother or Molly provided for our hungers and thirsts and John was always first to leave the table, much to the annoyance of Father. 'No meal is complete without cheese' versus 'Life's too short, Papa'.

Tuesday 21 August

At the Mews, shooting with cookbook writer Mini,
my client Kyla and a gay pug dog called Elvis

John had no interest in food other than as a fuel to function, to be eaten at speed, the table to be left as soon as manners dictated for an unoffended Father. When we were little and if I was annoying him at the breakfast table, John would build a wall of cereal boxes between us, sometimes as many as ten or twelve, a cereal Hadrian's Wall, and would get so upset if I breached the wall, the punishment was the silent treatment all the way to school. Poor Richard Eaton, one of our mutual best friends, sometimes called for John and I to walk to school with him and would then have to walk between us, a Richard Eaton wall replacing the cereal wall. John would still do the same in later life, the wall between our bedrooms, the closed door, a wall of silence, sometimes I'd annoy him enough that it would last for days. I'd sneak into his room sometimes and leave him little apology notes, which he would rarely acknowledge, but eventually he would bring the walls down, painfully, brick by brick, though they would cost me in humble pie. (He loved pie.)

Wednesday 22 August

A day spent in Andy Harris's Vinegar Shed near Pitshanger Lane, photographing him and his homemade lovage vinegars and his dried herbs and spices and his busy bees who are about to produce their harvest of urban honey. I spent a quiet half-hour sneaking inch by inch to the mouth of the hive. There were hundreds of bees, the hive full of honey, swarming and unpredictable, but I like to get so close and so calm that I'm 'part of the woodwork' and they ignore me. I love to film them in slow motion, so close you can hear every beat of their wings, and when they swagger back, legs laden in 'bloomers' of pollen, drunk and ungainly, bumping into the hive, trying to enter by the front door but aimless and woozy. Occasionally they get stuck in my hair and I try hard to ignore them in case they panic and sting my head, but mostly they just buzz around my eyes and ears, hundreds of them, focused on the job in hand and not the massive inquisitive interloper with his camera, a hive of activity bringing so much joy.

Thursday 23 August

Dinner with Paros and Ange at Colbert after a windswept shoot up The Shard, a day of several seasons. And more bees.

Friday 24 August

Shooting at the Mews today, clear blue sky, missing Tim on his sabbatical, all is calm and quiet. I feel a weekend of sitting on the boat coming on if the sun still shines. I've worked my way through the next family photo album, which covers the years 1974 and 1975 and our first day of school at Wallington. Summer 1974 was driving across Denmark after sailing on the overnight ship from Harwich, possibly at the time the most terrified I have ever been. There were rough seas, and John and me shared a cabin below the waterline, allowing two teenage minds to run riot with thoughts of icebergs and U-boats, sinkings and drownings. I seem to remember Father beneath the waterline too, the sounds and smells of the engines and the alarming lurching of the hull, although in photographs he remains the epitome of cool in dapper suit, tie and brogues. The pictures tell of a cultural trip across the islands of Denmark, visiting castles and Viking settlements, Elsinore, the Royal Palace, Roskilde and Legoland, John dressed in head-to-toe-purple, me in a rather stylish pair of flared cords and a white zip-up cardigan. It was the happiest of road trips, ending with a few weeks in Copenhagen. Father was in his element, freezing lakes and seas to bathe in, grand castles to explore and the wrecks of Viking longboats to peruse, his health good and the four of us behaving ourselves and not squabbling for a change.

The album then skips a year to the summer of '75 and what was probably his favourite road trip, though it did end with the autobahn pile-up that put me and Johnny off driving for ever more. Pictures of us bathing in the Moselle, Luxembourg, the Black Forest, the Danube, the Dachstein Glacier, Hitler's Eagle's Nest in Berchtesgaden, Toplitzsee, the lake of sunken Nazi gold, and then back via Belgium and a stay in Bruges. Though we were just thirteen I can remember the trip as if it was yesterday, particularly the grand hotels on the Mosel and the Rhine, the endless summer days and late evenings boating on the Austrian lakes, the reminiscences of Father and our Uncle Patrick, the tales of concentration camps, hidden tanks in the woods and the legendary gold sunken under layer upon layer of drowned forests. It was a *Boy's Own* dreamworld. There's the first picture of me using a camera, a Kodak point and shoot, a snap of edelweiss flowers growing on a mountain side, the moment

John started his obsession with pressing flowers in old books and flower presses. Worried that he had gained a hobby where I had not an iota of interest, I took to collecting small metal badges to nail to my newly purchased ice axe, which had the bonus use of terrifying Jean-Marian and Ian.

Saturday 25 August

The Mews

Carnival weekend in London, both Paros and Pascale will be dancing with a can or two of Red Stripe, with their chums, in the streets of Notting Hill. For some reason, in Chelsea, growing up, Notting Hill felt like another world, and when visiting London from The Beeches John and me saw the King's Road as our spiritual home. 1978 and the opening of Rough Trade Records saw our first forays into Portobello, queuing up outside for the new releases of bands like The Monochrome Set and Subway Sect, but there was always the warning that you shouldn't wander far from the main roads. I remember asking a policeman the way to All Saints Road where John and I were signing on with a film-extra agency for one summer and the reply being, 'Even we don't patrol down All Saints.'

We only got one decent job from the agency, but those couple of days' work earned us enough for our flights to Paros. The film set was the old Nine Elms railway station, then a vast semi-derelict terminus beneath Battersea Power Station, sprawling and atmospheric. John and me, along with Paul Allen and Richard Eaton, were soldiers, marching up and down, climbing onto steam trains, off to war. The actor Donald Sutherland was playing a spy, weaving in and out of us, *The Eye of the Needle*. Oh, the disappointment of the fleeting moments on screen when the film came out a year later, blink and you missed us, and of course we'd built up our involvement into virtually starring roles. Paul fared rather better, promoted by virtue of his good looks to platform conductor and therefore a uniform that stood out in a sea of marching khaki.

Today feels rather end-of-summery, it's colder and more unpredictable, sun and showers. Paros is already back studying, medical school holidays getting shorter and shorter as the years progress. Pascale, just returned from the Edinburgh Fringe, knows that this is her last-blast weekend before finding work for her gap year. It's funny how you never grow out of that end-of-summer-beginning-of-term feeling, even more than thirty years on.

Sunday 26 August

The Mews
Grey and cold

With Mother today. Smiling, in her corner chair, we talked of her time living in Naworth Castle and in Tarn End House, near her surgery in Brampton. We spoke of a time I came up to visit her after John had died and she had moved back to Brampton in search of the company and quietness of her old friends there. One time she found me at the tarn on my own. I was breaking off fat chunks of ice from the water's edge and skimming them across the frozen surface of the tarn, so cold and icy under a clear blue sky; the pieces would skim for ages, creating the most beautiful high-pitched song or hum. Mother watched me for ages, delighted by the sounds I was making, but her heart ached for me, I looked so heartbroken, so miserable. Thinking back, I can remember the cold, the beauty of the moment, and the extraordinary euphoric sound of each skim across the ice. I remember the mulled wine at Tarn End with Mother and her dear friend Bill. I don't remember it as a time of misery but as a time of great poetic beauty. It makes me realize how hard it must have been for Mother, a couple of years on from our loss, to see me there, where she had always seen two; a solitary twin making music with the ice covering her tarn, the same banks that she would sit on with her student friends and their admirers, carefree and happy, before Father, before us.

Today is the anniversary of the bomb with which the IRA killed Tim's twin, Nick. Upon the Bay of Mullaghmore in Ireland on a clear and sunny day a bomb was planted beneath the deck of *Shadow V*, Tim's grandfather's boat. It was detonated by Thomas McMahon, one of the IRA's most experienced bomb makers, as he and his team watched the family from the surrounding cliffs.

Lord Mountbatten was killed, as was Paul Maxwell (a fifteen-year-old local friend). Baroness Brabourne (Tim's granny on his father's side) was also killed, as was Tim's elder twin, Nick.

Tim and his parents John and Patricia, as I later knew them, were all seriously injured. Tim's eldest sister, Joanna, would later say to Tim in hospital, 'You woke up, Nick never did.'

Nicholas Timothy was an all-important twenty minutes older than his identical sibling, Timothy Nicholas, who like me was the younger, the very slightly lighter in weight. Like us, in scuffles and bundles the elder would always get the upper hand; like us, they started and finished each others' sentences; like us, there was a healthy competitiveness. Like us, people could sometimes tell us apart when we were together, but found it much harder upon meeting us individually; like them, we often took advantage of our being identical, particularly at school. Like them, we were often sick together, double measles, double mumps, double chickenpox. Tim, like me, was the more chaotic, more easily distracted, the more reliant on the leadership of our elder twin. And, like me, upon hearing the news of our twin's death, the underlying feeling existed that somehow the wrong twin had died.

In the immediate years after I met Tim I would spend that weekend with him and his parents either at home in Kent or we'd fly somewhere in his little plane – Scotland or France. At breakfast we would raise a glass to 'Nick and Grandpapa and Granny and Paul'. Somehow I believed that their collective suffering was so much greater than mine and I never admitted, other than to my own raised glass, that it was also a day that would haunt me for the rest of my life.

Tuesday 28 August

A grey and still day at the Mews

Feeling stagnated and downbeat, I decide not to write today, only the second time I've missed a day. Sometimes the mountain that I am climbing feels too steep, then it's time to pause, reflect, look at the view.

Wednesday 29 August

I do remember watching the BBC news report, the grainy black and white footage of the bay at Mullaghmore, the floating wreckage, listening to the fragments of information, which included, to John and my collective horror, that one twin had been injured and his elder twin killed. We walked away from the TV set and went to our separate bedrooms, unable to discuss it but knowing that if I tapped gently on the wall next to my head that I would get a reassuring tap-tap back again. We were a year older than Tim and Nick, at a familiar stage in our lives but worlds apart, but at that moment we felt the terrible break in their seemingly unbreakable bond, too painful for us to comprehend. Little did I know that years later I would be best man at Tim's wedding and he at mine.

In hindsight I went almost immediately from meeting Tim to us being in virtually constant contact. We met in the summer of 1989, and by Easter of 1990 I was flying with Tim every other weekend. I spent the Easter holidays with his whole family in Eleuthera in the Bahamas. It makes me sad now to think that I hurt my Mother by forming such a close bond with another family and I wish that I had been more sensitive to the situation. It was another mistake in the post-traumatic fog I was feeling my way through at the time.

I remember that he mentioned that his family used to wear t-shirts with their names on, and family photos taken just before the bomb often showed Tim and Nick in their orange-labelled tees. Where Tim and Nick were often dressed alike, for the most part it's the memory of mine and John's different clothing that allows me to tell us apart in photographs. As toddlers, to differentiate Tim from Nick, their mother attached a small gold bracelet around Nick's left wrist and later when Nick lost it Tim worried that there would be a lifetime of confusion, but actually, by then those close to the twins had noticed an easier way to spot difference, a mole underneath Tim's chin. For our nearest and dearest, it was John who created tiny differences in our faces, but one had to look very closely: the tiny scars from his fingernails as he drew blood holding me close to him in our cot, and later the slight twist in my nose where he had broken it by putting into physical action the rhyme, 'we all rolled over and one fell out'. It happened in our grandmother's Victorian bed so it was a long way to fall flat on one's face for a toddler.

Thursday 30 August

Surrounded at my desk by photos of John, it's hard to imagine how alike we would be now had he survived. The wears and tears of being a photographer means that my back twists and slopes in funny directions, a bit of scoliosis, a slight hunch, an over-developed muscle behind my neck from hand-holding heavy cameras. I try not to look at photos of myself and my mirror image still haunts me enough to avoid shaving, but if I force myself to look closely, to study my visage, I don't see much of the youth I was when John was alive. In my dreams we remain unaged, two twenty-five-year-olds frozen in time, and I prefer that image. The face that stares back at me doesn't quite add up and somehow I imagine John would have grown up a much better-looking version. The sun damage would probably be much the same, wrinkles and creases, freckles and liver spots everywhere, 'lentigo senilis', which sounds far too senile. The hair is thinner and streaked with grey, but not really balding like our father was, but it's the general pudginess, the rounding-off of the features that I find it hard to imagine John putting up with. I don't think his vanity would have allowed that! Maybe he would have sat at his easel doing facial exercises, jutting the chin, flicking the double chin, holding back the years. I feel he would. Recently, after Hak clean-shaved me for the first time in nearly thirty years, I checked to see if I could still see Johnny's nail marks in my skin, my tiny embrace scars. I think they are there, but when I find them hard to find I stop myself from looking, frightened I might be losing another of his legacies. The broken nose remains.

Friday 31 August

The Mews

At lunch yesterday at the Colbert with Bart, who was over from Amsterdam. I spotted Rupert Everett in the corner, still tall and elegant, but like us, a long way from his *Another Country* days when John so wanted to be like him. He sat under a Jacques Tati poster, reminding me that John thought him funnier than Laurel and Hardy, which caused many a breakfast wall-building.

Woke this morning to the sound of a wren outside the bedroom window, a real chatter of rattles, tweets and chirps, bubbling away, surprisingly sharp and shrill for a bird so little.

AUTUMN

Saturday 1 September

First day of autumn

Slightly hungover on my Middle East Airlines flight to Beirut, sweating it out in the overheated and slightly fetid atmosphere. Currently flying across a dark and misty Turkish coastline, the Greek islands only just visible, barely there, towards Lebanon and Beirut. Descending towards Beirut I find it strangely calming and familiar to hear the Arabic voices excitedly chattering around me. Father used to love Beirut, he liked that he could swim and sunbathe in a warm sea in the morning, dine on fine Arabic food at lunchtime and then ski in the mountains in the afternoon, to return to party in the city in the evening.

Sunday 2 September

Hotel Phoenica, Beirut

The level of excitement is so much higher when a flight feels like it's landing in the centre of a city as opposed to the suburbs. Low over the Mediterranean, the initial impression is that one is still high among the stars, until there is the realization that one is lower than the buildings, millions of tiny lights dotting Beirut's mountainsides, some so close you can see families sitting around their television screens.

Today troubled me. I travelled all over southern Lebanon and saw some amazing sights and met some lovely people. I tramped in 40°C around the Temple of Bacchus, but was offered Hezbollah t-shirts outside it. I was welcomed into the homes of goat farmers, cheese makers and za'atar farmers, but stopped at more heavily armed checkpoints than you can shake a stick at. But I did watch Grace, a beautiful eighty-year-old draining the whey from her sheep's cheese in ancient amphorae, as she has done for the last seventy years, her hands smoother than mine, telling me in Arabic, 'As long as I go away loving her a little, she will be happy.' The extraordinary paradox of the world we live in.

Five beautiful moments of this day:

Watching hundreds of storks flying slowly in V-shaped patterns along the Beqaa Valley against a hazy blue sky.

Crushing sun-drying bulbs of purple sumac in my hands, releasing their sweet scent, while remembering snoozing under the sumac tree at The Beeches.

Wandering around Baalbec, the ancient city stronghold of the Shia Hezbollah movement, home of the Temple of Bacchus, one of the grandest Roman temples in the world. Half an hour running around with my Leica wasn't not long enough.

Sharing fresh labneh, figs and Arabic coffee with the family of Grace, from generations of cheese makers, and her shepherds. Travelling up into Mount Lebanon to meet their goats and the sheep with 'fatty tails'.

Tasting the oil of za'atar, an extremely intense essential oil, so strong it hurt my tongue with just a drop on my fingertip; the deeply tanned, charming and laid-back herbalist

Abu Mohammed, sitting in a huge mound of drying rosemary and lavender, with Arabic coffee and za'atar water, a 'medicine for everything'!

Monday 3 and Tuesday 4 September

Lebanon

Beirut, heading north into the mountains in search of za'atar and sumac, honey and wine and all things fine.

Dawn rises over an orange and brown smog that seems to permanently envelope Beirut, dawn to dusk. The sun sets an hour earlier, not even reaching the horizon, the smog is so chokingly dense. It's Wednesday morning and I'm exhausted and physically broken though I can't help smiling as I follow a pair of hand-holding identical twins onto the plane. Matching pink shoes, pink dresses and rucksacks. Their only difference, for their parents maybe, is one wears pink spectacles, one wears blue.

I feel deflated after Lebanon and desperate to get home. Last night, feeling poorly, I sat sweatily on my hotel balcony on the twenty-fourth floor, watching the chaotic city going through various shades of *Blade Runner* hues as the sun faded as opposed to set.

Lebanon is not a huge country but so utterly chaotic and shambolic and disorganized that more time was spent in fear for my life on the half-built roads than wandering its ruins and villages. The Temple of Bacchus will remain a vivid memory, as will spending time high, high in the mountainous cedars and thistles with the beekeepers harvesting their honey, and the kindly and gentle za'atar growers, but I won't miss the countryside, its beauty under threat from corruption, building and mining, and abandonment and an ever-increasing and constant 'hedgerow' of plastic filth. Taking a landscape photograph was nigh on impossible without the backlit sparkle of shattered glass and the silhouettes of broken cars and bicycle frames.

I suppose India is the nearest I've been to a country of such contrasts, chaos and constant hint of danger. Standing in streets in the Hezbollah strongholds towards Syria and to the south of Lebanon with the posters of AK47s and ayatollahs and 'the martyrs' of war, the only European for days, I definitely got the feeling I was being observed. Being told it was dangerous to be carrying 'any form of camera or recording equipment', I did have to question why I was there. I travelled light, with no laptop, so haven't loaded the images yet and, jeepers, I hope it was worth the stress to the old ticker!

Wednesday 5 September

Evening. Home
A week shooting with Meera Sodha in London

The flight was delayed by two hours due to 'naval operations off the coast of Syria and the firing of missiles by the Russian Navy', not an excuse you wish to hear just before take-off. I probably shouldn't have gone straight from such a stressful flight to a shoot in North London, but Meera Sodha is such an uplifting and inspiring food writer that I just managed to hold it together, fuelled by milky tea and a constant supply of beautiful ingredients like figs and fragola grapes to launch into the air and catch in my awaiting *bouche*.

Saturday 7 and Sunday 8 September

Shooting at home, the wonderful world of eggs,
with lovely stylist Pip

I've been trying to face reading the transcripts of the operation John endured on 27 August but I can't do it. Mother is right, there's no need for me to read the dispassionate account of dissection and rebuilding of poor Johnny. The doctors could barely manage to describe what they were going to do so our dear mother understood. John listened, understood a little, but quite understandably failed to grasp the scale of the operation about to be performed. The surgeons did give John one choice to make, over the 'entry point' of the operation: it could go either through the side of the face, creating a huge scar, but potentially an easier route to the brain; or through the 'non-scarring' option, which sounds barbaric: to enter the face through the mouth, above his top teeth and up through the area behind his nose to the base of the brain. John and I spoke about it a few times and a scar-free option was chosen, though neither of us could really grapple with the logistics. He was just keen to get a move on as his double vision was upsetting him and his right side, particularly his right arm, was losing more and more feeling. Both of us had never been more scared or out of control in all our lives, but there was nothing we could do other than try to be positive. The twenty-seventh would be our longest day.

Sunday 9 September

Train from Paddington to Bodmin, Cornwall

Seeing dear Mother this morning with Ange, she was on such sparky form that I decided not to ask for any more details about that day.

Conversations covered included my trip to Heliopolis, the sumac tree at The Beeches, Brexit and 'that buffoon Boris', the importance of honeybees, and, very briefly and in her gentle manner, the reasoning behind me not reading the medical/surgical records.

'The longest day' was extraordinary in that we had so little control, so little news; it was but an elongated blur of inactivity. Ian and I sat together watching movies and playing snooker, fed and watered by a fussing Molly, not wanting to leave The Beeches in case the phone rang bringing news. The operation lasted for three uneaten meals, cooked by Molly, three barely watched movies including, inexplicably, *Platoon*, luckily with the music on silent, at least twenty games of pool and ten of snooker, many pots of tea, several bars of chocolate, a bottle of red wine, and the cricket highlights. It was evening when the phone eventually rang, Mother telling us that 'the operation had been long, but had gone as well as expected and that John was unconscious and in Intensive Care'.

Monday 10 September

Rock, Cornwall
Shooting Nathan Outlaw in Port Isaac

When I first saw John in Intensive Care, attached to all the tubes, drips, drains, monitors and wires, he resembled a victim of a front-on collision, his beautiful and still tanned face bruised and battered and swollen. Ten or twelve hours of pulling his face apart and removing the tumour had, apparently, been successful. There had been some frights but, according to his consultant, he was as good as could be expected.

Several weeks later, sitting under the damson tree in the late-summer sun, I asked John of his first memories post-operation and was surprised to hear that he had 'come to' between the operation and Intensive Care.

He said that he'd felt okay. One minute he had been having his preoperative injections, the next he was coming to on a fast-moving hospital gurney, trundling along, looking up at passing strip lights. He said he had realized things weren't quite all rosy when he saw the faces of the surgeons around him, their eyes of alarm. He remembered the rubberized smell of a mask and then nothing. Thankfully, much of Intensive Care was a forgotten blur after that.

I tried not to cry in front of him, but at times I barely made it to the ward door. The first time I saw him I cried for two hours, sitting on a bench on Wimbledon Common, hoping that my tear ducts would be dry by the time I saw Johnny. He cried every time I saw him for two or three weeks, frustrated by how awful he felt. He had expected a return of movement in his right-hand side, but if anything it was worse, and his vision was still 'crossed'. Plus, of course he had the mother of all headaches. Alarmingly, his teeth in his upper jaw and the upper jaw bone wobbled and seemed to be unattached and loose, which the doctors couldn't explain to me, just saying 'it will get better'. It did, slowly, and there were now long talks of weeks and weeks of intensive rehabilitation, physiotherapy for his right side, a possible operation on his sight at a later date. Also, for the first time, there was talk of radiotherapy to 'knock off tiny traces of the tumour left behind in the midbrain cavity'. And with that his fate was sealed.

* * *

Desperate for air this evening and ignoring the threatening skies, I abandoned my desk at the St Moritz and wandered down the tiny coastal path between the blackberry bushes and late-summer primroses, smiling at the rabbits as I passed, to just the sound of windswept flocks of oystercatchers and the increasing roar of the sea. I clambered down to the little cove of Daymer Bay, knowing that there would be no one there at high tide, while the beach was covered and there was a danger of being cut off by the incoming sea. I sat for over two hours on a jagged rock, a freshwater stream both sides of me, the crashing sea all around.

I closed my eyes tight and tried to connect with my senses of smell and hearing, but the sea was so loud it frightened me not to be able to see it. I was soaked through by the spray, so I concentrated on smell: fetid and wet, kelp and bladderwrack, dead crabs and skate eggs, cuttle-fish and salt. God it was beautiful, waves ten to fifteen feet tall crashing around me, buntings or pipits, flocks of them, singing in the freshly washed-ashore seaweed, hundreds of crabs. All around me, so noisy, so beautifully out of control, the sea was ferocious and dark. The clouds swirled ominously, but every now and then the sun, only just above the horizon, would blindingly flash its appearance, skimming the waves and reminding you of their true aqua-clarity; every pebble, rock and weed illuminated like tiny mirrors, utter uncontrollable chaos. I lay back, closed my eyes, and thought of John opening his eyes on the gurney, that moment of clarity and false hope, that feeling that actually, everything was going to be just fine.

Tuesday 11 September

Finished shooting Nathan Outlaw's book, train in
the thick fog to London, a 'pea souper'

I travelled back on the train from Bodmin Moor today, the weather moody and close, everything and everywhere faintly silhouetted by thick fog. I was woken by a wren outside my window this morning, a perfectly timed alarm, then photographed Farmer Hoare in his fields of kale and goldfinches, father and son oyster farmers down in Rock, and Nathan, smart and formal at his restaurant.

I feel much like the weather, drowning in a warm mist. I can't get past the thoughts of John's false hopes, his castles in the air. As I was distractedly photographing the oyster farmers this morning, the father was searching for the word for fish leather and kept saying the word 'chimera, chimera'. I think he must have been thinking of shammy leather, but he just kept rubbing his sunburnt head, repeating 'chimera'. Eventually I had to smile and tell him that no, that means 'false hope'.

Wednesday 12 September

Flying to Lapland via Stockholm for Niklas Ekstedt

I'm flying over the Swedish archipelago, accompanying my friend and lovely Viking friend Niklas Ekstedt, on an odyssey to Lapland to photograph the Sami people herding their reindeer off the mountains for the beginning of winter. Traditionally they slaughter some of the adult stags on the mountainside, then remove and then cure their hearts, and that's the merry task I have been asked to capture: the Sami removing the beating hearts of reindeer. So here I am, Lapland-bound, the lights of tiny dwellings twinkling in the clear air beneath me, another journey into the unknown.

After three flights and two long journeys by car, Niklas and I arrive after midnight in thick mizzle and complete darkness. Our Mountain Lodge Hotel is somewhere in deepest, darkest Lapland and we find no welcoming committee, just a shut-up and deserted hotel. Eventually we tried an open door, passed the deserted reception – unsure of the protocol – but, finding a couple of simple bedrooms furnished with reindeer skins and little else, we unpacked, called our wives and settled down ready for an early start. An hour later, as I was dozing off, I had a knock on the door from Niklas in his underpants, laughing so hard he could barely breathe. It seemed we'd broken into the wrong hotel . . .

Thursday 13 September

Saxnäs, Västerbottens län, Lapland
8°C

In the correct hotel, my room looks like an Edward Hopper painting, retro and so uncool it's cool, shades of dark green and brown streaked with actual sunrise orange. Pulling back the curtain reveals an extraordinary scene, the brightest orange sun streaking over an island, bizarrely called Japan, on a lake called Kultsjow. If it wasn't for an ancient Sami house by the water you would think it was Scotland. There's the clearest air, early-autumn oranges and the occasional bright, bright red maple; the sky is so vast and there's a rainbow, miles of shore line, rows upon rows of fir trees and Cairngorm-like mountains on the horizon.

We were picked up early by a lovely smiley Sami girl called Kajsa who guided us up to the mountains. Nothing prepared us for the utterly terrifying, exhilarating, heart-thumpingly beautiful madness that followed: a breakneck car ride through some of the most beautiful lakeland roads I have ever seen. We were in a desperate rush to catch the movement of the reindeer, which were charging in a clockwise mass of dust and sweat through the mountainous forests. Mist rolling across mirror-like lakes reflecting forests of bright white-veined plane trees, rainbows so bright that at one point Niklas, now like a child who'd eaten too much candy, exclaimed, 'They may have the Northern Lights but that is the brightest rainbow I've ever seen, it's actually got an extra purple in it!' Dark burgundy dwellings in the backlit mist, white antlers of moose and reindeer nailed in patterns that made their façades look like the wings of a butterfly. A moment of sadness flashed through me as I remembered John and how much he would have loved and been inspired by the scenes fleeting past me, coinciding with another flash, this time of guilt, as I realized in my tiredness I hadn't said my awakening 'good morning' to him.

The heart of the reindeer is why I had travelled all this way. Hopefully it's the nearest I'll come to seeing what is apparently the closest thing to a human heart. I know mine is broken, physically bruised by Johnny's death, and those bruises would be visible to intense X-ray, but at least my broken heart didn't send me to an early grave.

Friday 14 September

I kept the hotel curtains open, looking out over the lake and mountains beyond in the desperate hope of an early showing of the Aurora Borealis.

Today was spent with Kajsa and her husband Andreas, cooking and fishing for small green and speckled trout in an ancient, protected, fairly secret Sami village, full of their old wooden *gahti*, Tolkein-esque huts, conical, moss-covered dwellings, impossibly beautiful, dotted among the lushest and most verdant forests beside a clear water lake teaming with fish. I became obsessed with the woodland floor, the lichens and mushrooms, from the minute to the prehistoric and gargantuan, the Jurassic fungi and plants, a kaleidoscope of colours I dream of but never see. Tiny islands in the lake and streams reminding me so vividly of the 'Singing-Ringing tree' dreams of my youth, the calm and idyllic scenes of ultimate rest in my dreams of adulthood.

Overcome by a feeling of melancholy I played with their collie in the clear water, skimming flat pebbles, throwing him logs, building Andy

Goldsworthy-esque leaf patterns in the cold shallows, alone with my Lakeland memories. It was a stunningly beautiful day.

Saturday 15 September

Home is where the heart really is. Godson Buddy Oliver's birthday

Three flights; storms, rainbows, the sun setting over the endless Swedish archipelago turning thousands of lakes into mirrors, and home.

As I landed in the wee hours of the morning, the moment the tyres screeched on the tarmac, Tim called me from his sabbatical in America. I'm so happy to hear his voice, his promises of coming home soon; we'll have so many stories to share, so much has been on hold while he is away.

Sunday 16 September

Popped down to see Mother and found her teary-eyed and sad, missing John, mulling over what we could have done to prevent his death. This week Ange received a reply to her letter to Dr S. The original envelope had been opened but, unsealed, it had been marked 'return to sender'.

Monday 17 September

With lovely designer Andy, shooting a hotel in Canterbury. It was a stunning day, clear blue sky. From the train, I spotted a pair of herons courting in the middle of a field of corn. As I walked towards the cathedral, across the river with sixteenth-century buildings hanging precariously over its banks, small speckled trout swam in the weeds amidst vibrant greens and crystal-clear water. I stopped on an ancient bridge next to a friary garden and a kingfisher flew past, a flash of extreme blue.

On the train I took the time to read Ange's letter to Dr S. She was so disappointed to see 'return to sender', particularly as it had the correct address. It was opened but probably unread, maybe the name Loftus was enough to guarantee its rebuttal, its very 'return to sender' a statement of refusal to even acknowledge our being.

I know Ange, she would have pored over the writing of this letter for hours, analysing every sentence, every nuance. It outlines the last thirty years from the failing of my first marriage through grief, the effect on my mother's career and health, to the success of my brother Ian, through adversity, to become such a talented surgeon. It appeals to 'his heart' to not ignore the letter, to appreciate our loss and it asks him to be 'kind and understanding' as 'humanly possible'.

Tuesday 18 September

Shooting at the Wolseley
6.30a.m. start. Balmy day

Early start, early finish, so sitting at the Mews rereading Ange's letter to Prof S. I think that his return of the letter is his way of saying 'do not contact me again'. That's fine, I guess. It might even be the first time he's thought about John's death since the inquest, but I hope not. I hope he learned at least some sort of lesson from the whole sorry episode.

Wednesday 19 and Thursday 20 September

Crystal Palace and Colbert

Second day of a three-day shoot with Christian (DJ BBQ) and his madcap and merry band of bearded brethren. Much-needed hilarity, taking my mind off yesterday's bad day.

Friday 21 September

Last day of Christian's book shoot with his band of brothers, Forage Sussex Dave, Charcoal Matt, little Lizzy, T-bone-Chops Chris and various dogs and charcoal burners, chefs and spoon carvers. Much hilarity over burger flipping, controlled arson, swashbuckling, axe wielding, head banging, air-guitar strumming and wild drinking. Somehow we have made a beautiful book through the fug of smoke and mayhem and the threat of Storm Ali in a suburban garden.

Sunday 23 September

Shooting at home with Ange and cookbook author Rukmini Iyer a.k.a. Mini, editing my Lapland trip in the Cabinet of Curiosities.

Text received from Mother this morning, acknowledging our conversation about people in life who enjoy manipulating and causing trouble:

'Remember darling David, less said, soonest mended, and a soft voice turns away wrath x'

Monday 24 September

Shooting in N7, finishing the Lapland edit

The bullies we've endured in life, do they sleep the sleep of babies at night, dreamless and free? I dread my nights. Multiple awakenings, nightmares, the occasional night terror that awakens me thrashing and sweating, endless dreams leading into more dreams . . . sometimes I'm not sure whether I've actually awoken or have falsely woken into another never-ending chain of nightmares. It doesn't matter how exhausted I am, how accomplished my day has been, whether I am happy or sad, it's always the same.

I finished my shoot early today, edited it and sent it in, then went back to my Lapland edit. I'm taking my time as it was such as complex and frenetic shoot, on two cameras, one in each hand, and it needs my patient attention. The day is blissfully clear, blue sky, *Simpsons* clouds with silver linings, warm sun with a cold chill to the wind. I yearned to be on the boat but forced myself to work on for an hour or so, eventually heaving our enormous sheepskin pouffe out onto the roof terrace and plonking myself louchely face-to-sun for half an hour's quiet contemplation.

Tuesday 25 September

Finished the Lapland edit. A two-shoot day in London and then catching a train to Norfolk to shoot with Gennaro Contaldo

I realized yesterday was the anniversary of John's move back from Neurology to the oncology unit, a day that at the time was filled with positivity, that seemed like the beginning of the road to recovery. John arriving by ambulance, in a wheelchair, on a sunny day much like yesterday, no wires or tubes, tentatively walking to his bed to begin his physical therapy and his radiotherapy. Little did we know that meeting with the consultant radiotherapist would be the beginning of his fateful treatment there. Nothing much happened that day other than Samantha settling him into his bed and surrounding him with his teddies, cards and flowers, filling his drawers with pyjamas and smellies and pens and papers to practise his writing. He met his two fellow patients, whose names I'll leave, both charming chaps; the businessman having 'blood cleansing' and another young man who had just undergone chemotherapy and literally vomited between sentences of greeting. It was also our first meeting with Douglas, the gentlest and kindest nurse you could wish for at such a vulnerable time, and my first meeting with Dr S, a serious and unsmiling junior doctor, working under the consultant.

John's first visit to the oncology unit had been on 11 September, where he was due for 'moulding'. This was the fitting of a plastic mask that fits face down into a secure table, allowing the head to remain in a still position during radiotherapy. Mother believed that so soon after major brain surgery John should have been transported gently, in a stretcher, but the decision was made to sit him in the ambulance and walk him in, rather than carry him. As John walked unsteadily from the ambulance, he developed what appeared to be an extremely runny nose, with clear fluid running from his nostrils into his mouth and all over his pyjamas. It had an unpleasant taste and he was visibly upset. The liquid was then discovered to be cerebrospinal fluid, a clear and colourless fluid produced by the brain. The primary function of this fluid is to act as a cushion or buffer to the brain within its hard skull and to provide immunological protection to the brain. It fills all the spaces inside and around the ventricles of the brain as well as the central canal of the spinal cord. With the help of Mother I was learning fast, and realized immediately that one thing you definitely do not want is for your cerebrospinal fluid to have contact with the outside world, with all of its floating and invisible germs and their microorganisms. Basically, you are opening a fluid pathway directly to the centre of the brain and nervous system.

It was then decided that John could not be fitted for the moulding and, after several delays, including an inability to find him an ambulance, he was driven back to the neurology unit. During the delay he had contracted a potentially lethal meningitis, an acute inflammation of the protective membranes covering the brain and spinal cord. John was, eventually, treated with strong antibiotics. This is when, to my horror, I learned the exact nature of the lumbar puncture, a procedure John put up, with his usual lack of complaint and calm, resigned composure.

For this procedure John had to lie on the bed, on his side, with his knees tucked up to his chest, which was not easy in his condition. This is the position I often see him in in my dreams, tanned and foetal, in his white underpants, under the pine trees of Agios Fokas.

An injection of anaesthetic is given into the area of the lower back and then a thin and improbably long needle pierces through the skin into the small of the back, through the bones of the spines, into the space around the delicate spinal cord. The cerebral fluid then drips through the needle and into a tube, to be tested for infection. This is repeated to check whether the antibiotics are working, and also to relieve some of the pressure building up in John's brain, which was causing him severe headaches, nausea and, eventually, unconsciousness. The lumbar puncture is also known as the spinal tap.

* * *

Five things to remember about today:

Walking past the still-flowering magnolia tree beside the Mews,
I thwacked one of its branches with my outstretched hand,

dislodging a very disgruntled tabby cat preparing to pounce on a lone sparrow, now flying free.

The blood-red moon rising over the Essex marshes as the train trundles its way towards Norwich, the first flying 'V's of ducks beginning their long flights over the Thames Estuary to sunnier climes in the south.

The warmest of welcomes from Gennaro Contaldo, Liz, his partner, and stylist Pip Spence at Waterfall Cottage in the Norfolk countryside. The hug Gennaro gives me is that of a bear: long, close and painfully loving.

Tucked up in 'my usual room'. Gennaro likes me to sleep in his daughters' bedroom, as Chloe and Olivia, his fifteen-year-old twins, are back at school in London.

Falling, eventually, to sleep, all the windows open and my face pointed to the chill breeze, the blood-moon full and white and high in the sky, watching the bats dancing among the stars and listening to the hoots of the barn owls.

Wednesday 26 September

Waterfall Cottage

After breakfast Gennaro insisted on a pre-shoot stroll along the lanes that cross in all directions around his ancient cottage. The sky is cloud-less and clear, the air cold enough to sting the nostrils. Over several rosés the night before I had vowed to 'be like Johnny' and remain shoeless and sockless for my three-day stay, so I do get the odd peculiar look from my walking compadrés, who are dressed in appropriate attire of boots and jumpers as I stroll along the grass verges, pretending I am oblivious to the painful thistles and nettles. The bridge over the River Wensum in his village is stunning in its *Haywain*-like simplicity, the trout-filled waters clear and mirrored, fifty shades of reflective greens in the spangled, early-morning sunshine.

Gennaro, whom I've known for over twenty years, is one of the few people who can read me like an open book. Hunting for skimmers and feeling melancholy among the chattering girls and the sparklingly beautiful scene, he came over with two large red rocks he'd picked up while foraging for honey mushrooms. 'Launch them as far as you can into the millpond, Loftus,' he said, handing me one of the giant flints. A satisfying heave, an almighty splosh and thud as it hit the shallow bottom. He handed me the other one, identical to the first. 'And one for John,' he said, a tear in his eye.

* * *

On 26 September John was allowed to come home to The Beeches for the weekend. It seemed at the time terribly risky; he was so frail after both the operation and the meningitis, but that feeling of concern was tempered by the joy of having him home, sitting in his bedroom. Because of the nature of his operation, the entry point being beneath his upper lip, you could have been forgiven for thinking that there was little wrong with him. His Parosian tan had faded but there were still tan lines under his woven bracelets, his hair was foppish and, though he'd lost a lot of weight, he was handsomely thin rather than skinny.

That weekend we sat in the garden, under the damson and hazelnut trees, talking of his memories of the operation, his hopes and his fears. Sally, our corgi, spent her time curled by his feet as if sensing his early departure. He was obviously in demand. Samantha protectively fussed around him, friends popped in briefly so as not to over-tire him, he even, briefly, fell asleep in the sun.

I knew Mother was worried, I could see her watching us through the living-room window. She knew it was far too early and too risky to have him at home, yet acknowledged the pleasure he was getting from being back. It was during that first afternoon that John started leaking the cerebral fluid again, through his nose, like a clear continuous nosebleed. Mother telephoned both the neurology and oncology units, but was assured by both that there was no further treatment needed at that stage. She was told that he would be looked at upon readmission to Oncology on Monday the twenty-eighth.

During the week beginning the twenty-eighth John was treated for another serious, life-threatening dose of meningitis, which meant another week of lumbar punctures and antibiotics, violent headaches, vomiting and unconsciousness. Luckily, somehow, he later found it hard to remember some of the worst moments of this terrible week. Sadly, I do, a week that felt like a month, John often curled up amidst taps, tubes, drips and monitors, endless tests, probings, awakenings while trying, trying to sleep, sleeping while trying to be awake. But it was he who had to endure their constant discomforts, not me. All I could do was hold his hand and communicate with him in moments of lucidity, bed-tagging with Samantha and poor Mother. No mother should have to watch their beloved offspring endure such ghastliness.

Thursday 27 September

Under a clear blue sky, shoeless still, sitting watching the dewy dawn sunrise over the fields. Warming my hands around a morning tea, watching muntjacs nervously skirting Gennaro's garden, attuned to the crack as he fires his rifle frequently from the comfort of his dining-room table.

As my feet began to thaw I stubbornly remained barefoot as Gennaro took me for another of his little strolls around the neighbouring lanes and fields.

In the early evening, after our shoot, Gennaro bundled me into his rickety old Land Rover and raced, driving like a mad teenager, through the narrow lanes so we could sit quietly beside a nearby lake where he fished for trout and we watched the sun set over its mirror-like surface. Walking back later we picked fresh walnuts from a tree, a first for me, cracking them open with a pebble, soft and slightly bitter, ideal companions to the rosé waiting for us back at Waterfall Cottage. Well done Gennaro, my dear friend, you successfully distracted me for a whole day and I fell asleep slightly tiddly, a belly full of mushrooms and pasta, to the sound of the 'Barnsley owls' hoots', as he calls them.

Friday 28 September

Another gorgeous misty morning, day three of our shoot, grubby feet a testament to a third day of no shoes and socks.

During the day, my third spent almost constantly in various dappled corners of Gennaro's rambling garden, shooting combinations of him making pasta, picking mushrooms and courgette flowers, foraging or just smiling playfully at the camera, I am reminded how lucky I am to have refound photography post losing John.

Thank you, Father, for persisting with your mission to find me a hobby, because John had so many and I had so few. Twenty years of almost daily shooting, whether on a phone or a camera, hiding behind an inherent desire to keep trying to create beautiful images. Even today, in between set-ups, I wandered almost continually, my hungry eyes searching for pictures. Last night's walnuts and their dark green leaves; the vibrant turning leaves of the grapevine bruised with the deepest reds and oranges; conkers bursting from their prickly cases; backlit crocuses, impossibly pinkish-purple. Dahlias of every colour; flowering lemon balm and thyme; ripening white blackberries; tree stumps covered in honey mushrooms; medlars and quince trees laden with fruit . . . and all within whistling distance of a steady supply of milky tea from an attentive Gennaro, with his calls of 'Loftus! Loftus! Where are you?'

Day three over, his book finished and 'wrapped' to a toast over champagne and cream cake baked by his gardener, Penny.

Saturday 29 September

Another clear blue sky

Breakfast in Chelsea, mussels fresh from the fishmonger. Catching up with Ange, rarely more than a few feet apart.

A weekend of quiet contemplation, editing and reading, snuggling, spooning, kissing and chatting. Just what was needed. This period, between John's re-hospitalization and 5 October when eventually his deep X-ray (radiotherapy) treatment started, was an anxious time, toing and froing between The Beeches and the neurology unit. Mother trying to maintain her patients and alternating between hospital and surgery and The Beeches, with me, Molly and Samantha; Molly too upset to visit but holding fort at The Beeches, endlessly baking and cleaning. Somehow I had fitted in a few illustration commissions. Ironically my career was flourishing but my heart wasn't in it at all, it was pure distraction.

Sunday 30 September

I sent my Sami edit in this week, to Niklas and to the publisher. Niklas is over the moon. The removal of the heart of the adult stag, the Sami people, their fishing, farming and herding, is, in my mind, one of the best forty-eight hours of shooting I have ever accomplished. Of course, as ever, there is so much I could have done better – missed opportunities, focus not quite on target, fear overtaking technical speed of thought, under- or over-exposure, but I'm still happy with the results.

I photographed the heart, cut out of the chest cavity, as Kajsa's father ladled out its congealing blood with his father's old hollowed spoon. Laying in its bed of wild flowers it looked a lot smaller than I had expected and clean of the blood it had been pumping around the extraordinary beast. I placed my camera down upon the grass and picked it up with both hands. It was heavy for its size, clean purples and pinks mottled with sinews of white muscle, firm to the touch, almost like a miniature rugby ball. I inspected for the bruises of heartbreak. Of course there were none, just smooth flat colour, a perfect heart that had been beating frantically but ten minutes before, now lifeless in my open palms, in this small patch of sunlit cotton flowers, under a vivid rainbow shining through the rain; I felt an intense sadness.

Monday 1 October

The boat
A clear blue sky

A dreadful night's sleep, a night of utter madness, often waking in dreams, returning to bad dreams, awake until 3.30a.m., mind abuzzing and rampantly untired. God, I hate my own brain sometimes and wish it would just let me rest.

Barefoot again, sitting upon a Moroccan pouffe on the deck of the boat, I disturbed a heron on the front anchor, though the grace in which it took flight suggested that there was no feeling of fear, just a need for solitude. A pinch and a socking great punch, it's the first day of the month, a day so clear that you can see every inch of the Dickensian fore-shore, the odd early-bird mudlark larking about, pied wagtails wagging. I can just hear their chirp, more a 'chripp' than a chirp. There was even a solo grey seal hunting in the murky shallows this morning, ignored by all but me.

Tuesday 2 October

At the Mews, shooting for the British Heart Foundation

Card found on the boat yesterday, a rare written note from Ian. A picture of Paris in the mist. 31 October is now twenty-nine days away, our birth-day, always a silent and reluctant countdown.

> Dearest David
>
> I don't think it'll ever be a happy day again because it'll always be yours and Johnny's day. But it is a day for some happy memories as well as sadness.
>
> I'll be thinking of you and Johnny today on your 25th birthday, as I think of you every day.
>
> With all my love for next year, hoping it may bring a little more comfort and happiness. I'm so glad I've got you there – I think of you so much.
>
> From your Little Bruv, Ian xx

Life at this time of the year is a close-together batch of anniversaries from 1 October to 11 November, mostly unwanted and uncelebrated, but marked yearly. A countdown to the anniversary of John's death, but now also peppered with joyful anniversaries including Ange and my official and unofficial weddings in London and Marrakech.

Morning, Wednesday 3 October

Shooting at the Mews, British Heart Foundation

I dined with my brother Ian last night at the Colbert in Sloane Square, my usual table in the corner, an intense dinner of rosé and oysters and more rosé. The head this morning is fuzzy with over-drinking, lack of slumber and too many Solps but the mind is clearer and I chuckled at the memory of John's insistence that *Monsieur Hulot's Holiday* was funnier than Laurel and Hardy's *Sons of the Desert* – how wrong he was.

Such mixed emotions from the evening. There were laughs and hugs but far too many sorrows and tears. The postcard I found yesterday in the boat was written by Ian at Leicester; almost childlike really, a second-year medical student just managing to hold it together, excelling in his exams but detached from the family, Mother and me, at The Beeches. Year two of a seven-year medical education, the same education that my son Paros has now embarked upon.

That postcard-writing boy is now sitting next to me in the Colbert; little changed, really. John and me grew up teasing him about his hair, we called him Mushroom for his tendency to look like a large cep, much to his annoyance. It's a nickname John would still use in later life, knowing it always touched a nerve. I've no idea why John teased him so remorselessly and continued to do so into Ian's student days, often quite meanly. I did ask him but he didn't really have an answer. Yes, Ian was the annoying little brother who passed every exam with a clean 100 per cent, the gifted, Mensa-busting genius who followed my mother into a glittering medical career, but that shouldn't have warranted some of the abuse he took from John. Neither should the cheating at cricket, the annoying Sunday-night magic show he occasionally put on, or the 'Swap Shops' he used to open in his bedroom, swapping some excellent car-hee cars only to renege on his swaps hours later, or the fact that from a young age he kept audited accounts of his pocket money.

In the summer before John became ill, he invited Ian to spend the day with him at Nucleus. Ian watched him work, met his colleagues and boss Peter, had lunch in the pub by the river. It called an end to the teasing and constant ribbing and I think it was John's way of saying, 'Well done, little brother, now go forth and conquer.' John would be so proud of Ian now, a pioneering Professor of Vascular Surgery, with 'special interests including complex aortic repair, hyperhidrosis, thoracoscopic sympathectomy, popliteal enlargement, thoracic outlet syndrome, carotid surgery and varicose veins.' He's also the editor of a number of books on vascular surgery, has written over 200 publications, is the chair of many a vascular society and has saved countless lives on and off the operating table at St George's. Father and John would have been chuffed.

Sitting under *Monsieur Hulot*, he is little changed from that slightly chaotic and annoying, cricket-cheating younger self. Though four years younger, he has always behaved as if four years older than us, the brighter, more mature, more sensible brother. The 'mushroom' haircut is no more, his hair now short and spiky and thinning like Father's, much to his chagrin. His fashion sense still generates a gentle ribbing from me, looking as if he's just walked out from one of the Italian Gentlemen's shops you only see in Rome or Milan. Once a little brother, always a little brother. The emotional 'hit' of sitting together, just the two of us, for the first time in a year is immediate; tears flow, wine glasses rise, hugs are exchanged. He spoke, I spoke, we agreed on everything, even things we'd always disagreed on, we hugged some more, tears mingled with rosé, promises were made, secrets were undone, unravelled.

I told Ian that we had tracked down Dr S, now Professor S. 'Professor of what?!' – the same reaction as Mother. I told him that Ange's letter had been opened, but 'returned to sender'. More tears, 'All he needed to do was apologize, it's the lack of remorse that upsets me so much,' he said. I talked to him of Tim, and how missed he is on his sabbatical, his struggles with lone twindom, and again, how it's the lack of remorse that chokes him, the IRA bombers and their cronies.

I had thought that Ian and Jean-Marian were against me writing my elongated love letter to our lost brother, but I was wrong. What I had failed to do, in the thirty years since his death, is learn to communicate with them as a singleton, as their solo older brother. I thought my presence just upset them with reminders of John. It did, but what hurt them both far more was me isolating myself, cutting myself off from them. As they became closer to each other they felt that I was moving farther and farther away. As a result, they became more and more paranoid about saying the wrong thing, walking continually on eggshells, and texts and emails were misread and misunderstood, secrets were kept, tales untold, barriers raised. Where once a family had been so close, after the tragedy of John's death we became broken and uncommunicative. Those doctors, and their total lack of care, love and humanity, had driven in wedges where previously there had been none. From the moment of the injection to the coroner's inquest, these men who had trained to provide care to the sick and needy, through their collective arrogance and unsympathetic stance managed to leave our family broken, scattered, shattered and torn to this very day.

I left Ian last night with a long hug, and the promise of an attempt to return to our relationship of old, teasing and all, and he told me that all he hoped for me is that I find 'some sort of peace'.

Afternoon

Mother used to hear nightingales at Naworth Castle, and recognized the bird's song immediately. She believes she heard one in Cheam, we certainly heard one once at The Beeches. Today, as I lay restlessly awake,

I listened to a muted dawn chorus, thinking of the gorgeous cacophony at The Beeches. A solo thrush singing among the concrete patios in place of the finches, sparrows and doves of The Beeches.

Last week Ian had Mother checked over: heart, blood pressure, circulation and general wellbeing, but ignoring the cancer. He told me last night that her heart is barely functioning, she is so weak and frail that he is amazed that it works at all, and the circulation to her feet is nigh on non-existent. What is truly amazing is her lack of complaint. She is obviously in a great deal of pain but makes no fuss at all.

Thursday 4 October

Shooting at the Mews, British Heart Foundation. Tick-tock.

A photo album from Mother's to peruse, compiled in 1974. Highlights include:

John and me on our eighth birthday, at The Beeches. One cake but with sixteen candles, eight each, big front-toothy grins. I'm proudly showing off a new watch on my wrist, and we're both at the breakfast table in our pyjamas.

Ian's fifth birthday, his face so serious.

John opening a Meccano set at Christmas, Dad in a suit and tie and apron, cooking the turkey.

Mother on a steam train, looking so young at thirty-eight, John's back turned to the camera. I took the photo.

Me, skimming stones, head to toe in orange, John in a blue-stripe jumper, watching from a rock. The Kent coast in summer, a day trip to see Uncle Derek.

Nanna Nicholson, Mother's mother, rarely smiling, fearsome. 'Who's broadcast?' when she heard a fart. Once swiped me with a metre rule, it missed me and broke in half. She didn't like Father, which always upset

John and I. We called her Banana because banana backwards was 'ananab'. John and I were fluent in 'backwards', our private language.

'Uncle' Ronnie, suit and tie, looking always like *Dad's Army's* Captain Mainwaring, cuddling a young and very smiley Jean-Marian.

Jean-Marian, playing her recorder. ABBA and the recorder, her two annoying musical habits.

Christmas 1974, taken by Mother: Father holding Sally the corgi; Ian with newly opened 'explorers kit' including camera and binoculars; John, a new camera; me, the *Eagle* annual; Jean-Marian some Kenyan dolls for her doll collection, a present from her godmother.

Friday 5 October

Radiotherapy, day one

John started his deep X-ray treatment on 5 October 1987. The radiotherapy was to remove the tiny bits of the tumour that had been left from his operation. He was understandably weak after his meningitis and the week of lumbar punctures and heavy antibiotics and painkillers so I helped him down to the room. He opted for the stairs as 'that's what his physiotherapist had wanted', so progress was slow and painful. He was told to lie face down on the table, a torturous version of a massage table with a hole at one end to fit his head into. His face mask, moulded but hard plastic, was designed to allow him to breathe while holding his head rigid. I helped him up and lowered his head as delicately as I could into position. As he leaned forward some of the cerebral fluid ran from his nose into the mask, collecting in its grooves and in the nose area, causing him to splutter and choke. The radiologist wasn't in the room so we just got on with it but I was alarmed at his choking on the fluid so I got some help from Nurse Douglas, who tried to dab away the liquid.

Stepping back from the table, seeing him there, skinny and weak, his right side drooped and barely moving, face down, coughing into his mask, was heartbreakingly sad. Only four weeks earlier he had been fit and strong, happily playing cricket with me, Debbie and Peter and his Nucleus team, a designer at the peak of his ability, bowling spinners and thwacking balls for six. Happily in love with Samantha. It was beyond horrendous how far life had changed and how much he had suffered in such a short space of time. Suddenly I missed our father terribly. I was aware John couldn't see my tears, but might be able to sense them, so when I was asked to leave the room I did so with a gentle squeeze of his good left hand and went to call Mother. The vision of him lying there in the treatment room, strapped into place, choking on the fluid from his sensitive brain, coughing and spluttering as if drowning, is an image that is seared into the memory banks of my own headaches.

Afternoon

A quiet day of editing and a quick portrait shoot at the Colbert in the dull grey afternoon. Summer seems to have breathed its last.

* * *

The week of 5 October progressed painfully slowly. I'd work on my illustrations at night and in the early hours of the mornings I'd jump into a taxi up to see John. Sometimes Samantha would be there, and Mother if she could get a break from her patients, but between us at least one of us would try to be with him. He'd started a cycle of radiotherapy in the morning followed, while he had the energy, with physiotherapy. It was on one of these days that I found him, still in his pyjamas, coming out of the hospital chapel. He'd always been an atheist, at times uncomfortably vocal about it. I myself was a hypocritical agnostic Christian, i.e. praying when in trouble (as we were then), but disbelieving conversationally, not sure what to think in all other times.

John had been vocally anti-Catholic with me in conversation. I asked him about his visit to the chapel and he just said, 'Well, it can hardly do me any harm in here . . .' As I shuffled him back to his bed it felt like an eternity since Richmond Park and our game of cricket, but he was positive and we began to talk about things to do when he got out, which was something all the doctors and specialists were discussing. It very much felt that this was the beginning of John's recovery, that the worst was over, and now would come a period of recovery, treatment and physio to return him to his previous self.

As John mounted the stairs, I put my hand on his shoulder to steady him and noticed some long fine hairs on the back of my hand. As he had been warned about and dreaded, his hair had begun to fall out from the radiotherapy. I'm sure he was aware, but we didn't talk about it.

Saturday 6 October

The Mews
Rain, rain, tick-tock

Spent the day quietly, not leaving the Mews. Persistent rain falling today in London, for the first time in months.

We had a surprise visitor last night in the shape of Simon ('Farmer') Jones, one of my Musketeers and closest chums, beaming smile and ruddy face, always smelling subtly of fresh milk. He'd driven down from his Lincolnshire dairy to see me 'because he felt something was up'. We talked late into the night, polishing off a small truckle of his 'poacher' cheese and me a bottle of Whispering Angel to his small glass, Ange asleep in our bed, deliberately giving us space to chat into the wee hours.

Simon is as spiritual a person as one could meet, as good as a person could be. Listening to Simon reminded me of times spent in Windermere in the Bahamas, the four of us, Tim, our mutual best friend Jeff, Simon and me, talking later and later into the night, our girlfriends asleep, the sound of the crashing Atlantic waves.

We'd wander down between the palms and the casuarina trees to Atlantic beach to watch the sunrise. Christmas Day, New Year's Day, Easter Day, Midsummer's Day, we did them all. Simon's voice is like the waves, euphoric and lightly soporific, talking of out-of-body experiences, spiritualism and unconditional love, it's akin to being hugged. Some of the happiest times of my life have been spent in the company of these three chaps, whether lounging louchely about, zipping through the clouds or skipping through the waves. I was the happiest I'd been for years. It's a funny old world.

Sunday 7 October

Driving along the Thames towards Cheam and Mother, Ange and I were listening to an old episode of *Desert Island Discs* in which Kirsty Young asks Tom Hanks why he became an actor. He chokes back a tear and says, 'It was loneliness.'

I sit in the car, listening to Agnus Dei, the adagio for strings, my mind drifting, the passing treetops blurring, and thought about my own loneliness and how it has infected almost everything I have done.

I gave up a very successful career as an illustrator because of loneliness, swapping the solitary drawing board for the company of strangers, semi-circled behind one's back, watching the photographer's every move. I dated totally unsuitable but beautiful girls because of loneliness and the jealousy at John's settled and beautiful relationship with Samantha. And then, a month after starting to date a fellow illustrator, Debbie, John became ill, dying weeks later, and I was plunged into an ocean of loneliness so dark and deep that I thought I would never recover, never find my way to the surface.

I once read an article in *The Independent* that featured a 'Top ten types of people to avoid having a long-term relationship with'. It was meant to be lighthearted, and I seem to remember that pop star was number one. But identical twins was number two, and photographer number three. They jokingly even said that the only thing worse than an identical twin was a lone identical twin. My relationship with Debbie, according to the paper, was doomed from the kick-off.

I met her at the Seven Dials art gallery. Debbie was very bright, and a talented artist. She looked Greek or Italian, though thirty years later her actual heritage is still a mystery to me. The stress I suffered after John's death is such that there is little I can remember now of our courting days. John became ill and the amount of time I spent with him in hospital soon became an issue.

There I was, running between my gloomy bedroom at The Beeches, the oncology unit, the neurology unit and courting Debbie, who was about as bewildering and mysterious as one could imagine. After John died I felt under a huge amount of pressure, especially around her and my other chums, not to be sad. Be normal. It was a Herculean task. I'd often cry for two hours before I went out to meet them in the King's Road, to try to 'dry out my tear ducts', feeling that somehow if I cried enough beforehand there would be no more tears to cry.

Bumping into Dr S on the Underground was my first journey into town after Johnny was buried and it set me back a month or two. I made several trips to the Lake District with Debbie and Peter and Janet. I remember some climbing and walking, croquet in the garden, but mostly I remember drinking. In the pub, The George; in the garden playing games; late candlelit nights, the soundtrack of This Mortal Coil and the Cocteau Twins. Beer, red wine, vodka. Endless bottles, a river of alcohol, never-ending. Even up mountains, hairbrained risks at every corner. And then tears, tears in bed, on the stairs, in the forests. I was an absolute mess. And there would be another shout of 'Hurrah!' from Peter. More Pimm's lined up in the garden, more games, more wine, more fireside tears, more booze.

How I survived that road to self-destruction I do not know. Somehow my career continued to climb and I became established as one of a small handful of top illustrators in Europe. I commanded large fees, created book covers, album covers, wine labels, Tube posters. My images were everywhere, but I hated them. I felt like a fraud. I'd even begun to cut up some of John's painted backgrounds and use them in my illustrations. I told people they were mine.

I married Debbie in October 1990, surrounded by friends and family, in the Norman church behind John Loftus House in Thames Ditton. It says a lot about my state of mind how blurry my memory of the day is. I remember the late-October sun shone, and standing between Tim and Jeff, my cousin Edward and brother Ian, waiting for Debbie in her white Cadillac. Uncomfortable in my first-ever morning suit.

Tim, Jeff and probably Mother, also grieving, were the only ones who knew how terrible I really felt. They were my three rocks, my supports.

I was in no fit state, and neither was Debbie, really. She married a seriously damaged, incredibly lonely, highly emotional and needy, self-destructive lone twin, flailing in the dark of our relationship: desperate to be loved, silently screaming for physical and mental warmth. Debbie was beautiful, but enigmatic and aloof. Straightaway I insisted she kept her old flat as a studio to work in so that we could have our own creative spaces. There were immediate problems between us: me blaming her coldness, she blaming my abject misery. We were both right and we were both wrong.

At marriage guidance years later I had to laugh when she was asked to list the negatives of living with me. The list was so long that when she had finished the counsellor's chin had almost hit the floor.

It was sitting in La Delizia restaurant in the Fulham Road that she asked me whether she should move back to her mother's. Fearful of being left alone, I asked her what she wanted, how I could make life easier for her and she stunned me by saying, 'I want a child.'

Fear of being alone, fear of fatherhood, most of all, fear of losing a child; suddenly I was confronted with all my fears. Not to mention loneliness and mortality. I could barely function as an adult let alone be a good father. Nevertheless, just over a month later, I had a call at the Delano hotel in Miami Beach. I remember that No Doubt's 'Don't Speak' was playing on a vast screen of MTV, as Debbie told me she was pregnant.

Eight months later I got a call, in the same room at the Delano, to say that she was in labour and that our son was about to be born. I abandoned my shoot, jumped on a Freddie Laker flight, sitting in the cockpit as there was no room on board, and I still made it back to London with time to spare. Though we had both decided that I wasn't going to be there, I was at least nearby. Debbie gave birth to Paros, three weeks early, like her, sporting Mediterranean brown skin and dark thick hair. He was, and still is, furry all over.

That weekend at Chelsea and Westminster made the newspapers the Monday following, with a perfect storm of births, emergencies and deaths. One mother had died, one baby, and Debbie had only just pulled through a sixty-five-hour birth. With the utter chaos of blood loss and screaming, she had survived what the doctor called 'the equivalent of a major car crash'.

Paros, however, looked, and has forever looked, totally unfazed by anything. Paros, the island of my and Johnny's youth, a name given to him by Debbie as a nod to John, a gesture greatly appreciated. Paros Erik Loftus, now a third-year medical student at St George's, where his uncle Ian is Professor of Vascular Surgery, and where the coroner at John's inquest trained to be a doctor.

Where Paros was a dark and swarthy baby, Pascale was the polar-bear opposite, pale-skinned, blonde and blue-eyed and three weeks late. I wasn't present at either birth but, after the near disaster of Paros' birth, my mother was with Debbie when Pascale was born. I was on the boat, cuddling the two-year-old Paros who had flatly refused to sleep since his birth.

Pascale and Paros – the two Ps – two peas in a pod. It is they who saved my life and I do thank Debbie, with all my heart, for persuading me into fatherhood. By then I was sharing a bedroom with Paros and something had to give, so I bought a tall terraced house beside Battersea Bridge, a stone's throw from *Candy Coloured Tangerine*, the narrowboat we were then living in.

Debbie and the Ps moved into no. 31 but I kept the boat and began to spend more and more nights there, while Debbie became a full-time mother. It was around this time that a neighbour, a barrister called Paul, popped in to take the piss out of me. When he walked onto my house-boat I was half-naked, doing pull-ups on the roof of the boat, with crazy unwashed hair, skin the colour of the river, a half-smoked joint in my mouth and a bottle of rosé half-empty beside me. In my defence, it was the first and last time I have ever smoked a joint, your honour, and, being a non-smoker, I was choking like a hound.

Settling me down into a deck chair, he invoked 'barrister's con-fidence'. I told him how desperately unhappy and lonely I was, how I thought that I needed to learn how to be a singleton, to spend time on my own. I pointed to one of the many small whirlpools that eddy around the boat's hull and said, 'That's how I feel!' I was lost, swirling aimlessly in life, unhinged and unstable. If I'd been asked to write a 'be thankful for' list at that moment it would have read:

My mother.

My Ps – Paros and Pascale.

My photography, particularly, at that time, my work with Jamie.

The boat, *Stow*, that I'd moved in to, a.k.a. *Candy Coloured Tangerine*.

Rosie Scott, my PA, my assistant and my rock.

Debbie was still a big part of my day-to-day life, but she had become a mother, and a great mother too. I was, understandably, second fiddle to the Ps. I was the depressive mud walker, and actually it was okay, living apart gave me the space to breathe as a photographer, to travel on commissions without worry of upsetting Debbie. She once told me how much easier it was when I was away, the kids always getting the best of me upon my return.

It couldn't carry on forever though. I so desperately needed human warmth, love and kindness. I began to date a stream of beautiful but totally unsuitable young ladies, each relationship involving far too much drinking and over-neediness, usually by me, turning to feelings of crushing claustrophobia and paranoia, particularly a fear that the relationship might affect my time spent with my Ps, which inevitably it did. That metaphorical whirlpool was getting bigger and bigger, faster and faster, sucking me under.

Meeting Ange changed it all. Debbie likes to tell me that Ange is lucky, she has inherited the 'good' me, the 'recovered' me, whereas Debbie had the impossible, sick me. It's not as simple as that; I'm still prone to prolonged bouts of darkness and at times I teeter on the edge of something much worse; my nights are a continuous battle of good and evil, evil often winning through. I am, as I have said before, over-emotional, incredibly needy both physically and emotionally, prone to manic happiness and extreme darkness, certainly not a walk in the park. I do, however, have a strong survival instinct, ambition in my craft, and a maturity that I didn't have when I met Debbie. I regret many of my relationships in my life, but how could I regret a relationship that ultimately brought me the Ps, and the freedom to work as I now do?

* * *

In Cheam with Mother, she can barely walk, but, as ever, endures it with little grumble and good humour. I've noticed that she has started wearing her 'Do Not Resuscitate' bracelet and necklaces outside of her clothing. She cheerfully sits with us over tea and flapjacks, anointing her aching limbs with a mixture of olive and hemp cream, her pale skin incredibly smooth but painfully thin over her brittle bones. I often photograph her hands. The way her long and elegant fingers intertwine, the way she holds her forehead in moments of anguish and despair: Brexit, Boris Johnson, Gerry Adams, Donald Trump, Martin Amis, all warrant a clasp of the forehead. As ever, subjects are diverse and the Good, the Bad and the Ugly are all covered, from nightingales to the Hornseys, to the Lake District, dear Tim and his sabbatical, Hadrian's Wall to Heath Robinson. Smiles and laughs and tears, an average hour spent with our dear mother, like riding a joyous roller coaster.

Stunning, cloudless skies, the clearest light. I watch a high-in-the-sky 'V' of migrating geese flying south, so high I could only just hear their call. They seem happy in their formation; I'd be happy flying south for winter.

My sister Jean-Marian just wrote to me, including a letter, a poem really, to John, as follows:

Dearest John

Do you still remember?
The long summer days on the Orkney Sands, collecting cowrie shells and cycling in the dunes?
Building dams in the rivers of the Lake District, and swimming in the icy water of Hynam Pool?
Playing potato tennis over a Northumberland farmhouse, catching a mouse in a lampshade, tossing hay bales at each other?
Barbeques in the garden, whatever the weather, at any time of the year?
Picnics at Rottingdean?
Inter-railing?
Old Greece?
New friends who came and stayed?
Dad sat in the corner of the kitchen as we all came in from school?
Smoke rising over the shed door?

Do you still see?
California poppies?
The autumn colours of the chestnut trees brightened in the late sunlight?
Collecting conkers?

Fireworks nights wrapped up against the cold evening air,
exploding in the sky?
Watching Guy Fawkes at the top of the immense blaze?
Birthdays?

Do you still feel?
The excitement of waiting at the door as Dad put the final
touches to the Christmas morning?
The cold snow against your face?
Standing in the rain?
The wind against your face on your motorbike, or standing on
the end of Brighton Pier?
Pebbles under foot?

Can you still hear?
Sally barking, and pushing under your legs?
Childhood memories of happy days?
Playing and fighting?
'Boys being boys'?

Do you still play?
With toy hand-painted soldiers
Strawbod?
And draw at a large table in the window, beautiful, lasting images?
Watched over

In the windmills of your mind

Your face moves along in the breeze
Over houses and places
And memories
Lasting forever.

So when the clouds pass over
And darken my eyes
When the past seems so sad
When I sit in the park on an autumn day
Surrounded by the mighty chestnut trees
The sun will still set
The moon will still rise
The birds will still sing and the grass still grow
When the memories of losing you still seem so close

The wind blows through the trees

I see, feel, hear
And remember

Love always,
JM

Jean-Marian 9 October, at home in Cheam.

Wednesday 10 October

Day three at the Mews

I've read and reread my sister's poem. I've cried and instigated the foetal position for an hour or two. My overriding feeling is that I've been the crappiest of brothers to both Ian and Jean-Marian. I was so very lost after John died that all of my focus was on Mother, so that I didn't have to think about myself and the guilt I felt over my part in poor John's death. Guilt at not preventing the injection, guilt at being the surviving twin plus an overwhelming feeling that the wrong twin had died. Ian was a student and Jean-Marian an overworked nurse, Ian in Leicester and Jean-Marian in East London, he with a girlfriend and she with her husband. I guess I felt that, emotionally at least, they were being well looked after. I feel awful now, that John and I formed a team within a team, and that upon his death I remained solo rather than rejoining the team. Our family.

Thursday 11 October

Tick-tock runs the clock. Dinner at Colbert

This is my 'difficult time of year' when anniversaries are coming along, thick and fast. But this year is different, with the sorting of drawers, unopened documents, portfolio cases and photo albums. John was obsessed with Sir John Soane's Museum in Lincoln's Inn Fields in London and he created an identity for the museum as a project when he was at art college, using his gouache-style of hand-painted typography, script and outline paintings of sculptures and interior details, cornices and borders. Yesterday, in among the drawings, I came across a small contact sheet of 35mm black and white photos. Images of busts and clocks, interior and exterior details, and there, hidden among them, frame 18A, there is a blurry but smiling Johnny. Frame 36 is a portrait of Samantha so she must have taken the pic of John, big chunky jumper as usual, scarf around his neck, passing a huge Grecian bust of an unknown god, Zeus-like (the bust, not John). Finding a picture of John that I have never seen before feels very special indeed, however soft and ghostly.

I often leave music playing on shuffle at the Mews. I like to come in to lights and the sound of music, it stems from living alone at the boat. Tonight, when Ange and I wandered in, Jean-Michel Jarre's *Oxygène* was playing. Synths and blips and the sounds of a Francophile 'outer space', so ahead of its time when it was released. I bought the album, my second only to Mike Oldfield's *Tubular Bells*, at a tiny record shop in Hove near

Brighton with John. We thought we were oh so cool, paying with record tokens on one of the picnics in Rottingdean.

It's hard to put into words the enormity of the sudden awareness of being a 'crap brother'. I guess in my subconscious I felt they were covered, as long as I could persuade Ian to stay at college, to find good in the medical ethics of our mother rather than the confused and blurry ethics we had just experienced. That he could use the appalling time we were going through to remember that most people go into medicine to do good, to care, to heal, to cure, not to act like God, for money, for power, for ego.

Friday 12 October

Day five with Mini at the Mews

On 12 October John was readmitted for radiotherapy, but that evening he again developed a severe headache and was in obvious discomfort. At Samantha's request, Dr S saw John but he decided that no further action was needed other than observation and painkillers. Dr S's first response to Samantha's request for help with John's headache was to 'try slapping his face'. Samantha was desperately upset. Unable to get any help from Dr S, she telephoned Mother at her surgery. When Dr S was cross-examined at the Coroner's Court, he flatly denied ever saying this, despite it being a criminal offence to lie when giving evidence under oath.

I spent the evening of the twelfth with John. He was in pain but sleepy, and I remember that Samantha was incredibly upset at what Dr S had said, as was Mother. I believe complaints were made. The general feeling among our family was that Dr S was not fit to be a doctor in any hospital, let alone a cancer hospital where so many are so desperately ill. Nurse Douglas, Johnny's favourite nurse, was also visibly upset by Dr S's comments. Sadly, none of them were called to witness by the coroner at the inquest. A lie is a lie, and a lie under oath is a crime, but ultimately a crime no one cares about but one or two people. And it wasn't the only lie that Dr S would tell that day.

Saturday 13 October

The Mews
Balmy October days

On 13 October, against Samantha and Mother's wishes and despite their concerns, John was sent home. He was still suffering from severe headaches, and he was put straight to bed. Samantha made it very clear to the nurses, to Nurse Douglas and to Dr S that she was upset about John's treatment and that she was not happy about his condition. She was particularly worried that the course of intravenous antibiotics had been stopped and that they had not given sufficient time to see whether the headaches would subside and ensure that the meningitis would not reoccur.

That night John had the cow bell beside him and he rang it several times, complaining of terrible headaches. I barely slept, one ear always alert to the bell's ring. Mother and I looked after him as best we could. We were exhausted and worried, and overwhelmed with a sense of fear. Running along that corridor to the toll of the cow bell is one of my many recurring, lying-awake nightmares.

Sunday 14 October

The Mews
Rainy Sunday bloody Sunday

Visited Mother this morning and we talked about restless, madness-filled nights, lack of sleep and whether, ultimately, after extreme trauma, one ever sleeps a full night again. A night can be filled with so much love – Ange, the Ps, John, Mother, Father – but is often coupled, particularly with those who are recently grieving, the left-behinds, with feelings of guilt, self-loathing, rage, self-pity. The difference with me, as a lone identical twin, is that those feelings have not lessened. Mother said today, out of the blue while trying to spot jays in the trees, 'You know that to say one can "come to terms" with one's grief is frankly ridiculous, one never "comes to terms" with it, not at all, one just learns how to live with that grief, that's all one can hope for.'

Mother asked me about Jean-Marian's poem and I told her how touched I was by it. 'Darling boy, do you think all this delving into your memories is proving a cathartic experience?' I don't know the answer yet and I told her so. 'But I think it'll make me a better brother to Jean-Marian and Ian. I feel that as the surviving twin, I have neglected to be a good brother.'

'Dear, dear David, you couldn't have been anything other than as you were and you must have no reproach. I, however, feel that I have been less than the perfect mother. I should have known, I should have noticed signs. John once asked me if there had been any family history of cancer in the family, and I said no. I had a feeling that he knew.' I told Mother that it wasn't anything but a fear of brain tumours, the horror of them, Billy from Ontario's tumour.

On Wednesday 14 October, after another restless night of sleepless nursing, painkillers and cold compresses on poor John's aching head, Mother and I helped him into the car and drove him slowly to his radiotherapy appointment as an outpatient. He was still suffering from severe headaches, and Mother asked Nurse Douglas if John could be seen by the on-duty doctor. Dr S was on. He said he was too busy to see John, but he asked the nurse to carry out some tests and John was taken away into a side room. He should have been seen by a doctor, and Mother was unhappy. John was quite clearly suffering from meningitis and in any other hospital and circumstance would have been seen by a doctor immediately. But Dr S was still too busy. Mother noted in her legal statement later that if 'the diagnosis of meningitis had been made, the subsequent tragic events may have been avoided'.

We were told to give John analgesics (painkillers) and to wait to see how he felt the following day. Mother and I were sick with worry. Somehow, as I sat with John until Samantha arrived, Mother went back to her surgery to check on her own patients. She was under enormous strain, was limping badly from a previous broken hip, rushing backwards and forwards, frustrated beyond belief about the way S had been.

That night John barely slept, a terrible night of awful headaches, nausea and a temperature, an unnecessary night of horror for all and extreme pain for John, the drugs barely scratching the surface of his discomforts. It was the first time, other than the 'slap his face' comment, that I felt fury towards the hospital. I couldn't comprehend the sheer incompetence, the lack of respect and the lack of care they were giving John. At that point it felt almost personal, deliberately cruel and I couldn't bear it.

Monday 15 October

Shooting in London, which is as grey as London can be,
easy to forget after an endless summer.

Awoke after another restless night to the song of a wren outside the bedroom window. Tiny mercies.

After John's atrocious night, Dr S refused to see him and then went home. But we insisted that he was seen by a doctor. Mother had to force the issue as John's headache was desperately bad. Another doctor had seen John in the afternoon, far too long after we had reported his extreme headaches, but she, too, was too busy. She told us what was by now blatantly obvious, that John probably had meningitis. They didn't have a bed for the dreaded lumbar puncture so he was again transferred to the neurology unit. I stayed at home, trying to finish a commission. I must have made a terrible job of it, I was so distressed. Meanwhile it was confirmed that poor Johnny had another serious bout of meningitis. He was immediately placed on intravenous antibiotics and he remained there for another fraught night. I saw Debbie and Peter that night but I must have been awful company, I was so upset that John had endured so much additional pain, and later that evening I suffered one of my worst-ever migraines. I took three Solpadeines and went to bed tearful and frightened. That night I prayed more than I'd ever prayed in my life, since the days when John and I prayed together, in our red cotton dressing gowns with tassels that we would chew on, with Strawbod and Ted.

Tuesday 16 October

Sitting on the boat in Chelsea

On 16 October poor John was transferred by ambulance, back to his familiar nurses, under Nurse Douglas, and back into the care of the doctors on the oncology ward. Sitting now on the deck of the boat in the October sunshine, with the clearest blue sky, the water silky and mill-pond flat, watching the herons and the cormorants drying their wings, I no longer feel the intense anger of the time, just an immense, unhealing bruise of sadness. Anger just eats away, infects other feelings and memories. With time, somehow, one learns to deep-breathe through those moments and they lessen and lessen. Visiting John on his return to the oncology ward, half-asleep but suffering, it really had begun to feel like a 'them and us' situation.

Poor Samantha was now on an almost constant, exhausting vigil to make sure John was treated correctly and with gentle care and respect. Mother was backwards and forwards between hospital, The Beeches and surgery and I was filling in as many gaps as I could. We knew, collectively, that John's current suffering was the result of a lack of care, and Dr S came in for most of our ire. We desperately wanted him to be treated by someone else and his bosses vaguely agreed to this. The neurology unit, meanwhile, had become the place, in our mind, to patch up the errors of the oncology department, always on the end of a phone, monitoring, asking and caring.

A few friends popped in to see John. He was too ill for any more radiotherapy and the focus was on trying to cure his meningitis. They often brought books and magazines, but reading was too difficult, so he looked through a *Tintin*, *Asterix* or two, and a biography autographed to him from cricketing legend Sir Len Hutton. I would read the odd feature from *The Independent*, fill him in with the cricket season, but he spent a lot of this time heavily sedated and sleeping.

At one point his lovely boss Peter popped in, as he often did, and sat with him. John told me later that he was going to carry on with driving lessons and give up riding the Monkey bike (too dangerous!). He pointed out of the window. In the car park was a VW Golf, very trendy at that time. Peter had apparently lifted him out of bed, carried him to the window, and pointed at the car, saying, 'See that car, it's yours. Your company car waiting for you when you are well again.' I had brought him some of his favourite Molly's apple pie, which she was now baking on an almost weekly basis. John was so funny, he ate most of it, but then hid the plate because he didn't want to offend the hospital kitchens by appearing to prefer Molly's fare.

* * *

I bumped into a friend, Jeremy King, at The Wolseley over breakfast this morning and he kindly asked if I 'was really all right?' I answered 'No, not really, but I shall be fine.' We talked of perfect storms where all the conditions come together at the wrong time, in perfect harmony, to create a perfect storm. Just now a red admiral butterfly fluttered past the boat, risking its delicate all by flying low and fast over the water. That moment, watching its chaotic flight across the rippling Thames brought back memories of the night of 15 October 1987, the Great Storm, when the beech trees all around The Beeches swayed alarmingly, groaning down to their roots, the night the old plum tree came crashing down and the night that, somehow, the ambulance men battled their way through falling trees and crushed cars between Banstead and Wimbledon, all because a doctor was 'too busy' to see a young man with meningitis.

Wednesday 17 October

At Fortnum & Mason for the launch of their Christmas book, written by Tom Parker Bowles and photographed by me. Shoot on the thirty-sixth floor of The Shard for Shangri-La Hotels and in Bermondsey with the beekeepers, the fudge makers, the sausage makers, and the vegetable suppliers – a full day in which the rain did not stop falling. A classic perfect example of a day where, however ropey I feel, I can hide behind my profession and I realize how lucky I am to have that luxury.

17 and 18 October were quiet days for John, uncomfortable and painful with endless headaches. I remember at one point he said, 'I thought the operation had been to get rid of these headaches,' and I couldn't have agreed more. He had a few visitors but wasn't well enough for any more radiotherapy. He was fed up and restless but, as ever, uncomplaining.

Thursday 18 October

Shooting with my dear friend Andy Harris for his company Vinegar Shed in his Pitshanger Lane garden

I loved today's shoot. It was good to be with Andy, chewing the fat, teasing, reminiscing, taking pictures, filming his bees, harvesting his honey, his vinegar, his quinces and medlars. He's like Richard Briers in *The Good Life*; he even made me urinate outside as apparently it stops the foxes crapping on his vegetable patch.

Friday 19 October

By the nineteenth John's condition had deteriorated. He was at times semi-conscious and in constant pain. After another lumbar puncture, it was decided to again transfer him by ambulance back to Neurology where he could receive more attentive and specialized treatment. He was now, once again, seriously ill, but at least the focus was now on his meningitis and getting him over it. He had been looking forward to our birthday, still twelve days away, and we'd planned some gatherings of chums around his bedside. Though he was so ill, we tried to feel positive as we weaved our way through the fallen trees in the roads, some still impassable, back to the neurology unit, but it was hard. Every time John seemed to be on the mend another setback slapped him down.

As soon as John was admitted he curled up and went to sleep, only to be awakened continually for his vitals to be taken. He was weak, thin and in pain, although he still had a faint tan and his hair had stopped falling out with the break in his treatment. It was painfully hard to watch him like this.

* * *

In the last few days it feels like autumn has at last begun to arrive, leaves are turning, cold mornings when the cover of the duvet makes getting up that little bit harder. As the trees turn through reds and browns I will forever be reminded of the walk up from the station, up the hill to the hospital, legs like battling against a sea of treacle, heavy-hearted and stressed, shoulders and head drooped against the wind, the carcasses of fallen trees everywhere, the year autumn came with an almighty crash.

Saturday 20 October

The Mews, a clear blue sky

Each day that week I'd take that lonely walk up to the hospital that had done so much to try to save poor Johnny, to find him no better, and often slightly worse. For four days he had daily lumbar punctures, now not to test the infected cerebral fluid but to relieve the pressure the fluid was causing on his brain, intensifying his nausea and his headaches to such an extreme that often he was barely conscious, just curled in a ball and looking more and more like a frail and poorly child. Each day was gut-wrenchingly, heartbreakingly awful. I was worn out with tiredness and worry, but this was always unsaid and unshown. Compared to the suffering poor John was going through, which was beyond my comprehension, it was nothing. Samantha was also exhausted, almost permanently by his side, stroking his hand, his hair, cooling his feverish brow.

The last day he'd spent in Oncology, John had asked me to shave him. I'd made a couple of fairly timid attempts before, mainly with an electric, but his whiskers were quite long and it's not easy to do to someone else. He was worried that if the hair on his head was falling out it might start getting patchy and we talked about shaving it from his head too, but he hated the thought that he might look like a cancer patient, which he still didn't. As he lay there in the neurology unit I was glad that I'd managed it, he looked so young, and I thought the younger he looked the more care they'd take of him.

When Hak wet-shaved me a few months ago, it was the first time that I had been completely clean-shaven since John died. When our father died we had kept all of his shaving gear in the bathroom cabinet at The Beeches, old badger-hair brushes and deep wooden soap bowls, so much cooler than our crappy foam squirters and disposable razors. So I brought his razor, with new blades, one of his favourite brushes and his bottle of 4711 up to John's bedside. Using a hand towel soaked in hot water and a few drops of the tonic, I shaved him as delicately as I could, warming and softening his whiskers, pulling his delicate skin this way and that with my fingertips, desperately afraid that at any moment I might snick him and cause him to bleed, painfully aware that if I did catch him, with the painkillers he was on, he would bleed and bleed. It was a slow process and as the soap dried on his face I would wash it off with the hot towel and re-lather him. I found under the nose particularly difficult and as I pulled at his top lip I realized that the area above his top row of teeth, where the surgeons had cut open his skull, was still sensitive. John pulled back against my touch and with abject horror I saw the aftermath of that incision, the wobbliness of his upper jaw. So many god-awful memories in such a short space of time, from the cricket match in Richmond Park to this tender moment.

He could sense my distraction and told me, quite cheerily, to 'Get on with it. If you think I'm worried about the scratch of a razor after what I've been through . . .' I could see his point. So I gently raised his chin and tackled the delicate neck area, checking each time for the grain, the way the hairs grow. He wanted a close shave as opposed to a smooth one. It took me a while, trimming his sideburns so they were the same length, trying to remember how I instinctively shaved myself, aware that if I did the exact opposite, the mirror image of my shaving self, then I should be able to move the blade without snicking the skin. Though a slow endeavour it was successful. I cleaned his skin, dabbed him with moisturizer and a splash of Father's cologne. He told me it reminded him of Papa.

After I left his bed I cried for what seemed like an eternity, walking all the way back to The Beeches. Down Pine Walk, where his first girlfriend Liz lived with her twin brother John, its famous pine trees looking like a fallen Jurassic forest, tree upon tree upon tree felled by the storm, a sea of moulted pine needles to wade through. The world felt mad, bad and unfriendly. From that day on I have found it impossible to wet shave my own face, the few times I've tried I've nicked and cut myself. I've lost the instinctive feel that one gains from shaving again and again in the mirror, but I've ingrained the minutiae of John's face to my memory, every tiny mole, freckle and chickenpox scar. His lack of fingernail scars, they were my unique markers of Johnny's early presence; his crow's feet and his smiling dimples. I learned, much later, that I had most of these too, but at the time they felt like the minute details that made his face different to mine.

Sunday 21 October

The Mews

Jean-Marian came to the Mews for brunch, served by Ange, sourdough toast with avocados and smoked salmon and scrambled eggs, another clear blue sky, crisp and stunning. She pointed out that it was the first time she'd been invited in over eight years, a fact, I told her, I am not proud of. Conversation was quiet and reserved, strained at times, but jolly enough until I told her that I had come to the conclusion that I had been a pretty lousy brother, a crap friend, an absentee sibling, uncle and godfather, rebellious, aloof, and at times downright arrogant. She cried into her hands where she sat at the dining table while Ange quietly cleared away around us. Barely revealing her face, gently sobbing as I held on to the heaving of her shoulders, my face pressed to her head. After a while she left for home, not disagreeing with my self-examination but with a 'I guess none of us handled it particularly well', before she left the table. I solemnly promise to be a better brother.

Last night I eventually fell asleep, on my front, holding my forehead with one hand, Ange's bunny with the other, halfway through a relatively mild migraine, dreaming that I was pretending to be asleep so that I could sleep in John's room as he worked beside me and he pretended to ignore me to allow me to sleep. Sleeping and dreaming of trying to sleep and then dreaming some more.

Monday 22 October

The King's Road, Chelsea

22 October 1987. John's condition continued to deteriorate, and the lumbar punctures continued to try to relieve the pressure on his poorly brain. Tim, Samantha's caring father, had provided us with a mobile phone, basically a metal briefcase with a phone the size of a brick attached, the first of its kind, so that we could alternate the vigil at his bedside.

* * *

22 October 2018. I awake after another restless and dream-filled night to the call of a robin on the window sill, another clear London sky, chilled

and blue, warmed by my hot-water bottle of a wife, snuggling closer to whisper a happy anniversary in her ear.

* * *

22 October 2016. I awoke early and alone, to a similarly clear blue sky. Stretching lazily, an English breakfast tea in bed, I stuck my head out of the window to check the morning temperature and to share the dawn chorus, with possibly the same robin chirping merrily. Beside the bed, white shirt, white trousers, blue velvet Nehru jacket, and a pair of unworn Preventi desert boots in dark green suede, designed for me, named after me, and with my signature embossed on their sole.

I joined my best man, Andy Harris, at Hak's in the King's Road. Hak and his able assistant Saf smilingly awaiting us. They massaged, coiffed, caressed, sprayed, washed, polished, buffed and trimmed the two of us, side by side, pressing Turkish coffees and delights into our newly manicured mitts.

Smelling like a pair of Turkish spice merchants we then wandered down the road of my youth to the small jamón bar next to Chelsea Town Hall, Casa Manolo, where we ordered iberico hams, anchovies and cold glasses of Albarino and awaited our chums and my wife-to-be.

Mother arrived, with my sister Jean-Marian, driven by one of our old drivers, Pepe, and a handful of other guests to make fourteen of us in total, enough to fill one of the smaller rooms at the registry office. The service was lovely. This was to be the official signing before the main event later in the week in Marrakech, but it was much more moving and special than I had expected. I carried Strawbod throughout, his head poking out through my jacket pocket, Johnny's knitted scarf around his well-worn neck, his moth-eaten brown ears and well-sucked nose, one orange beady eye missing, the other shining like amber, my little bit of John with me through both weddings.

Tuesday 23 October

The Mews
Cold, hazy sunshine

The afternoon of 22 October 2016 was spent being entertained with rosé and oysters and cake at the Colbert with our gang of fourteen, just missing Paros who was revising for medical exams and Ian who was on holiday, but with the knowledge that both would be with us in Marrakech. We followed our long lunch with snoozes and languid love-making inside Antony Gormley's ROOM, the robotic sculpture perched on the outside of The Beaumont Hotel in Mayfair, more oysters, more rosé and a night of inseparable spooning, 'one of you and one of me, we'll be joined so tight'.

* * *

The afternoon of 22 October 1987 was much like the afternoon before, no better but not obviously worse, a desperately tense waiting game. Intravenous antibiotics, monitors bleeping, wires, liquids and lumbar punctures, temperature constantly dangerously high while we shivered around him, Mother, Samantha and me, taking turns.

Wednesday 24 October

Shooting for Andy Harris at his Vinegar Shed

Over the years the number of people who remember John with a card or a text have of course lessened, particularly after the Ps were born, and now I've added two wedding anniversaries to the end-of-October mix I expect them to lessen even more. I'm aware also of my diary running its natural course, starting on 1 January and ending on the anniversary of

John's death. And I still have so many things left to do, intentions I had, at the beginning of writing, that I have failed to complete . . . tick-tock, so little time left.

Yesterday I spent an hour tackling the folio of papers stuffed behind more papers, and frames, and broken glass. The A1 folio is there, the same one that either John or I would walk to school with between the ages of sixteen and eighteen, just too big to carry without scuffing the ground. The marks still there; heavy enough, over the space of two years, to leave us both with identical right-sloping shoulders. The smell of damp and mould was sneeze-inducingly strong but the squashed folder was so well rammed in that, luckily, it wasn't in contact with the cold floor, saving it from eight years of weather and London filth swirling in under the heavy wooden doors.

After lots of my own crap, instantly binned, I struck gold. John's screenprints of Sir John Soane's Museum, sketches of some of the treasures in the sarcophagus room there, beautifully drawn in Caran d'Ache pencil, painted architectural details, a drawing of a grotesque, an ancient moulding of the devil, in gouache-painted line, creating an imaginary 'identity' for the museum. To find anything new to me of John's gives me such a thrill, and this find is utterly priceless. 'John' is even there in his own signature, the same signature that adorns the front window at Nucleus in Thames Ditton. I sat there, cold-bottomed and sneezing in the dust, overjoyed with my find, bent double and contorted under Father's desk as I continued my archaeological dig.

I know now that is possible to smile and to cry floods of tears at the same time. It's a unique experience, probably preferably surrounded by loved ones, not rammed underneath a desk coughing up damp and dust, but I hugged my treasures close to my chest and wept for England.

Endless clear blue skies, shooting in the City

On the thirty-sixth floor with endless views over Old Father Thames, bronzed and silty, flowing east as far as the eye can see, 'like a rod of rippled jade . . .'

Letter from Ian, arrived yesterday.

My dear brother David,

It's thirty years since John died, and you asked, in advance of finishing your book, if I would write something. I'm not sure whether you wanted me to write about my memories of John, my feelings about the events surrounding his death, or what happened since, so perhaps I will write a bit about all of it.

While I agreed readily to write to you, I cannot promise to be able to express everything that I feel. There are so many thoughts in my mind and contrasting feelings in my heart, that I am sure all of us in the family share, but have never been able to fully express.

Firstly I should say that there are many things that I regret. Many of my emotions, especially related to the profession I found myself in, are still difficult to rationalize and I find myself challenged on a regular basis. To the point where, on many occasions, I have questioned my ability to continue. One significant and lingering regret is the way we have all drifted apart. Tragedy should bring loved ones closer together, but it seems at times to have fractured our bond. Perhaps now is the time to try and heal those fractures? I have always felt that a better ability to share our feelings and our emotions would help.

Specific to John, I have much guilt, as I think we all do – for not being there enough before, but especially during his illness. For not being there to stop things happening. And for not pushing for more to be done afterwards. I will come back to that later.

But thinking then of the memories, each year with frustration I find that they become more blurred and hazy. Some of the overpowering memories though are the funny times. In particular, I think of the potato fight at the farm in Cumbria. Mum's and Dad's faces when, coming into the courtyard, they found the entire farm littered with potatoes that you, John, Edward and I had hurled across the roof at each other. I think we dug the entire garden up. It still makes me giggle. I also think of John dropping the hay bale on Tracey's head. I know it shouldn't be funny, but boy it makes me laugh. And lobbing huge rocks into cowpats, trying to splatter each other. That holiday for me was a defining moment in the family, all I remember is sheer joy and fun.

I know there were times when John found me an irritation, and we didn't see eye to eye. I also remember that there were times when he could be a bit mean to me. I'm sure most youngest siblings have this, and I'm pretty sure I was a real pain at times, especially when any games of sporting activities were involved, I was never a good loser. John was usually pretty good at just letting me win, but I know I pushed his tolerance. This especially applied to car-hee. You will remember spending hours on the landing at The Beeches, chasing each other around with model cars. We must have done so much damage to the skirting boards. But John would always give me the benefit of the doubt as to whether we had made 'contact'. And let me have better cars.

He also had a pretty low impression of my friends, especially my girlfriends. In retrospect he had a point about some of them, so

I should have listened a bit more, and saved myself a bit of bother. Also my hair. I shall always be known as 'Mushroom'. And he used to take the mickey out of me for being 'Nana's boy', because I used to help with the washing-up after Sunday lunch. Little did he know that Nana used to slip me some sweetie money afterwards; I've always been a bit sneaky like that.

He was always the popular one at school, teachers, boys from other years and peers alike. And at art college and at work, when he joined Nucleus. He could be very sensitive and this attracted people to him. I recall how much *Midnight Express* affected him. It depicted graphically the harsh brutality of life, and the strength of the human spirit to overcome cruelty. He was able, so beautifully, to express this in his art and his animation – the stills of which hang next to me in my office. Art gave him that very different perspective of the world. I used to be jealous of the way he saw things and could express them in such a way.

There were certainly times, especially when he was a student, that we felt rather distant. But I will never forget an occasion when he started at Nucleus, when out of the blue, John invited me over to Thames Ditton to see his work, to meet the team and take me for lunch at the pub opposite. He was so gentle, so kind, and so thoughtful, and we felt like true brothers again.

I also remember with clarity taking John for his first outpatient appointment, not long after my visit to Nucleus. It was obvious as we walked from the car that something was very wrong. But he was so brave, he seemed to take the whole thing in his stride. While we fell apart, he looked ahead and was determined to get through it.

One of my last memories is looking down the corridor in Beeches Avenue, seeing him standing in his room, after his surgery, looking rather helpless, weak and battered. But still smiling. He was so positive – like Dad used to be – finding the best of things and managing a smile at the darkest of times.

I don't need to document what happened after that, but perhaps I can share some of my perspectives, which I still reflect on regularly to this day.

The fact that the doctors involved left behind so many broken lives, so much pain and anger, and never saw it in their hearts to just say sorry is bewildering. I have had a number of very difficult experiences in the Coroner's Court that have brought this back to me with renewed clarity. I have had to sit next to grieving families in court, aware of the multitude of emotions they face looking across at me. Distrust. Anger. Grief. Frustration. These patients and families never go away – they continue to shape my life, my career and the way I am, both at work and at home.

So while I think about these cases almost every day, and the multitude of conflicting emotions, what about the doctors in John's case? Did they just move on? Was John just another patient, replaced by the next one that came through the door?

I like to think not, but without a recognition of the pain and anger, the loss, and the shattered lives left behind, without the slightest apparent sense of regret or reflection, we can only imagine how they feel. So many people were changed forever, fractured souls and broken hearts. We like to think that most people are rational and civilized but of course we expect it more of the medical profession. It is a necessity. We expect a level of empathy that outweighs any personal introversion and inability to say sorry. What can have been justification for such an apparent lack of empathy?

Of course they did not set out to kill John. But they didn't take the care and attention to detail required to protect John from harm. Accidents happen of course. But at best the doctors involved with John were careless, we might perceive as negligent, maybe worse. Nowadays there is a low threshold to charge doctors with manslaughter. It's a very controversial area and one I fear as a practising surgeon who is not averse to taking on the high-risk patient and procedures. I have to perform at all times to the very highest level, not tolerate error or bad practice, and above all, put the patient, not me, first. They didn't do this in my opinion. They didn't follow the order and method we expect of members of the profession.

Who knows if they had, either at the time or subsequently, simply said 'sorry'. Perhaps given us some assurance that it could never happen again. Would we all be in a different place now? We can never know. But one of my big regrets now is that, in the absence of an acceptance of error, an apology, and a reassurance, we should have taken it further. I should have taken it further.

It is an extraordinary thing that a moment in time changes a lifetime for so many people. Every death does this, every accident, every serious injury, and each one is different. For you, as a twin, it has been especially shattering and has painted your life's path forever. But it changed us all beyond recognition. It is there, every day, every minute, affecting the way we see things, interpret things, feel about things, and respond to things. And so it will be, forever.

Deep grief, tinged by all the other associated emotions that come from the individual circumstances of such a loss, have had the spiralling effect of distancing us over the years. None of us can want that, and none would have predicted that. But we have always since that day struggled to express our emotions and feelings.

It has also brought out some of our best qualities with others, especially kindness and an ability to think of others in a different light. As Dad would say, for us to be 'gentlemen' in the true sense of the word.

Going forward we can never forget, and we can probably never forgive until we hear the word we have wanted to hear for thirty years. But I hope we can listen to our hearts and bring ourselves back closer together. Perhaps use each day to value what we have, to find a reason to laugh and be happy, but still allow ourselves to remember and to cry. I hope beyond everything that we all find our peace together.

I love you dearly.

Your little brother.

Mushroom

Friday 26 October

Shooting for the Sunday Times, *Tom Kerridge, in North London*

The night of 25 October 1987 was awful, a restless night at home at The Beeches. Mother was very late back and Molly and I didn't really know what to do with ourselves. I spent hours at the snooker table just thwacking balls aimlessly at corners trying to create any distraction possible. When at home I was deliberately not drinking, trying to keep my mind clear, aware that the phone could ring at any moment. When Mother eventually came home she was fraught and exhausted. John was not conscious any longer and again I prayed late and long that somewhere and somehow they would save him. During the morning of the twenty-sixth I worked at John's desk, another overdue illustration. Mother had gone up to the hospital alone, not wishing me to see what John was going through there. The pressure in his brain was far too high from the meningitis, the headaches and fever so bad, and the lumbar punctures not working to relieve that pressure, so the decision was made to insert a reservoir into the ventricles of the brain to relieve the pressure and enable the doctors to give John his antibiotics directly into the reservoir.

It's called an Ommaya reservoir and I can understand Mother's keeping me away that day. Like the initial surgery to remove the tumour, the surgical notes are too graphic and impersonal for my perusal; it all seems impossibly barbaric to the uninformed like me. A neurosurgeon makes an insertion, under general anaesthetic, through the top of the skull and inserts a catheter into the gap between the ventricles of the brain, attached to a small dome-shaped device just beneath the scalp, attached to the catheter. This allows the doctors to deliver medicine into the cerebrospinal fluid and take samples, directly into the area of the brain that makes the fluid and so relieve the pressure on the brain.

Saturday 27 October

Clear and cold, pyjama day at the Mews. 4°C
Dear Ange out shopping for my birthday presents

The broken folio case in the print room at the Mews had one final gem to present me, after much tugging, pulling and contortionism. An A3 spiral-bound, bent and wonky sketchbook, the watercolour paper jaundiced with time. Page after page, beautiful sketches on Paros, the view of the Castro church from my window at Jane's, several more of the boatyard at Naousa, a drawing of the view across the fishing port towards its grand church, the ancient Castro arches at the end of Jane's street, the higgledy-piggledy architecture of Parikia and Lefkes. Each sketch is annotated with notes, each word, even his name, 'John Loftus' a little gift to me, marks I have never seen before now, extraordinarily precious for me to find when I have so little of his.

* * *

On 27 October 1987 I was eventually allowed to see John, curled up in his tell-tale protective foetal position and still unconscious. I was able to study what the neurosurgeon had done to the top of his head. He had to shave a bit more of John's precious hair off, right at the top of his head, and I had expected to see something more gruesome, a Heath Robinson contraption for the head. Instead there was a small bandage hiding the entry point and a small valve in which the doctors could inject and sample. My immediate thought was of his hair, that and the painful thought of catching it on his pillow if he moved. I stroked his head, which still felt alarmingly hot, and anointed his lips with lemon balm to try to keep them from drying out. He was terribly frail and there was absolutely nothing else we could do but sit, stroke, whisper to him in the hope that he could hear us while his brain battled to recover.

* * *

On 27 October 2016 we had breakfast on the rooftop of Riad El Fenn in Marrakech, listening to the call to prayer from the Koutoubia Mosque, the snow-capped Atlas Mountains on the horizon. Flocks of sparrows swarmed around as we awaited the arrival of our friends and my Ps, and I couldn't remember the last time I had been so excited, so full of life, so happy.

Sunday 28 October

The Mews and the boat
Cold day. The first frost, hailstorms and sunshine

The twenty-eighth was a quiet day for John, who was still very poorly though his temperature had lessened a little. He was still in Intensive Care but the neuro-doctors were feeling a bit more confident. I did at one point hear the sentence, 'It's really up to him to fight it', and looking at his weak and unconscious body I felt desperately helpless. The idea that he might be well enough for a birthday party now seemed totally unrealistic. Samantha was by his side most of the time and fiercely protective of him, overwrought and overtired and understandably tetchy. So I only stayed an hour or so to give her a break and whispered in his ear that I'd found him 'the best birthday present'.

* * *

25 October 2016 was a glorious day in Marrakech. In the warm sunshine, Ange and I spent the day welcoming guests. Her parents and siblings had arrived from Australia and I met them for the first time and we settled them in a neighbouring riad. We spent the day rushing around, meeting and greeting; friends were landing from London, New York, LA, Australia and all over Europe. El Fenn was now exclusively ours so it was a merry scene of drinking Sahari Gris rośe and Moroccan teas, poured from a great height, to the soundtrack of the sparrows and the call of the mosques. Tim and I toasted to John and to Nick and to absent friends and partied into the evening.

29 October 1987 saw the first improvements in a while in John's condition. He was conscious for a while, tired and weak, thankfully not remembering the pain of the past few days; I even got a frail smile or two, which raised my spirits considerably. I got excited enough to suggest reinstigating our birthday party, but, quite rightly, I was reminded that there was still a long way to go yet. I remember walking back down Wimbledon Hill with a little more bounce in my step, more confident than I'd been in a while. I spoke for a long time with Mother that evening while Molly baked in the kitchen; I'd bought John and Samantha a holiday for his birthday present, Easter weekend in Venice, travelling on the Orient Express, returning on Concorde, and she was quietly confident that, as long as there were no setbacks, he'd be well enough to travel then. It cost me every penny I'd earned.

Poor Mother was exhausted and both of us were knocking back painkillers. I'm pretty sure I had a permanent tipple in my hand as I spent the evening playing solo snooker in the dining room, tinkering on the piano or playing Devo songs on my double bass. I had the overwhelming feeling that I was treading water, though not in a relaxing way, only just managing to keep my head up and out. I was late on several commissions and my agents really didn't understand, Debbie was impatient with me to go out and play, as were my chums, but I was so desperately worried for John and utterly helpless to aid him in his recovery. I was lost. People I know love autumn. But to me autumn is the leaves turning, trees falling, wind howling, time moving slowly, that shared childhood fear of Halloween, John's and my fear, aged five, of witches. Twins born on Halloween, hiding behind our beds, curtains closed, fearing every movement of shadow and light.

* * *

29 October 2016 was my wedding day in Marrakech, possibly one of the most joyous days of my life. Here are some of my more memorable moments:

Tim, Simon and me hilariously trying to sort 140 place settings, all hand-drawn by me, on the floor of our bedroom, the sight of which reduced Ange to tears.

Champagne countdown beside the fireplace, with Jamie and Tim, my two best men. Adjustment of flowers on my linen Nehru jacket and tucking Strawbod into my left pocket.

Wandering down to the courtyard below, filled with smiling friends, Moroccan mint teas and biscuits among the trees, tortoises dodging unintentioned kicks around their feet. Sigur Rós playing to the background chant from the Mosque. Hugging abounds.

Jason Flemyng, master of ceremonies, always so smart, a man who can wear a scarf with aplomb in any temperature, fussing Tim, Jamie and me into the orange courtyard, under the fruit-heavy bows. A sea of rose petals, thousands scattered everywhere among the rows of chairs and pouffes and cushions, a more romantic scene impossible to imagine.

140 hugs and kisses of welcome.

Paros and Pascale, Paros in smartest of suits, fitted the previous week with his Papa at Hackett on Sloane Street. Pascale in charge of her small portable record player, essentially a suitcase with a turntable, needles and speakers, a crappy microphone pointing at the speaker. Playing 'Into My Arms' by Nick Cave and the Bad Seeds.

The sudden drama of Tim Etchells, who had been warning the guests not to mistake the petal-covered pond as anything but a long and deep pond, disappearing up to his groin in said pond, Jamie screaming with laughter, recording every moment on his camera, chum Neil laughing so much he shatters the chair beneath him. The wonderful El Fenn ladies all in head-to-toe red, rushing around with mops and buckets of rose petals.

My wife, arm in arm with her mother and father, either side of the pond, walking towards my open arms, unbearably beautiful in an ivory dress, designed of course by herself and based upon a Sandro dress I once gave her, layers of French Chantilly lace with flowers and swirls and curls everywhere, backless and breathtakingly serene.

A kiss, the holding of hands, smiles everywhere as the music stops.

The readings: 'Castle in the Sand' by Norman Lourie, read by brother and sister Morris, Rebecca and Luke; 'The Blessing of the Apaches', read by Jason Flemyng; an extract from *The Count of Monte Cristo*, Alexandre Dumas, my favourite book of all time, read by Johnny's old boss and dear chum, Peter Matthews:

> The friends we have lost do not repose under the ground . . . they are buried deep in our hearts. It has thus ordained that they may always accompany us . . .

Pascale plays 'Windmills of Your Mind' by Terry Hall's The Colourfield on her little player to silence and tears from all. I hug my brother Ian.

More readings: Katie Millard reads an extract from *Winnie-the-Pooh*; Jeff Bennett reads from *The Little Prince* by fellow pilot

Antoine de Saint-Exupéry, spoken so softly it was almost said just to Ange and me.

Ange and I exchange rings, me receiving the amber ring she once bought me from The Great Frog, a homage to my days as a punk, my hands already cluttered with silver skulls and fiery hearts, Ange with a silver heart of her own, her rings having been 'lost' by the Australian postal service. Instead of traditional vows we perform an exchange of roses, in which we hand each other a perfect bloom, in front of a beaming Jason and Tim and a snapping Jamie, my two groomsmen.

Jason reads 'The Art of Marriage' by Wilferd Arlan Peterson, one of the greatest odes to matrimony.

To tears, laughter, smiles and roses, Ange and I walk slowly, either side of the petal-strewn pond, accompanied by the birdsong of the sparrows and 'Perfect Day' by Lou Reed on Pascale's player. For a quiet moment it's just the two of us, knowing that hers is a hand I will never let go of.

A rainfall of rose petals and 140 hugs, cuddles and kisses, handshakes and high fives, champagne and Sahari Gris flowing to a soundtrack of a lifetime of our music.

We climb the winding staircase up to the roof garden, the tables stretching to every corner, thousands and thousands of rose petals in fifty shades of oranges and reds, a milky setting sun, the Kartoubia Mosque framed against the snow-capped Atlas Mountains, storks rising on thermals and the sparrows, in their hundreds, murmuring like starlings, filling the orange trees for evensong.

Tables filled with happy friends on kilims and cushions and lounging on pouffes, candles lit everywhere, vases overflowing with roses, glasses overflowing with rosé, peppered with delightful tales of Ange's childhood shared by her sister, Mon. And I discover the nickname of Ange's youth, 'Moth.'

Plates of aubergine zaalouk, taktouka mixed peppers, khobez with green olives, confit pumpkin with honey, sesame and walnuts. Carrots in chermoula, salads with orange, walnuts and orange-blossom water. Moroccan breads and Sahari Gris. Then chicken and lamb tagines, slow-cooked local beef tanjia with Moroccan herbs, couscous with seven vegetables, curled mhancha, oranges in cinnamon and b'stilla with chocolate sauce, crème anglaise, fresh fruits and almonds.

As I stand to read my speech the mosque call to prayer launches at full volume, and I await the end of its beautiful chant. I talk of John, of being a twin, of my happiness as a father, my happiness as a friend to all present, the love that was missing in my life until I met Ange, and I read to everyone our favourite passage from *The Amber Spyglass* by Philip Pullman.

> And when they use our atoms to make new lives, they won't just be able to take one, they'll have to take two, one of you and one of me, we'll be joined so tight.

Ange gets up to say an impromptu speech, a surprise to me, thanking her family and friends who've travelled from Australia to Morocco, and Paros and Pascale for accepting her into the family, telling me, 'The vows we shared today are ingrained in my heart and I'll do everything I can to honour those words.' Pascale giving

a heartfelt, tearful and beautifully eloquent speech, welcoming Ange to being a Loftus, telling all how happy she is to see us happy with each other.

In the best man's speech stakes, Tim raises the bar impossibly high, then Christian Stevenson, a.k.a. DJ BBQ, takes over my rooftop playlist, my indie and miserablist music replaced by James Brown and Aretha Franklin and a call to join him back beside the pool for the first dance, 'I Need My Girl' by The National. I've changed into a vintage Comme des Garçons linen number emblazoned with an overblown image of busby-wearing brass bands in full march, looking better than it sounds.

Dancing around the pool beneath the huge palm trees, candles everywhere and fire pits in the marble tiles, the hot ashes rising into the warm air creating a 'firefly' light show of their own.

Wandering up to our room in the wee hours, following a trail of thousands more petals, pinks, whites and reds, all the way to our bed where Ange, exhausted, slept peacefully on a bed of roses.

Hyper after such an extraordinary day, I watch Ange fall asleep in our enormous four-poster, the room heady with the fragrance of flowers. Its like a field of roses.

Tuesday 30 October

30 October 1987 and John was slowly improving. He had been moved from Intensive Care onto one of the wards. This was a mixed blessing for poor Johnny as it was a hospital for those with serious brain injury, and this was a particularly disturbing ward, noisy and quite chaotic.

Most of the patients were quite young and very sick. One was a young scaffolder hit on the front of his head with a falling pole, another a youthful City banker who had crashed his Porsche driving too fast around a blind corner. Both had returned, upon awakening after their accidents, to the mental age of four or five, maybe even younger, their stunned and disbelieving families around their beds completely unable to handle the human tragedies unfolding in front of their eyes. At one point John and I watched a junior nurse trying to take the stats of one young man while he exposed himself and pissed directly into her face, not intending any harm, his brain having been shaken to a mush.

* * *

30 October 2016 was a quiet and sunny day spent on the rooftop of Riad El Fenn, head to toe in white linen, no shoes all day, even in the evening chill, a wedding breakfast of bread dipped in oil, and honey and, my choice, shakshuka, a tomato and egg tagine. Many chats of the day before's events, more hugs and kisses and quite a few goodbyes, the beginning of a sad post-nuptials exodus back home.

Wednesday 31 October

Halloween. Our birthday
The Mews and Cheam

31 October 1987 was a sober affair. John managed to open a couple of presents, we had a piece of birthday cake each and a small smuggled tipple. John's birthday card to me was heartbreakingly simple, written while suffering a wobbly left hand, double vision and a cracking headache.

Such a lot of effort had gone into that writing and it sits beside me now at my desk. I got Johnny to open my present to him; I'd collaged a homemade card with images of old Venice, Italian stamps and historic railway trains. He was shocked but delighted and that moment, sitting on the covers of his bed, I felt sure he'd be okay for the Easter departure. He was still having his drugs, gentamicin, administered through the reservoir in his head and he asked me to describe it to him. I was being honest when I told him that it didn't look as bad as it sounded. We stopped opening presents soon after as he was terribly weak and emotional. We agreed we'd leave the bulk of his present opening, and there was quite a pile, until he was a bit better and away from the chaos of the ward, which was truly horrific.

* * *

31 October 2018, a card bearing a painting of a barn owl saying:

> 31 October 1963 Twin boys were born, John and David
>
> 31 October 2018 All love to David today and for the future, Mum

Since John died my birthday has been a reluctant affair, a yo-yo of emotions, laughter often followed by guilt and tears, although there have been some memorable ones.

This year Ange grabbed a day off and we drove down to Mother's. She was quiet and frail but on good form; there's an inherent sadness that envelopes the day, it never goes away. Ange and I had breakfasted at Colbert on scrambled eggs and hugs, and The Wolseley had baked me a beautiful scripted birthday cake so we shared some rich, chocolatey slices. I topped up Mother's bird feeders and opened her present of a book; she always gives me books, which I love.

It was also a day of sweet messages on text, card and Instagram. Ange cooked a lovely dinner as a surprise, with a few chums including Andy,

Nick and Rosie, Pascale dressed up for a Halloween party later, Paros with a gorgeous new girlfriend on his arm. We toasted to Johnny and to absent friends. I missed Tim's presence.

Thursday 1 November

This day in 1983 John was poorly but brighter, making the odd tentative walk to the bathroom, and the neuro-doctors decided that tomorrow, despite his frailness, he should be readmitted to Oncology. They were worried it had been a while since radiotherapy had been administered to blast the tiny particles left post-operation, which now seemed like an eternity ago. John's bed was surrounded by flowers and cards, some even from the oncology nurses who missed his gentle smiley face.

* * *

Today Jamie and I started the process of shooting our new book, exploring not just recipe ideas and culinary direction, but props, backgrounds, lighting and technique. Our Italy book is still top of the charts, the previous two books still in the charts, but this one will need to be different from Italy and it's always the aim to make the new one our best yet.

After our shoot Jamie and I dined at Cornerstone in wildest Hackney, their chef Tom Brown is the hottest foodie ticket in town. We ate crumpets with shrimps, lemon sole in chicken sauce, scallops and mackerel pâté with treacle buns washed down with funky organic wines.

His message to me yesterday read, 'Happy birthday mate, a bitter sweet day today I know. But I wish you a truly wonderful day, look forward to tomorrow, it's a chilled day, then a birthday treat dinner and some giggles and a cheers to Johnny boy who sadly and regrettably I never knew. Shame, such a shame, anyway fella have a great day with Ange. xxx'

Shooting at the Mews

On the morning of Monday 2 November 1987 John was taken by ambulance from the neurology unit and, although very frail, was readmitted to the care of the oncology unit. Weak as he was, he was happy to be going back to get on with his treatment and to restart his physiotherapy. Before he left Neurology, he was given an intrathecal injection of gentamicin into the small reservoir in his head. Mother was very anxious at the thought of the injection being given in the oncology unit and she had asked the neurology staff to make sure that the oncology staff knew what to do and how to do it.

I was astonished to learn, in the afternoon, that John had been administered his first dose of radiotherapy in some time. He was too weak to walk and was carried to and from the radiotherapy department. Douglas and all of John's favourite nurses were all there for him and welcomed him back with genuine love and care.

Mother was with him during the afternoon and she asked who would administer the intrathecal antibiotics into the reservoir. When she was told that it was going to be Dr S, Mother told them that she lacked confidence in him, that we all did. The answer was that the hospital were aware of our concerns.

On the same afternoon Samantha spoke to Mother at the hospital, worried sick that she was having to monitor every moment of John's time in Oncology, to make sure he received the right care. It was an awful situation for her to be in and so wrong that between the three of us we were having to watch his every waking moment. Earlier in the day she had stopped a nurse from giving him an injection incorrectly. John had already received an intravenous injection earlier in the morning and was not due another until later in the evening. She'd also noticed that a doctor had removed John from the steroids he was on and it was vital that he remained on them while undergoing radiotherapy. When Mother spoke to the nurse in charge he assured her that he would see to it that John would be rewritten up for the drug immediately. No reason was given for either, other than that they were mistakes and they would be rectified. Our confidence in the doctors was at an all-time low.

Friday 2 and Saturday 3 November

Tick-tock. Saturday at home at the Mews

A quiet day at home on what would have been our father's birthday. He was forty-nine years old when he met our mother at that party in Knightsbridge, twenty years older than our mother. Eric John Loftus, buried with John, born 3 November 1910, dying on our parents' wedding anniversary in 1984, breaking the hearts of John, me, Jean-Marian and Ian. We missed him terribly, and still do.

I sat quietly with Ange, not allowing her to drift more than a few feet from my side while I try to summon the courage, the words to accurately explain the events of 3 November 1987, the day the world that we knew came crashing down, changing us all for ever.

As I sat at my desk she made what seemed the oddest suggestion.

She handed me a square box with the Eiffel Tower on its face, a small glass of rosé, and the words 'Just take a little break and build this.' Hundreds of tiny pieces of beautifully modelled and designed LEGO; we spent an hour and a half sorting, snapping together La Tour Eiffel, a structure we both adored, in awe of the complicated joints and hinges. We had so much LEGO as children, John and I, that we never fought over it, it was a game always shared, if still competitive. 'How tall can you build a skyscraper before it falls?' 'Can you build *Thunderbird 4* only using yellow bricks?' 'Can you build a vehicle with sixteen wheels that can survive a tumble down the stairs?'

La Tour Eiffel is now on my desk, next to a small red and white rocket, the one from Tintin's *On a Marché sur la Lune*. The rocket was the last of the gifts from Ange that I opened on our birthday this year, Ange unaware that it was also the last present that John opened sitting on his hospital bed, 3 November 1987. It was a present from one of his two best friends, Tim L-S and Nick H-H, I forget which one, oh the small coincidences of life.

* * *

Mother arrived in the early morning of the third and John was sitting in his bed having breakfast, better and brighter than he had been for a while, glad to be restarting his treatment and his recovery. Mother brought him his post from The Beeches, letters and birthday cards, even his payslip from Nucleus, and he opened them with her as they sipped their morning teas. Some more parcels had arrived but he wanted to wait until I arrived to open them together.

When I arrived, Mother left to attend to her surgery in Sutton. John was sitting upright, smiley and positive, excited about opening presents together. I joked that they seemed to be all for him and he admitted that one of the few positives of the situation we found ourselves in was that he'd really upped the ante in the gift-giving-and-receiving stakes. He was surrounded by cards and flowers and teddies, artworks and notes, the nurses fussed over him unlike the other patients, there was genuine care and love and a sense of positivity. We talked again of Venice, the Orient Express, Concorde and staying at the Cipriani, and he kept asking me, 'Have you really, really booked it for us?'

What happened in the next twenty minutes is etched so vividly upon my brain.

I was sitting on John's bed, gently helping him unwrap his presents. We had decided to go from the biggest to the smallest and I arranged them that way. It was like being children again, and he was genuinely excited. There was a *Tintin*-esque theme going on between his chums and we chuckled about Papa sitting on the bog watching our socks-inverted cricket ball whizzing past the door as he read his *Tintins* and *Asterixes*. The largest present was the rocket, an enormous wooden red and white *Explorers on the Moon* rocket that Tintin, Haddock, Snowy, Calculus and the stowaway Thompson twins travelled to the moon in. He was delighted and he made me stick the card with the present to remind himself who to write the thank-you letter to.

John had asked me again about the reservoir in the top of his head and I reiterated that it didn't look nearly as bad as it sounded. He told me that he couldn't really feel it, but then at that time his headache was almost constant, just slightly less intense now the gentamicin was doing its job. I placed the rocket on his bedside table and sat in the chair next to him, and as I passed him the next present to open, Dr S walked into the room to administer John's intrathecal injection.

The nurses were around, but not in the room at that moment and I said to Dr S that I believed that someone else was to give the injection, to which he replied that he was the only one that could. Normal practice, if a nurse prepares an intrathecal injection of gentamicin, is for another nurse to check it. Dr S had prepared the injection himself, without informing the nurses and there was no 'routine' to follow, apparently. Dr S was cold, unfriendly and sheepish, but this was what we had come to know and expect. He said he knew what he was doing and he sat beside John to inject the drug into the reservoir via a tiny valve that I had earlier hidden by gently combing his wispy hair around it.

Mother said later, in her statement via the lawyers, when she was pressurized to get things down in writing, that she believed that I wasn't there when the injection was given. I was. As the last of the drug was administered any normal doctor, one would hope, would check to make sure the patient was okay. Particularly when that drug had just been administered to a reservoir with access to the central recesses of the brain. But Dr S stood immediately and walked out of the room. And I knew straightaway that something was wrong. I called Dr S, but he had disappeared. I called the nurses. John's eyes were wandering and he told me he felt nauseous and that his head was spinning. I knew, without a doubt, immediately, that something had gone terribly wrong with the injection. John vomited everywhere, vomited like nothing I've ever seen before or since. I told him to breathe deeply, I remember saying that if you are breathing it's impossible to vomit, but it was no good, he vomited all over the birthday wrapping paper, over me. I held his head, screaming to the nurses to help me. Two rushed in. I had a potty from under the bed, they helped me with a bucket, he was looking up at me, gazing at me, but the vomit was awful, it just kept coming. All John could say was,

'I'm so, so sorry, David.

I'm so sorry,

So, so sorry, David.

I'm sorry, David.'

Again and again, his face as close to mine as I could hold him, the nurses running around in a panic, calling for Dr S, again and again. The nurses later attended the inquest; they wanted, all of them, to give their experiences of that moment, but they were not 'required'. One of the senior nurses eased John from my grip and he closed his eyes. As the nurses started to clean him up I was very aware that no one knew what to do, and that John was now losing consciousness. As I looked through the open door to the corridor outside I could, to my horror, see

Dr S at a desk, doing nothing. I asked him if he'd done something wrong. He said 'No.'

I knew I had to get Mother. I ran out into the corridor, telling everyone to get into the room to help John, white coats, blue coats, anyone, just please, please help. I could see S, unmoving at his desk. I knew then that he knew what he had done. He was looking at something, a phial or a box or something small, his head was in his other hand. If I knew, he knew. The first huge mistake was giving the injection, the second mistake was what the hospital did afterwards. But I had no time to spare, I ran to the phone.

I got Mother immediately on the phone, I told her that I believed something had gone terribly wrong, that John had become violently sick and that he was losing consciousness. I was in full panic mode by then, Mother knew immediately that this was really bad and she dropped the phone and ran to her car. I raced back past the still stationary S into John's room to find him just awake but breathing very weakly, he again said, 'I'm sorry, David.' I ran to Dr S and told him that John's breathing was getting incredibly weak and that he needed to see him, I then ran down the ward looking for anyone that I could find. No one was there. All I had was Dr S, who had no intention of helping, he wouldn't even acknowledge my existence. I've relived the slow-motion nightmare of what was unfolding again and again; what more could I have done at that moment? I ran back down the corridor towards John's room and as I drew level Dr S had, at last, risen from his desk and wandered in to examine John. At the same time Mother turned the corner and ran past me to see him.

I sat in a chair, my heart pounding. Holding my head in my hands, I could just see into the room but there still seemed to be little activity around John. Mother was talking to the charge nurse and was visibly upset and worried that John was unconscious. I told Mother that it was the moment the injection was given, that Dr S had refused to help, and, that I had seen him looking at something on his desk. I believe that the phial and box were never found.

As Mother was with John and I was outside the room Dr S walked in and administered another injection, not into the reservoir, but his arm. Mother asked him to clarify what he was giving him and he told her it was a steroid, to 'ease his condition'. Mother asked him about the intrathecal injection and he told her that he had given John the 'correct amount, 2 millilitres'. Mother didn't leave John's room. Again and again she expressed concern at his condition. She was told by the charge nurse that the registrar had been sent for, but was at another hospital. Mother was by now so alarmed at John's condition that she called the neurology unit from the ward telephone.

The registrar eventually arrived and contact between the two units was promised to monitor his condition. There was no mention of the injection that had been given, other than between me and Mother and the nurses. Several were in tears. Later in the day the unconscious John was seen by the consultant, still surrounded by our half-unwrapped presents, Tintin's rocket, Strawbod and his scarf. The consultant decided, at last, to move John to a high-dependency unit. Still there was little sign of Dr S, and no talk of the injection. The consultant suggested that John's brain should be scanned, but the oncology unit's scanner was out of action, so they gave him an MRI scan. Mother was told that John had 'probably had another brain haemorrhage' and that the timing with him receiving the injection was 'pure coincidence'. Mother then asked him if we, as a family, could have confidence that the injection was the correct drug, correctly given, at the correct dose, and he assured her that it was the first thing that they had thought about.

By this time Samantha and her parents had been called, and I was beyond consolation. Mother was talking to the doctors and holding John's hand in Intensive Care. It was suggested that I go home to The

Beeches and call Ian and Jean-Marian. I can still recall the cold wind off Banstead Downs as I walked up the hill and then down again towards Carshalton Beeches. They were still clearing the fallen trees, the ground was thick with rain-sodden pine needles. I saw Liz Piper's house, the road up to the Oaks park where we played as children, the old oak that gave its name to the place now also fallen and being shredded into firewood. Past Mr Frank's house, its heavy oak door that John and I would bash and bash with our 'Mr Frank' stick. Past Jayne's house, my first-ever girlfriend. The old Victorian pillarbox and home to The Beeches, to a tearful Molly, squeezing my cheeks and holding me tight for an eternity.

I sat at the piano, vaguely tinkering, the dining room cold and dark and I wept and wept and wept for John. His music, Moonlight Sonata Third Movement by Beethoven, was laid out to play. God, I was cold. That was the moment when the crashing, thundering realization came to me with absolute clarity: that I could have stopped him. Why hadn't I? Because John didn't want to make a fuss and, as a result, neither did I. I ran to the hall and called the ward, but no one answered, so I called the Intensive Care unit and spoke to Mother. There was no change and she would call me if she had any news. I went to my bedroom, lay on my futon on the floor and cried for as long as I can remember.

That night John was transferred, seriously ill again, still unconscious, to the high-dependency ward in the neurology unit. He would not return to Oncology. They were still maintaining that John had suffered some sort of haemorrhage, which I, as the only witness to what had happened, knew was complete bullshit.

Sunday 4 November

A quiet day at the Mews. Ange barely left my side, I hugged her for over an hour at one point. I briefly dozed in the autumn sun.

* * *

4 November 1987 was grey and bleak. We were back at the Intensive Care unit, which was a dark and sombre shrine to high dependency, high tech, deliberately dark, the most seriously sick, brain-injured or brain-damaged patients. All men, mostly the result of high-impact trauma to the head, except John, in the second bed from the end, tubes and monitors, drips and catheters.

During the day John was operated on by a neurosurgeon and a cerebral shunt was inserted into his brain to try to relieve the pressure of cerebrospinal fluid in his brain. During the afternoon our hopes were raised as John showed a slight improvement and could just about open his eyes and recognize us by his bedside. These moments were but minutes long but at least gave us the belief that the worst might be over. I had taken to using lemon-flavoured moisturized cotton buds to gently anoint his chapped lips and even at one point got a little smile, though I think he may have been dreaming.

Monday 5 and Tuesday 6 November

Two-day shoot with the *Sunday Times*, prepping for a big shoot with Jamie this week. Lovely FaceTime chat with Tim in America. Planning has started for the next Niklas Ekstedt adventure in Sweden, and Marrakech is booked for New Year, the Lake District with Ange next week and several other new adventures have gone into the diary.

* * *

John continued to respond to my gentle stimulation of his lips, and he could feel if I stroked the inside of his arm, something we both liked. I was told by the nurse that this, though reassuring for me, didn't mean he definitely knew that I was doing it, but didn't stop me believing that he could feel every stroke. During the fifth and the sixth Mother phoned the oncology unit several times, speaking to several people and again and again about the injection. They continued to say that it had been the correct dose and had been administered by Dr S correctly. Mother asked the registrar to check the drug on the ward and the neurology unit asked them to do the same.

The neurology unit had by then also spoken to the manufacturer of gentamicin and to the Committee of Safety in Drugs and apparently there had been no previously recorded incidents with this type of drug before.

Elsewhere, in Wandsworth, Peter Matthews and his wife T. J. were nervously awaiting the arrival of their firstborn, a baby who was due to be John's first godchild.

Wednesday 7 November

7 November 1987, Mother was still calling the oncology unit, but receiving no information from them. She hadn't had any replies to her queries and her continued questions about the injection were falling on universally deaf ears. The neurology unit continued to monitor and probe John's condition in Intensive Care. It was a quietly busy place, quite surreal in its relative darkness, the seriousness of the head injuries meaning that the death rate of these young men around us was alarmingly frequent. Walking in on the seventh, I passed with horror a 'bereavement room'. There was a shell-shocked family, all young, sitting with one of the

neurosurgeons, heads in hands. The patient in the bed next to John must have died in the night.

Dr Henry Marsh, one of the best known neurosurgeons in the world, was now on John's case, in the best neuro-centre in the country, but there was still confusion as to how we'd found ourselves back at the neurology unit with Johnny so desperately ill. It was the first time that I overheard the mention of John being in a coma and at one point he was wheeled away to surgery and another shunt was inserted into his brain to try to relieve the pressure.

When he came back from the operation I remember thinking how young he looked as I soothed his lips with the lemon-balm cotton buds, his head now swathed in clean bandages, peaceful but seemingly totally unaware of his surroundings, his skin smooth and untroubled. During the day another young man died and I was glad that John was unaware of him being read the last rites by a priest while a family waited in the bereavement room.

Thursday 8 November

Second day of the new book, shooting at Jamie's studio, long days, really full on, which I like. At breakfast I ask the team to be patient with me, reminding them that I am in a week of anniversaries and struggling to hold it together.

* * *

T. J. Matthews, Peter's wife, gave birth to a daughter called Clio and I called Peter to tell him that I'd tell John as soon as he regained consciousness. Samantha, Mother and I had again become a revolving presence around John's bed, stroking, whispering and soothing his unmoving body.

In the afternoon of that day hope was restored. John awoke from his coma. I had left the hospital to get back to The Beeches and to Molly. My illustrations were now in a state of limbo so I had nothing to go back for other than keeping Molly company and checking the answerphone, which told me to come straight back.

Oh the joy of seeing him among the prone and unconscious, eyes open, awake and responsive, smiley even. I rushed to his side, brushing the wispy hairs from his eyes, full of too many questions, I knew, but I wondered if he remembered what happened. He didn't really, he remembered being very sick, the vomiting, he remembered my present to him and Samantha, he seemed surprisingly lucid for a while. But, as the minutes went by, minutes rather than hours, I could see things weren't quite right. I was still bathing his lips in lemon balm to keep them moist and he started biting the cotton bud, just gently, almost jokingly, but it seemed strange. I told him about Clio being born to T. J. and Peter. He was, he said, 'chuffed' to be named her godfather and I told him he'd make an amazing one – the first of our godchildren. I remember feeling slightly jealous that this big deal had been bestowed on him.

As I was talking to John, I became upset at his biting of the cotton bud. I know that sounds odd, but he'd bite it and not let go. It was unsettling. I could see he was a bit agitated and restless, his movement more and more erratic. Gradually he fell asleep.

Telling John he was a godfather to Clio was the last conversation I had with him.

Dear Johnny,

Despite the fact that we were robbed of the opportunity to meet,
I feel as if I've always known you. As a child I remember seeing you
often, imagining your presence by my side, perhaps because you were

spoken about so frequently, so fondly, and with great love. You left an indelible mark on some of the most special people in my life.

You have been, and always will be part of my world, not least because in your place I have David, your other half. I call him the godfather sent from heaven, and I feel very lucky to have you both. Two for the price of one.

I hope you and mummy are looking after one another.

All my love,
Clio

T. J., Clio's mother, would die from cancer herself just a few years later, having sacrificed her remaining treatment so that she could provide Clio with a sister, Sibby.

As the afternoon passed into the evening of 8 November 1987 it became apparent that John's condition was deteriorating and that he had slipped back into his coma. I tried to speak properly to Mother about it but, even as eminent a doctor as she was, with the absence of information, she was struggling to understand what was going on in his brain. She did say that it was obviously fighting, hence his awakening. Again I left Mother and Samantha beside his bed, illuminated theatrically in the long, dark room.

That night I lay on my futon and prayed and prayed like I've never prayed before, no longer for stopping the incoming Ice Ages and volcanic flows, nor for protection from Billy's brain tumours. Instead I begged for forgiveness for letting Dr S complete his injection, I begged that Father was unaware, I begged that God think of my mother who had saved so many lives in her own eventful life, I begged and begged that he would 'make John better'. I must have slept eventually, but I would never sleep a whole night's sleep again.

Tick-tock go the hands of the clock

It's day three in Jamie's studio, shooting the new book. I feel fragile and sad, but at the same time positive, lucky that my inner world is strong: Ange, Paros, Pascale, Mother, Tim and my friends I call the Musketeers. Today is Friday, and this weekend I shall look at the last of the photo albums. I'll hug the children, I'll spoon Ange, I'll dine with Mother and Jean-Marian and Ian and their partners, I'll sit on the boat and read and write. I'll breakfast at The Wolseley and take Ange to Sir John Soane's Museum, I'll plan the walk next weekend up from Eskdale, along the River Esk and over the stepping stones to Boot, then up to Blea Tarn to write a final letter to my dear Johnny. Then, my job here will be done.

* * *

Monday 9 November 1987 saw John slipping deeper into a coma. We were all desperately worried and between us we maintained a permanent watch at his bedside. During the day Dr Marsh asked to see Mother. He told Mother that they had found eighty – EIGHTY – times the therapeutic dose of gentamicin in John's cerebrospinal fluid. The neurology unit had called the oncology unit over the weekend and, unbelievably, they had been told that John was in fact given intravenous gentamicin instead of intrathecal gentamicin, which would account for the huge amount of drug in his brain, an enormous overdose of one of the strongest antibiotics directly into his head. Far too late, the oncology unit had admitted their mistake.

Dr Marsh made the decision to operate again on John's brain to try to relieve some of the pressure but both he and Mother knew it would be hopeless. At this point she knew that her firstborn son was dying, and that now there was nothing any of us could do about it. I was in a state of total shock and disbelief, the information from the oncology unit, the admission to Marsh that they knew that the wrong injection had been given, was a thunderous punch in the gut. I knew the moment it had been given that it had been either wrong or given wrongly, I knew that I had let John down badly, and, seeing S motionless at his desk with something small in his hand, I knew that he knew that he had done something terribly wrong.

If they had admitted this instead of making out that John had a haemorrhage the reservoir could have been emptied. But no, they chose inactivity, fudging and lying. When John was scanned upon arrival at the neurology unit there was obviously no sign of a haemorrhage, and ultimately, upon post mortem, there would be no sign of the cancer that had made him so sick in the first place.

The ninth and tenth of November became a twenty-four-hour vigil, praying for a miracle, Henry Marsh and his quietly conscientious team doing all they could to make John comfortable. John's lips were no longer reacting to the lemon-balm buds but I kept up the hope that I'd see another twitch or flicker of a reaction as I anointed them, stroked the inside of his arm between the needles, and whispered in his ears.

Remembrance weekend 'The poppies are in the fields'

Over dinner of trout and mushrooms on toast and a fine rosé I apologized to Ange for being a bit under par, to say the least, during the week. We spoke of the tough weekend ahead, the tough week past, our plans for the next few weeks, the Lake District and Marrakech.

Breakfast at The Wolseley with Ange, a stunning cloudless day, boiled eggs and soldiers like Mother used to make, runny for me, well done for Ange.

As we got in I had a note from Pascale.

For Papa, to John.

Dear John,

When I was little, I asked my dad, 'If you could have dinner with anyone, living or dead, who would it be?' We were sat in my room and I think he was brushing my hair after a bath. I can't remember his response (maybe it was Alexandre Dumas, but I may have created that memory to fill a gap), though I remember my answer clearly. Without understanding of death, or my dad's experience, and with only a few photos and stories, I answered my own question with the statement, 'I would have dinner with John.'

It has taken a long time since that day to realize why my dad's eyes became foggy and why he hugged me so. It also took me a while to realize why that was my answer. I know and think of you as an extension of my dad. I can't tell you apart in photos, and I can't even see a difference in your handwriting. What I am able to see is how important you are. You've shaped my life and my relationship with my dad. I think it's why my dad loves us so much. That's why that was my answer.

Initially I struggled with the situation and was scared to ask about details, as if my questioning would loosen the stitches of an old healed wound. As I've gotten older, I've realized that talking about it helps my dad. You don't ignore a wound. When he talks about you, I can see a change in his face, and his posture, he looks just like you looked in all those photos I used to look at when I was younger. That's why I talk about it, and that's why I am proud of my dad. I am thankful for everything you did to make my dad the person he is today.

xx Pascale

If you ever thought you loved someone so much that it's impossible to love them any more, and then they do something that makes you do just that, then you'll know how I felt as I read that note.

To my mother's, and the nearest restaurant that can seat eight on a rainy Saturday night. Jean-Marian and Ian and their beloveds, Ange and Mother either side of me. I know now that I'm looking across at my siblings in a different way, more protective, more brotherly, certainly more emotionally involved. The love and care had never not been there, it just feels like an enormous gap has been closed. It feels good to sit at the head of the table next to Mother, my hand with all its rings of amber and skulls covering her cold and frail one, as she softly smiles at all who surround her. Small gifts are given to all, a toast is raised to Johnny. It is suggested that Mother makes a speech, quite rightly she decides to say nothing, as do I; there is nothing to be said that does not already exist, it's a mist that envelopes our every moment, an ever-present bruise on our broken hearts.

Sunday 11 November

Armistice Day

One hundred years since the Armistice was signed between the Allies from World War One and the Germans at Compiègne in France. It is also the day that Johnny died.

It was at 8.45a.m. on Wednesday 11 November 1987. The phone rang in the hallway and I rushed to sit in Mother's old Orkney chair. She was calling from the Intensive Care unit to tell me that John had died twenty minutes earlier and that I was to come immediately to be with him. All the false hopes, the failed fightbacks, everything was shattered. I was utterly, utterly devastated. I walked slowly into the kitchen to embrace and tell Molly the awful news. Poor Molly, she cried and cried, her teacup fragmented on the kitchen tiles, while I tried desperately to hold it together. She just kept saying, 'No, oh no, no.' Somehow, as if walking through thick mud, I managed to get myself a taxi to the hospital. Mother was sitting in the bereavement room, the room where we had dreaded to tread. Today that room was ours.

When a patient dies it is the staff's duty to attempt everything to resuscitate them, as they had done just an hour previously with John. Mother had to beg them to stop, knowing that his brain had been destroyed by the levels of gentamicin. While the chaos of attempted resuscitation had been going on, in an act of utter vileness, the mother of a desperately ill youth who had crashed his motorcycle was seen stealing my mother's purse. Mother was utterly exhausted, having been at John's bedside for forty-eight hours with little or no rest, the staff were doing their duty to try to save him once more, and during that moment of ultimate horror and grief, she was robbed. Mother begged the woman to give back just one thing, she could keep the purse, the cash and the cards, but the purse contained a letter that I hadn't known to exist. It was a letter Father had

332 • David Loftus

written at his desk, just before that final operation, just in case he never made it. The woman refused and Mother never saw it again.

I felt such dread as I walked towards John's bed. Mother went first, holding my hand, telling me to sit on the chair beside him, to hold his hand. All the tubes and drips had been removed, just the bandage around his head remained, his wisp of hair curling towards his closed eyes. Anyone who has experienced this moment knows that it is not easy to explain. Emotionally I was sapped, drained of all energy, the situation just seemed too unreal, it couldn't possibly have happened to my Johnny, my stronger, firstborn identical twin who had gripped my face so tightly that it had scarred my face for life. My world had fallen down, I was a singleton, no longer 'Mark I' and 'Mark II', 'Javid and Dyon', just David. The confusion and horror of it all would take a long time to sink in. I looked to my mother, knowing that John would expect me to think of her first and foremost. As she went to meet Samantha, I stayed by his side, holding his hand. It was warm and there were still little shades of tan lines between his fingers.

Other than the bandages around his head, his painfully thin body showed no signs of the horror he had endured in the past few months. The skin around his eyes, the crow's feet that both he, me and my son Paros inherited from Father had softened and faded. I kissed his forehead, tucked the curl of hair into his bandages, stroked his lips once more, the inside of his arm, said that I was sorry, sorry for everything, and as I turned I saw Samantha and her parents rushing towards the bed. She was inconsolable and broken, utterly devastated and in disbelief. I made way for her as she collapsed heaving and sobbing at John's side.

I sat in the bereavement room for a while. Ian had been called, Jean-Marian and her newlywed husband Philip arrived. Peter Matthews had arrived, unaware that John had just died. I can remember little of the next few hours, of the passing of faces, hugs, tears; just a numbing fog of disbelief. Someone must have driven me back to The Beeches at some point, I remember Molly's worried face at John's bedroom door as I lay on his bed and she replaced cold undrunk cups of tea with fresh hot ones. I remember that the doorbell kept ringing, Molly answering to florists and messengers. I saw no one, only moving eventually from John's room to my own.

I remember Mother running me a bath. I hadn't heard her come home but it must have been mid-evening. I heard the comforting sound of running water. Clean pyjamas were laid out. Molly tried to feed me but I couldn't eat. I lay in the bath and cried for an hour. Everything was John, his toothbrush, his hairbrushes, our wet shavers, never to be used again, our 4711 inherited from Father, the oversized bath, fitted so that twins and their two little siblings could all be bathed together, sharing bathwater, measles, chickenpox and flu. John and I would spend an inordinate amount of time in that bath, hours on end, hogging it from the rest of the family. Our favourite was to drain the bath, I was always at the tap and plug end, then we'd lather each other up with Imperial Leather and sit as close to the taps as possible, me facing them, John with his arms and legs wrapped around me, tight as possible. I would push off with my legs and our lathered bodies would shoot, like a pair of reverse-sitting bobsleigh pilots along the overlong bath and up the slope of the back, faster and faster, gaining height with each thrust, tears of hysterical laughter echoing down the corridor, occasionally pushing so hard that we would launch like skateboarders in a board park, over the rim of the bath. Mother told a story last night that one night, aged three, we had been suspiciously quiet, having not yet learned the naked bobsleigh game; one of us had done a small tuddy (little poo) in the bathwater, a tiny floater, and we had made it into a little boat and were gently guiding it backwards and forwards with our toothbrushes, much to her chagrin.

The bathroom was deafeningly silent that night. Eventually I got out, put on my father's lovely clean, striped cotton pyjamas and sat for a while with Mother quietly on the edge of her bed. She had a notebook with her; she had been ringing relatives and friends but she was exhausted and as devastated as I had ever seen her. She suggested I try to sleep but I told her I couldn't so she came with me into my room, tucking me into bed, stroking my hair like she did when we were kids. That night she gave me a hospital preoperative dose of temazepam, enough to knock someone out.

I lay on my back, looking up at the ceiling with a creeping blackness, as desperately sad as I could imagine ever being, completely destroyed, like someone had sucked me dry, like half of me had died. As I lay there, I willed my other half to die. It was like falling deeper and deeper into a black hole, the ceiling getting further and further away, my breath shallower and shallower and then I was aware of myself above, watching the real me, lying there, still and peaceful . . . and I awoke with an almighty intake of breath. I was frightened and terribly confused, but I had realized what I was doing, what so many with a newly broken heart do, what one in two identical twins when losing their twin does: I had given up. Fourteen hours after John had passed away I had decided to die too. I was furious, furious with myself, furious with S and his cronies, and determined, determined that I wouldn't let John down, that I would care for Mother, that I would prove his faith in me correct.

That I would live.

CODA

My dearest Timmy,

I'm sitting in an uncomfortable corner of the deck, between the mast with its peeling varnish and my old Alaskan canoe, on an even older Moroccan pouffe, a childhood gift from a distant nomadic godparent. I'm sheltered, just, from the early-spring wind off the water, warmed by a small patch of sun caught between two buildings rising from the shore.

You always knew where to find me when I hid from everyone, knowing it was 'my way', the far corner of the terrace at Villa Marco in France, where the sun fell behind the house, under the casuarina trees on West Beach in Eleuthera, or the garden bench out the front of Strathcarron or Georgie's place. Sometimes reading, often just at one with my thoughts, face tilted to the setting sun, the one person determined to see the sun set, finding solace in that fading moment, you were the one who always loved to see it rise.

Being born eleven months apart, I'm older and wiser, by the way. Both with our identical others, both in Knightsbridge, you the last-borns, us the firstborns. I like to think that we met as babies, Molly pushing us along in our pushchair in Kensington Garden, bumping into your nanny, sharing a cup of tea over their common bond! I wonder sometimes if we would have met if our twins hadn't been so cruelly taken. Maybe, but I wouldn't have been the same person now if I hadn't met you thirty years ago, back home in Knightsbridge. Windmills of Your Mind.

As you know, I quickly came to know your parents like surrogate god-parents and we shared so many laughs, tears and tears of laughter. I miss your father like a favourite uncle, like a dear friend.

As your best man, standing proudly by your side, I described to your family and friends, us, with Jeff and Simon, running through the waves at sunset on Atlantic beach in the Bahamas, and it being the happiest I had felt since my youth, it was a moment of time stopped, all else forgotten, indescribably magical, tragically happy.

It's been a tough year for both of us, and I know that my writing this memoir has not been easy for you, and I have edited out much that I could easily and joyfully have sung from the rafters, but I appreciate that, amazing though so many of those memories are, many of them are extraordinary because they are private, shared but with a few not the many. Shared between two of the closest friends, lone twins, 'identical twins, just not each other's.' I love and adore you, Timmy, more than most can comprehend and more than I can share, and I thank you from the bottom of my heart for all that you have done, all that you have shared with me, and all that we are yet to share and do together.

As aye, David

Saturday 17 November

My dearest Johny,

I've spelt it like you do, not like we all do. I've just wandered, not 'as lonely as a cloud' but with Ange, up Miterdale to Burnmoor Tarn on the clearest, warmest November day that I can remember. You'd have loved it, the little Mitre in full flood, peaty and moss-bound, all the waterfalls like elven heavens, the constant company of finches and the sounds of bubble and brook. So many damming possibilities, and now, sitting with Ange beside Burnmoor Tarn, mirroring the most perfect palettes of orange, blue and green, I'll hunt down a perfect skimmer and skim a few for you under the clear blue sky.

I started to write this book for you, but also for Paros and Pascale, a love letter to you, but also to help them know you a little better, understand what made me who I am, why our shared DNA was so important to us, why deep down I'd never be a singleton but always an identical twin.

I miss you more than the sea misses the rain. I was lost without you, but sitting here, held in the arms of my Ange, I've found a degree of peace that I never felt I could discover. You never really agreed with my girl-friend choices but I know you would have loved Ange like a sister. When I first met her she found a patch on my upper back that gave out such an extraordinary energy that when we need comfort she rests her palm on it, night and day, even when I am asleep, and we are almost immediately calmed. She's resting her head on my shoulder now, left hand pressed to

340

the spot. The only sound is the tiny stream bubbling up next to us; it's an extraordinarily peaceful spot and where I always intended to write to you.

I think the energy patch on my back is part of you. I think it's where you soothed me in the womb and where Ange spoons me now, and it makes me happy that she is the only one that can feel it. The water is so flat now it's begging for a skimmer. There was a time when we would have loaded our rucksacks with skimmers on Wastwater and walked them all the way up Mitredale with them.

When I asked Ian and Jean-Marian (Mushroom and yellow pants girl) if they'd write a word or two for the book, they both spoke fondly of the Lake District and our youth there, the damming of streams, playing of pooh sticks; they even miss that we used to drop rocks on cowpats next to them and splatter them in fresh green dung – you sailing off has romanticized even that to the youngers. Both mentioned the time we dug up a farmer's potato field and launched a barrage of tennis racket-propelled missiles over the farmhouse, hundreds and hundreds of them, raining down on them in the courtyard beyond. Led by Cousin Sarah they responded in kind and the hour-long 'Battle of the Lakes' that ensued has gone down in Loftus folklore as a classic 'boys will be boys' moment. I miss the beachcombing in Greece most of all; I'd have loved to have taken you to the Bahamas, we would never have stopped! Collecting St Cuthbert's beads in Lindisfarne, cowries in Orkney, urchins in Paros, Thomas clay pipes, shiny crystals in the mountains of Austria (and edel-weiss for your flower press), fossils in the Lake District's fellsides. I think of you every time I comb the shores and these are still some of my happiest times.

The rest, I think, is here in this book. Paros, Pascale, Ange and Tim, those who never knew you but those who have made me live my life to the fullest and have brought me a happiness that I hadn't felt since the moment you cracked your head at the cricket field. (I checked *The Independent* this morning, Joe Root – you'd like him, a Gower/Robin Smith kind of chap – hit a century against Sri Lanka in Galle.)

I'll never forgive myself, whatever anyone tells me, for letting Dr S perform that final injection as we unwrapped our presents. I know if Mother or Samantha had been there, he wouldn't have been allowed, and I've gone over that moment millions of times, day and night. I was scared, scared to say 'No, you can't do it' and I am so terribly, terribly sorry. If our roles had been reversed I know you would have stood up to him. I know it, but I did not.

My dear, dear Johnny, what can I say? I miss you all night, I miss you when I look in the mirror to contemplate whether or not to shave, I miss you every time I close my eyes, but, and it's a big but, I am happy. This little fellowship keeps me happy and on track. I can't change what happened, but I can try to make you proud. You were my biggest champion, as I was yours. My heart is so full of you, but it's also full of Mother and Ange, Pascale and Paros, Tim and my Musketeers, and luckily my post-traumatically stressed heart is a big one, one with space for you all.

Love, David x

Papa: 'No meal is complete without cheese.'
John: 'No, no meal is complete without baked beans.'

I overwrote by 75,000 words – I guess that's the nature of writing a diary, there is day-to-day waffle of interest to no one but a few. Daily moans and gripes that are easily lost in an edit. I wrote several lists of goals, many of which remain unaccomplished, but I did take Strawbod and myself flying over Iceland with Volcano Pilot and after two days of constant flying I felt like I'd been to heaven and back. I took the last photo album with me and on a sub-zero ice field I browsed and mulled over our final years, rarely shot together forging forth, trying our best to be singletons. I did also give up Solpadeine on 1 January 2019.

The object of writing this memoir was firstly to write a love letter to dear Johnny. I called him John, but he called himself Johny, others spelt it with two 'n's, he spelt it with just one. I gave myself days to weeks to write it but as the time passed and with the words flowing, unforced, in ink, so unedited, no crossings-out, the weeks turned to months and what had begun as a love letter to Johnny morphed into a lettre d'amour to all those that I have loved, but especially to our parents Jean and Eric, my brother Ian and sister Jean-Marian, to Tim my best chum, to my children Paros and Pascale, and to my darling wife Ange.

Acknowledgements

Ange, what can I say, my bunny, my one and only, my love. I am sure you quietly dread the moment in Marrakech, every year, when I turn to you and say . . . 'I have a plan . . .' This is one of many of my life projects that I couldn't have done without you gently whispering lovingly in my ear, or holding my hand from near and afar. I love you to the moon and back.

What shall we do next . . . I have a plan . . . xx

My darling Mother, my best friend, we share so much love and so much pain together, we both feel we are partially to blame, that we failed John somehow, but you were and are the most extraordinary and the most loving Mother I can imagine, and John and I were the happiest boys alive with you and Papa. I so adore our time together now. You have devoted your life to the care of others, saved countless lives, including the lives of your own husband and daughter and grandchild. My super hero.

Paros and Pascale, my two 'Ps', loves of my life, my 'raison d'être', all I am is you and this book is for you.

My brother and sister, Ian and Jean-Marian, I know it's not been easy having a lone twin as an elder brother, but I love you both unconditionally. Your letters this year have meant so much.

Nicola Brooksbank my master and gatekeeper, what would I have done without you the last few years?

344

Posthumously, my dear Father, Eric John, the kindest, most gentle of gentlemen, if I am half the man that you were then I would feel whole. I have missed you more than ever writing this book. The only positive in loosing you is that you didn't, two years later, have to witness the cruel loss of your first born.

My old best chum Harry Dagnall, the first person to say to me 'you should write all this down', during our long nights at the Reform Club, me your Passepartout to your Phileas Fogg. So many secrets shared and kept.

Lord and Lady Brabourne, I miss you both, JB, you were a colossal rock to me at such a seminal part of my life and were as much a friend as a surrogate Godfather. So many laughs shared.

Trevor Hopkins, Marrakech feels empty without you.

John 'Hammy' Hamilton. Twenty years of making books together, and you were beside me in Mumbai as I struggled to find my voice amongst the mayhem. You were in New Orleans when I was attacked, in Wyoming eating Prairie oysters, LA with the Bloods, and cruising the avenues and alleyways of the Cote d'Azur. So many adventures, so many bottles, so many memories.

TJ Mathews, for being so very loving to John, for giving me Clio, and for, as you were dying, promising to 'scare the shit' out of Dr S by adding him to your 'haunting list'.

Carole Tonkinson is what every writer embarking on such a perilous literary journey needs, a calm commander but with enormous stores of empathy, patience and kindness, I feel blessed and lucky to have met you and to have you in my life, as a friend for life. Hockley, as second in command you have held the tiller through both calm and rough waters, your calm and considered messages to me have meant more than you can imagine. All those at Bluebird, Zainab Dawood worked tirelessly on transcribing my diaries, which, having not realised that 'authors' wrote on computers these days, I wrote by hand, then Jess Duffy my PR, Jodie Mullish my marketing director. James Annal and Lindsay Nash, my designers and Sarah Badhan who kept it all under control as it headed off to print.

Samantha Connolly and your dear father Tim, I miss you both in my life.

The Musketeers, Timothy Knatchbull, Jeff Bennett, Simon 'Farmer' Jones, Andy Harris and Peter Hornsey. I'm so happy to have you all in my life. Rosie Scott, if Musketeers were ladies, you'd be one!

Peter Matthews, for everything and beyond, and for entrusting John's 'godfatherhood' of my darling Clio to me. To Clio, and Sophie your dear beloved wife.

My culinary ambassadors, Jamie Oliver and Gennaro Contaldo, we've climbed some mountains and taken a few tumbles together.

Bart von Olphen, so many adventures my friend and so many more to come!

I'm so lucky to count as best chums and supporters when I need them, Nick 'the' Pope and Sammie Bell, Rebecca Frayn, Jack and Finn Harries, Jason Flemyng, Dexter Fletcher and Dahlia, Jonah and Jeremy King, cousins Sarah and Edward, Leila and Marten Lindholm, Rachel Khoo and her Swedes, Meera Sodha, David Flint Wood and India, Christian Stephenson, Charlie and Liz Berman, Charlie Boorman, Ian Bickerton, Pete Winterbottom, Sir Johnny Scott, Nicklas Ekstedt, Guy and Dorothy, Nathan Outlaw, Johnny Yeo, Barney Harwood, Isabella and Amber Knatchbull, Janet and Theo Hornsey, Ben and Katie, Ed and Jen Henderson, Liz Cocozza, the Foxes of the Mews, Karin Grainger, Charlie Forté, the Zambelettis, the Cloakeys, Colette and Bradley. Kevin at ChaChaCha, and all my lovely boys at Riad El Fenn. Richards, Sinclair, Clatworthy and Eaton and Eleanora Galasso.

My lovely Danish crew, led by Anne and Ditte. Soren, you are in my prayers.

To Dr Debbie Street for keeping my oversized heart ticking along.

To Timmy Cooke and Codie Proud for joining us on our Parosian adventure to find our Shirley Valentine, Jane Apostopolous, with flowers in her hair.

And to all who I work and play with of whom, luckily for me, there are many.